D0162415

ARCHAEOLOGICAL THEORY
IN PRACTICE

ARCHAEOLOGICAL THEORY
IN PRACTICE

Patricia Urban

Edward Schortman

Routledge
Taylor & Francis Group

LONDON AND NEW YORK

First published 2012 by Left Coast Press, Inc.

Published 2016 by Routledge
2 Park Square, Milton Park, Abingdon, Oxon OX14 4RN
711 Third Avenue, New York, NY 10017, USA

Routledge is an imprint of the Taylor & Francis Group, an informa business

Copyright © 2012 Taylor & Francis

All rights reserved. No part of this book may be reprinted or reproduced or utilised in any form or by any electronic, mechanical, or other means, now known or hereafter invented, including photocopying and recording, or in any information storage or retrieval system, without permission in writing from the publishers.

Notice:
Product or corporate names may be trademarks or registered trademarks, and are used only for identification and explanation without intent to infringe.

Library of Congress Cataloging-in-Publication Data
Archaeological theory in practice / Patricia A. Urban, Edward Schortman, editors.
     p. cm.
Includes bibliographical references and index.
ISBN 978-1-59874-628-0   (hardcover : alk. paper) —
ISBN 978-1-59874-629-7   (pbk. : alk. paper)
1. Archaeology—Philosophy—T extbooks. 2. Archaeology—Research—Case   studies. 3. Archaeology—Fieldwork—Case   studies. 4. Excavations (Archaeology) I. Urban, Patricia A. (Patricia Ann), 1950– II. Schortman, Edward M.
CC72.A635 2012
930.1—dc23

                         2011038614

ISBN 978–1–59874–628–0 hardcover
ISBN 978–1–59874–629–7 paperback

CONTENTS

LIST OF FIGURES AND TABLES

Figures

Tables

PREFACE

THIS VOLUME IS A RESUL T OF OUR EFFOR TS, over more than three decades, to convey the nature, goals, and uses of archaeological theory to undergraduates. Whether in a classroom or under the unforgiving sun of northwestern Honduras (where we have directed a field school since 1983), we have been impressed by our students' intelligence and commitment to the field. Even the brightest of this very good bunch, however, have tended to view learning theory as something akin to taking medicine: important but nothing to look forward to. Let us assume for the moment that the several thousand undergraduates with whom we have had the good fortune to work were not unusually reluctant to engage with theory. Why, then, were they so averse to approaching the realm of ideas? We suspect that there are several reasons for this mild antipathy toward matters conceptual.

First, most people are not attracted to archaeology by the prospect of studying ideas. We want to learn about the ways in which people once lived, understood the world, and thought about themselves. The role of theory in this essential process may be easy to miss. The problem seems to be made worse when theory is taught, as it often is, in stand-alone courses in which the outlines of different conceptual structures are described and their histories traced. Such classes are certainly valuable. Their true utility, however, may well be appreciated only in the future when students apply those abstract concepts in a research context. Theory, like a language, must be used to be appreciated.

Second, the association of particular conceptual frameworks with specific scholars tends to give the impression that the realm of theory is exalted: only a few gifted thinkers—and not less prominent individuals—have roles to play in developing concepts. It is easy to lose sight of the very real truth that everyone who takes up a shovel or examines a potsherd is using theory. More than that, each of these applications of the abstract to the concrete changes theory; in addition, each use contributes to general debates about what happened in the past and how those events can best be understood. Theory, in short, is a tool all of us employ and, in the process, shape to our uses.

In other words, considering conceptual frameworks in isolation may help to clarify their particular features, but doing so reinforces an artificial and ultimately inaccurate distinction between archaeological thought and practice. In this book, we attempt to make explicit the link between theory and the conduct of archaeological research. We begin with a general consideration of the nature of theory (Chapter 1), and how it is used in the social sciences (Chapter 2) and in archaeology in particular (Chapters 3–4). These chapters define an essential part of the research structure within which archaeological studies are pursued—that is, the body of thought on which investigators can draw in asking questions and interpreting their finds.

There are at least two other parts of that research structure, however: the data to which theory is applied, and the interests and predispositions of the archaeologist who does the applying. Theory, as noted above, becomes meaningful when it is used, and it is always used by very real individuals to interpret equally real materials. The bulk of the book is therefore taken up with seeing how the abstract concepts outlined in Chapters 1–4 have been put to work by researchers to make sense of the past. We do so by considering the various ways theory has been employed in three cases: explaining the appearance of political hierarchy and centralized rule in southern Mesopotamia between 5000 and 2000 BC (Chapter 5); investigating the social and cultural significance of Stonehenge in late Neolithic Britain, from 3000 to 1700 BC and in more recent times (Chapter 6); and, in an extended case, pursuing our own research in the Naco Valley, northwestern Honduras (Chapters 7–9). These narratives show the creative interactions among data, method, and theory that shape our understanding of the past. The points made throughout the book are summarized in Chapter 10, along with an invitation for you to take part in theory building. A glossary of key terms is also provided at the book's conclusion.

To guide readers in following up some of the points raised in the discussion, we provide full references for further readings at the end of each chapter, together with a brief discussion of the significance of these articles and books. We selected these sources with several considerations in mind. In some cases, they present overviews of a broad topic, such as the nature of archaeological reasoning or craft production, along with references you can use to broaden your understanding of the issue in question. The sources listed in Chapters 7–9 are also designed to give you a sense of what concepts were available, and particularly attractive, to us during our Naco Valley investigations. The articles and books cited in Chapters 7–9 will, we hope, convey how we viewed the theoretical literature in archaeology at any one moment and how our views of that body of thought changed with time. The sources provided here are not meant to be exhaustive. Rather, they should help orient you toward debates in the field that are just touched on in these pages.

Perhaps the main point of this book is that theory is not an exotic phenomenon but a body of ever-changing thought to which you can contribute. In fact, if our argument elaborated here is correct, you may have no choice but to add to the ways in which theory develops and is used as you apply it in your research at all levels of study. Every time you use ideas to interpret a body of data, you change that conceptual structure in subtle ways. The insights derived from that application can contribute to general discussions of theory. To do that, you need to pay attention to what you are learning about the past *and* what you are learning about theory. This book is intended to help you see those connections.

Acknowledgments

We have been aided throughout our careers by far more people than we can mention here. Robert Sharer, our mentor in graduate school and now a friend, helped us chart our original path, though he might be surprised by the direction it has taken. Professional colleagues and friends, especially Wendy Ashmore, Janet Beatty, George Hasemann, Gloria Lara Pinto, Hayden Schortman, Aeleka Schortman, Joyce Marcus, and David Sedat, have cheerfully put up with our ramblings over the years, constructively criticizing and encouraging our ideas. We are also grateful to Jennifer Brown, Brigid Donahue, Kara Pellegrino, Katia Roque, Emily Smith, and Laura Yakas, who provided insightful commentary on an earlier draft of this book. Mitch Allen demonstrated remarkable fortitude in his several careful readings of this volume and critical acumen in the many very help-ful suggestions he made for improving the text. It is virtually impossible to list all of those authors from whom we have drawn inspiration, though the works of Wendy Ashmore, David Clarke, Kent Flannery, Ian Hodder, Joyce Marcus, Thomas Patterson, Colin Renfrew, Bruce Trigger, Eric Wolf, and Alison Wylie have been, and remain, important to us.

The Naco research discussed herein was generously supported by the National Science Foundation, National Geographic Society, National Endowment for the Humanities, Fulbright Foundation, Wenner-Gren Foundation, Margaret Cullinan-W ray program of the American Anthropological Association, and Kenyon College. We are very grateful to these institutions which made our explorations of Naco Valley prehistory possible. Directors and staff of the Instituto Hondureño de Antropología e Historia (IHAH), the Honduran government agency that oversees archaeological investigations, have been unstinting in their support of the Naco Valley research. Those who have been particularly generous with their time include the directors Olga Hoya, Jose Maria Casco, Ricardo Agurcia, the late Adan Cueva, Margarita Duron, Victor Cruz, and Dario Euraque, as well as IHAH staff, including the late George Hasemann, Carmen Julia Fajardo, Vito Veliz, Eva Martinez, and the late Alberto Duron.

It was through the hard, conscientious work of the Naco Valley's contemporary residents that the data discussed herein came to light. We owe a great debt to all of our collaborators in the field, especially to Luis Nolasco, Samuel Nolasco, Dagoberto Perez, members of the Posas family (Margarita, Edith, Elena, and Enrique), Rolando Rodriguez, and Jorge Bueso, with whom we had the good fortune to work for so many years.

The Naco project has served, since 1988, as a context in which 114 undergraduates and 32 graduate students from a variety of institutions learned the fundamentals of archaeological method and theory. In the course of working with such a uniformly bright and highly motivated group, we learned a lot, these insights filtering into the remarks that follow. Undergraduates are often not credited with the ability to conduct serious research. You will see in Chapters 7–9 the significant contributions these young scholars made to unraveling Naco Valley prehistory.

We are grateful beyond words to all those named above and the many others who have enriched our understandings of the Naco Valley's past, archaeology in general, and teaching. Needless to say, any errors of logic and fact that appear in the following pages remain our responsibility alone.

CHAPTER 1

THEORY, PERCEPTION, AND EXPLANATION: WORLD VIEWS AND SCIENCE

Introduction

IT WAS MARCH 5, 1988, AND VERY HOT. We were working on a drawing at the site of La Sierra in the Naco Valley, northwestern Honduras, and things were not going well. We were trying to capture in 2-D, on graph paper, a complex set of 3-D relationships: the vertical relations between a complex sequence of walls, floors, and earth layers. This set of constructed and natural features resulted from extensive remodeling of a rather large building that took place between AD 600 and 800. The structure was winning. In the midst of this ongoing battle with heat, humidity, and stratigraphy, one of our undergraduate colleagues burst through the brush and thrust forward several fragments of white material that had just been unearthed in the excavations he was directing nearby. "What is this stuff?" he asked. We expected to see little bits of white plastic that had accidentally been mixed in with prehistoric materials. Instead, we were very surprised to find him holding fragments of conch shell. The most likely source of this material is the Caribbean, at least 35 km from La Sierra in a straight line that crossed mountains. Nothing like this had ever been found in the Naco Valley before, and, more to the point, we had never *expected* to retrieve imported, exotic shells. The Naco Valley is, after all, an interior basin, not a coastal plain. After saying something useful like, "You found shells?" we struggled to make sense of the materials. What our colleague held—seashells—was clear enough, but what they meant was a mystery. Little did we think, as we stood there perspiring and furrowing our brows (warning: wrinkling your forehead makes the sweat and sun block get into your eyes even faster than normal), that our whole view of Naco Valley prehistory was about to change.

But how could a handful of marine shells have such a major impact? And, even allowing for the adverse effects of heat on mental processes, why did two professional archaeologists have so much trouble grasping the significance of what they were seeing? Addressing these very reasonable questions and understanding our confusion requires braving the realm of ideas: we needed to look at the preconceived notions that we carry into the field and use to make sense of what we find. By themselves, there was nothing particularly odd or outstanding about those bits of shell. Instead, their significance rested in their surprising presence in a place and time frame where we would not expect them. The conjunction of objects, place, time, and expectations gave them importance far beyond their physical qualities.

Some of the factors and processes that condition what we see and expect to find in the world around us are the subjects of this chapter. In particular, we examine the role **world views** play in shaping our understandings of reality. The advantages and limitations of these culturally constructed guides to thought and action are outlined; then we contrast them with scientific theories. We argue here that world views and theories make reality understandable by simplifying its events and processes. There are real differences in how this essential goal is accomplished, and these distinctions are the subject of the chapter's concluding pages.

The Power of World Views

What do you see when you look around? Take a few minutes and write down what you perceive in your immediate environment. Now, ask a friend who's there with you to do the same; better yet, get several friends involved. Compare the results after finishing your lists. To what extent are your inventories the same? How do they differ? By combining your observations, can you arrive at a clear agreement about what's all around you at the moment? Each of us **sees**, or takes in visual stimuli, more than we consciously recognize, or observe. Our brain busily filters all the input captured by our senses, arranging the information into recognizable categories (tables, chairs, books, for example). The brain then selects some aspects for particular attention while ignoring others entirely. Our observations are then organized into a coherent structure. We see the wall but may not immediately (or without thinking about it) register the texture of its surface, the patterning of paint drips, or even its precise color. We probably could not process and make sense of all the sights, sounds, smells, and physical sensations that confront us on a minute-by-minute basis. At the very least, we would find ourselves frozen into inactivity if we had to take into account consciously every possible bit of information that could be gathered from our surroundings. Consequently , our brains provide us with a selection of elements and their relations to which we can devote our attention; other possible observations are dumped in the dustbin of perception. Since we can only **describe** what we observe, and only **explain** what we describe, the screen through which we view reality powerfully influences all aspects of how we understand the world around us. What goes into this selection and structuring process? What determines what we observe from all we could possibly see? A whole range of factors can be named, including everything from potentially universal features of the human brain that have been selected for over millennia of evolution, to individual tendencies based on how we feel on any given day. The world looks different when we have the flu than when we are healthy. Observing is a very complex process; here we consider the significance of only one set of factors that condition perception.

We begin with the notion that what we observe is what we expect to be there. Those expectations, in turn, are founded on a **model** of the world and how it works. This model is based on formulas we share, to some extent, with other members of our culture. This conceptual framework is also shaped by individual inclinations resulting from our own life experiences. Such a model is a work in progress, built up and modified over the life-span of each individual. At its core are certain fundamental assumptions around which all other ideas are organized. These core beliefs and values are learned as we grow up within our families and communities. Acquired by watching and getting advice from those in our closest circle of relatives and friends, these central principles tend to lodge in our unconscious and are resistant to change. They impose a strong and extensive influence on how we perceive, describe, and explain the world. The degree to which our childhood experiences are shared by others in our culture shapes a common conceptual model. The model is known as a world view; it positions us to see reality in similar terms.

Try thinking of life as a continuum of experience with no obvious divisions among its constituent parts. In this case, trees are not clearly different from bushes, which, in turn, are not distinct from large perennials with thick stems. Humans do not generally take to such a view. Instead, we divide up life's unity into categories that are related to, but distinct from, one another. These categories, to which we assign names, are the basic **concepts** of which our world views are composed. We use them to describe what is going on around us. We also seize on certain *relations*, or causally significant connections, among these units in our attempts to explain what we describe. As an example, think of how we conceive of our political life. Most of us divide politicians into major categories that correspond to named political parties. We can then treat these parties as distinct entities, each characterized by a body of clear principles. We may know, on some level, that there is really a continuum of values and beliefs within the parties, making their boundaries unclear. Nevertheless, political parties are among the basic concepts by which we divide the complexity of political life into neat, manageable units. We use their presumed adversarial relations to explain to ourselves and others how our political system works. Many of us think in a more complicated manner than is implied by these categories and connections. Lurking in the back of our thoughts, however, are those basic divisions and relations that influence even the most knowledgeable political commentator. We think this way not because early 21st-century politics is naturally divided into clear positions. Rather, these are the categories we have encountered since birth in our interactions with close family, friends, and our constant companions, the TV and Internet. Most of us are therefore disposed to think in these terms, basing our actions on these understandings.

There are numerous other examples of how world views subdivide life's essential unity. Place of origin, gender, social and/or economic status, race, and ethnicity are used in many societies to classify their diverse members. Each social category, as defined by the intersection of these factors (e.g., African-American middle-class woman; Guatemalan upper-class man), is supposed to be characterized by certain distinctive features (sometimes called *stereotypes*) that are used to describe and explain the behavior of its members. Life is not that simple. When confronted with people who violate our expectations, we may even admit that things are not as straightforward as our world view suggests. In general, however, we are prone to employ these concepts unthinkingly, day in and day out, creating a simplified version of a complicated reality.

Evaluating World Views

The named concepts and the relations among them that comprise world views, therefore, are important elements of the filters through which we see and understand the social and physical environments in which we live. Using them helps us recognize and make sense of the forces, people, and phenomena we confront on a regular basis. World views also allow prediction of crucial events, such as when the rains will return so crops can be planted, or when to arrive at work to avoid losing wages. It almost goes without saying that these models must mesh tolerably well with the reality they confront. A world view that consistently fails to identify the season in which wild plants would bear edible fruit would not be a practical one for foragers dependent on those resources. Similarly, a world view that encourages you to take unannounced days off from your job would likely get you fired fairly soon. In this sense, therefore, we can say that world views are regularly tested against "hard" data. Major disjunctions between expectations and events may cause us to change our understanding of the world and the concepts by which it is grasped, if only because this is the sole way to survive.

Such dramatic and unpleasant confrontations with reality aside, world views are not subject to systematic testing; as long as they work at least tolerably well, we rarely question our unspoken rules. Adopted during our childhood years, these models and the concepts and relations that make them up have strong emotional associations with hearth and home which get in the way of efforts to view them rationally and objectively. Such linkages are strengthened when perceptions and values seem to emerge from the actions of sacred forces. If the categories by which we observe and understand the world are the gift of, say, a deity, there is little motivation to doubt their truth. Such questioning is not only unasked for, but would almost certainly be emotionally wrenching to the questioner and those around him or her. Galileo was put under house arrest because he would not accept that the sun and planets rotated around the earth. This was a basic conviction, suffused with sacred meanings, of the late medieval European world view; questioning it was more than an academic exercise. Many others have been shunned, imprisoned, or burned at the stake for publicly doubting supernaturally sanctioned world views.

Even without religious associations, these conceptual models are strikingly resistant to being rejected. It seems that we are very good at ignoring contradictory evidence. We selectively recall only those instances that conform to the values and expectations of our models. Alternatively, unanticipated events may be seen as special cases, explained as exceptions, not threats, to general rules. Existing conceptual categories can also be protected from questioning by enlarging them to accommodate new phenomena. Native American populations throughout what is now Mexico and northern Central America, for example, adjusted to the arrival of the Spanish in part by redefining their basic religious concepts to accommodate Christian ideas. Sacred Precolumbian figures were combined with Catholic saints, the resulting spiritual beings having elements derived from both religions. In this way, the core concepts of indigenous Native Americans were preserved; and foreign ideas and rules were modified to match these preexisting principles. The new Spanish overlords might have been comforted by the crosses they saw going up within and around indigenous towns. What they did not grasp was how that traditional Christian symbol was viewed by those who raised it: for most indigenous residents of Mexico and Central America, for example, a cross represented the great world tree that held up the heavens. Such misunderstandings were sometimes revealed in dramatic fashion, as when a talking cross led the Maya of Yucatan in a lengthy revolt against hispanic authorities during the 19th century. Never is human creativity more in evidence and more effectively used than when trying to maintain a cherished world view in the face of contradictory evidence.

World views, therefore, are essential companions throughout our lives. They make the overwhelming complexity of daily existence manageable and comprehensible. Their concepts and assumptions provide a framework for making observations, prioritizing their significance, and determining the reasons why things happen as they do. These models are not only functional, but, given the emotional, often supernatural, associations of their core principles, impart a psychologically satisfying vision of the world. Our ways of observing and understanding are not simply useful but "right" and "proper" means for conducting the business of living. As long as our world view and reality mesh fairly well, understandings codified in "common knowledge" yield productive interactions with a person's social and physical environments. Each time an important objective, such as finding a spouse, getting food, or attending a cocktail party without embarrassment, is attained, our world view is essentially and profoundly confirmed.

The Limits of World Views

As important as world views are, these conceptual frameworks have a wide range of drawbacks. Problems with determining their validity through empirical tests have already been mentioned. Accepted more on faith than on proof, these models may not be sound foundations on which to build a systematic understanding of the world. Even though European scholars once thought of their planet as the center of the solar system, the earth really does revolve around the sun.

Another drawback is the close linkage between world views and the conditions that exist in the particular times and places in which they are created. That is, their concepts and relations may not be easily generalized to other circumstances and periods. These models, therefore, are poor guides for coping with radically novel situations. Their unexamined assumptions often yield behaviors that are out of keeping with new conditions. If you have ever traveled outside your home country for a protracted period of time, you have probably experienced "culture shock." Your hosts' behaviors might well have seemed unpredictable, and their meanings mysterious, especially if you did not speak the local language. Concepts, beliefs, and expectations appropriate to your home culture are not likely to have offered much help in these very different circumstances. While you may not have chucked your world view out the window as a consequence of such encounters, some changes were probably necessary to get along in the new environment. Whatever satisfaction you legitimately felt after having adjusted to your novel surroundings, the process of reaching this new level of awareness is sure to have been difficult and emotionally unsettling. These difficulties result from problems encountered in questioning and changing your entrenched world view.

In some cases, world views can threaten the very existence of people facing rapidly changing conditions. For example, as described in *A Welcome of Tears* (Wagley 1983), the Tapirape, who live in the Brazilian rainforest, limited the number of children any couple could have to three. Restricting family size successfully kept Tapirape populations well below the level where they would overwhelm their fragile environment. This image of the ideal family was an important part of the Tapirape world view, one to which they clung even after the spread of Western diseases among them led to dramatic population losses. By 1953, there were only 51 Tapirape left and yet the survivors still insisted on maintaining families of no more than five individuals. It was only after a long, hard struggle that this view was changed and the Tapirape could take advantage of newly available medical services to increase their numbers.

World views, therefore, are guides to life that often do not bear close scrutiny. Composed of emotionally charged concepts and assumptions that exist largely out of awareness, their basic principles are not easily called to mind, evaluated, and modified. We go through life blissfully unmindful of just how much of what we see and think is predetermined by the cultural and social conditions in which our world view developed and functions. While fine for making sense of frequently repeated daily encounters, the unexamined precepts of world views offer distorted pictures of broader patterns in nature and human behavior.

Scientific Models of Perceiving, Describing, and Explaining

Scientific theories operate at multiple levels of generalization and abstraction (Figure 1.1). At the low end, they include statements of regularities based on direct observations (e.g., all kiwi birds are flightless). Closer to the other end of the continuum are high-level theories composed of precepts that explain a wide range of phenomena, including those empirical generalizations identified in low-level theories (e.g., the synthetic theory of biological evolution can be used to account for the kiwis' unusual anatomy). Middle-level theories fall between these extremes, explaining relations among observed phenomena by reference to principles drawn from high-level theories (e.g., the kiwis' flightlessness might be accounted for by demonstrating how its inability to get airborne is an outcome of processes of adaptation through natural selection operating within the specific environmental conditions of New Zealand prior to human occupation of that island). We focus throughout this book on higher-order theory examples, reserving the term *theory* for them unless otherwise noted.

High-order theories, like world views, are filters through which reality is perceived, described, and explained. As world views do, theories identify concepts and relations that account for why a particular event occurred. Those mechanisms involve specified relations of causation and dependence among a set of variables that the theory singles out for particular attention. Unlike world views, however, scientific theories require (1) an *explicit* statement of basic concepts and their relations, and (2) re-

High-Level Theories

Explanations of phenomena based on principles of broad application.

Middle-Level Theories

Explanations of recurring patterns noted in field observations by reference to principles derived from high-level theories. It is through middle-level theories that high-level theories are evaluated against field observations.

Low-Level Theories

Specification of regularly recurring relations among variables observed in the field. These patterns comprise the data that are explained by high-level theories through the application of middle-level theories.

FIGURE 1.1 A synopsis of relations among the different levels of theory discussed in the text.

peated testing of conceptual frameworks against data derived from observations in the physical world.

You have almost certainly been exposed to scientific theories in classes you have taken in physics, biology, and chemistry, and we cite just one simple example of such a theory here. Newton's Second Law of Motion proposes that force equals mass times acceleration ($F = ma$). Force, mass, and acceleration are core concepts, each of which is carefully and clearly defined within the theory. The above equation elegantly and without ambiguity specifies how these elements are interrelated. Using this theory, you can describe and explain what you see happening around you (the rate at which objects fall within the earth's atmosphere). Compare this set of concepts and their relations to the earlier example of the distinctions we commonly make among political parties. The political affiliations are rarely defined with any precision, and relations among them are certainly not the sort that can be expressed in a straightforward equation. This short exercise illustrates that the explicit statement of concepts and relations in physics makes for a far clearer description and explanation of the world than do the often vague expressions found in most world views.

Just as important to the definition of scientific theories is the requirement that they be tested. Ideally, expectations of what should happen under specified conditions if the scientific theory is correct are matched against what actually occurs. This determines how well the theory predicts the course of observed events. That said, theories are rarely tested directly. The concepts and relations that theories employ exist on such an abstract level that it is often difficult to evaluate them against actual observations. Theories are therefore examined by testing **hypotheses** derived from these larger conceptual structures. Hypotheses apply a theory to specific cases in ways that are testable and designed to make sense of what is observed. These *falsifiable* propositions (statements that can be proven to be untrue) fall within the domain of middle-level theories. As noted above, such formulations usually apply the abstract concepts of high-level theories to the observed regularities identified in low-level theories.

Take, for example, the case of northern England's peppered moths, *Biston betaluria* sp. This nocturnal insect lives near Manchester, England. Prior to industrialization in the middle 19th century, most peppered moths were a light gray. About the middle of that century, members of the species with genes coding for a black color increased rapidly in numbers, soon comprising about 90 percent of all peppered moths in the area. One hundred years later, light gray members of the species were again on the rise, gradually replacing the darker-colored variants. How was this to be explained? Biologists proposed the hypothesis that the shifting colors were a specific example of general evolutionary principles operating within specific environmental circumstances. During the 19th and early 20th centuries, industrialization in northern England produced tremendous quantities of soot which darkened the trunks of trees in the moth's habitat. Those individual moths whose genes created a dark gray coloration blended in with this pollution-soaked environment. The darker moths lived longer and produced more offspring than did their peers with genes for the lighter color. Pale gray moths were easily spotted by predators and eaten early in their lives. As smokestack industries gradually disappeared from Manchester and its surroundings, the environment changed. With less soot on the trees, now it was the dark gray moths that were easily seen and eaten, while their lighter-colored fellows blended in far more effectively. Patterned regularities recognized in the changing colors of moths (low-level theory) were therefore explained by a hypothesis, or middle-level theory, that linked variables of moth color, environmental pollution, and predator behaviors. These correlations, in turn, were accounted for by using principles of natural selection through differential fitness, derived from the high-level theory of biological evolution. The hypothesis could be evaluated by continuing observations over the coming years to see if the relevant variables were related in ways predicted by this particular application of the principles of adaptation through natural selection.

If a theory's expectations are consistently met through the successful testing of its hypotheses, then a researcher can say that the theory is supported by available findings. Few would assert that the theory is fully established until many additional tests are completed. There is always the possibility that new data will overturn a long-standing theory. Predictions that are not met in the observed data can indicate several things: (1) a theory that is seriously in error; (2) a misinterpretation of the theory in the hypothesis based on it; or (3) a flawed experimental design. This is an approach to reality that stresses doubt and uncertainty, as opposed to the unquestioned acceptance of world views. There is, ideally at least, no room or excuse for becoming emotionally attached to your theory and the ideas that make it up. All is to be explicit, objective, and precise; nothing is to be accepted until it has been rigorously tested and retested.

An approach to the world founded on doubt and uncertainty lacks the emotional appeal of world views that assure us of the built-in, possibly god-given, rightness of our basic understandings and beliefs. Clear statements of basic principles and an insistence on evaluating our ideas against physical data do offer some advantages, however. Knowledge obtained in this manner is likely to be a more reliable foundation for understanding the operation of the world around us than that provided in most world views. Further, scientific theories are not limited to describing and explaining events occurring within one particular area during a single moment in time. Instead, they are attempts to comprehend the operation of forces in a wide range of places and periods where similar conditions exist. Newton's Second Law of Motion, for example, was not intended to explain rates of falling objects only in 17th-century England; it was meant to apply all over the world at all times. By questioning everything, scientists attempt to create a solid understanding of general, timeless processes, such as gravity. This knowledge, it is hoped, will become the basis for a better understanding of the world and for controlling some of its forces for human benefit.

Theories and World Views

It is important to bear in mind several features of scientific theories. First, they are the products of people working with ideas and assumptions that are available to them in specific places at particular moments in time. That is, like world views, theories are culturally constructed and historically contingent. Newton's work cannot be fully understood outside of its historical context. Where theories differ from world views in this regard is in the efforts of scientists to actively and consciously make their theories applicable over a wide range of circumstances, thus going beyond the specific circumstances of their creation. Newton certainly worked within the culturally and historically contingent context of 17th-century England, but he sought to speak of processes that had existed throughout time and across the globe. His successors living in different times and cultures also sought to apply, test, and evaluate Newton's insights, making those ideas, for a few centuries at least, core principles of the science of physics.

Second, scientific theories and their associated hypotheses, also like world views, constitute simplified models of reality: a theory describes or accounts for, through its hypotheses, a limited aspect of what happens in the world. Traditionally, scientific theories derive strength from their concentration on the effects of a few variables operating under a limited set of specified conditions. The more factors involved, the more complex their relations are likely to be; therefore, the less clearly will we be able to discern the chain leading from a particular cause to a specific effect. For example, imagine that you are evaluating a theory about the factors affecting growth in bean plants. It would be much easier to test a hypothesis that temperature was the most important of these factors if you kept other variables—humidity, soil fertility, and duration of exposure to light—constant. Any differences among the plants at the end of the experiment would therefore have to result from the divergent temperature settings in which they developed (assuming that each specimen was genetically identical). A researcher who considered the impact of different temperatures, humidity levels, soil nutrients, and light exposures *simultaneously* on the development of bean plants would get results that are hard to interpret. Did Plant A grow faster and taller than Plant B because A germinated under warmer conditions than B? Or was B's development held back by getting too much water, growing in poor soil conditions, and/or being exposed to less light? Answering those queries would require conducting at least four additional experiments, in each of which only one of the variables under study (heat, humidity, soil fertility, and light) was allowed to change, while the rest were held constant.

Scientific theories, therefore, promote an understanding of events by providing a set of concepts and assumptions we can use to observe, describe, and explain those phenomena. Even more than world views, theories narrow our focus, encouraging recognition of some factors while disregarding others. Scientific theories are, in this sense, like flashlights whose narrow beams clearly reveal certain aspects of reality but leave the rest in shadow. Without theories to direct our attention and filter out "non-essential" perceptions, we would be overwhelmed by an abundance of possible observations that might be made. Like the unfortunate researcher attempting to grasp the factors controlling rates of bean growth, we could never be sure what variables, in what combinations, had what consequences. Learning guided by science, therefore, involves paying close attention to the operation of the relatively few factors and relations to which a theory draws attention. Perceptual screens are essential to any engagement with the world, to describing and explaining what we perceive. Scientific theories and world views provide these screens but differ in their precision, general applicability, and testability.

Summary

Making sense of what is going on around us depends on turning all that we can see into a manageable set of observations. Next we explain those observations by focusing on a few variables and the relations among them. World views and scientific theories both serve as means for converting the seen into the observed, the mysterious into that which is understood. In a real sense, world views and scientific theories exist at two ends of a continuum. They are separated not by their ultimate goals, but by two other factors: the extent to which the variables that compose them are explicitly defined, and the degree to which relations among these factors are rigorously tested. They are also separated by how much emotional commitment people holding these perspectives invest in them. Never lose track, however, of something world views and scientific theories share: they are both simplifications of life's remarkable complexity. Such simplification is essential to getting on with the business of perceiving, understanding, and acting. Nevertheless, it is important to remember that every description and explanation of any event, no matter what its source, is incomplete. While scientists are trained to be acutely aware of such restrictions in vision, most of us do not question our world view's completeness until we are forced to confront such gaps. These confrontations are rarely pleasant.

It would be comforting to believe that approaches to understanding life could be neatly divided between world views and scientific theories. That perception would, however, leave out most theories used in the social sciences, of which archaeology is a part. Coming to grips with where archaeology and the other social sciences fall within the science-to-world-view continuum is the topic of the next section.

Further Reading

Case Studies

Reed, N.

2001   *The Caste War of the Yucatan*. Stanford, CA: Stanford University Press.
   This overview of the Maya rebellion led by a talking cross mentioned in the text gives you an idea of how people can adjust their world views to drastically new situations while still preserving something of their own distinctive understandings of reality.

Wagley, P.

1983   *Welcome of Tears: The Tapirape Indians of Central Brazil*. Prospect Heights, IL: Waveland Press.
   It is from Wagley's account of the Tapirape that the example of relations between world view and population loss among members of this group was drawn.

Theory, General Discussions

Hempel, C.

1966   *Philosophy of Natural Science*. Englewood Cliffs, NJ: Prentice-Hall.
   Archaeologists fell upon this slim volume written by a strong proponent of Positivism and used it to create Processualism. Positivism was an approach to understanding the structure of scientific inquiry that stressed rigid adherence to a model of covering laws by which all phenomena could be explained.

Nisbett, R., and L. Ross
   1980   *Human Inference: Strategies and Shortcomings of Social Judgment.* Englewood Cliffs, NJ: Prentice-Hall.

   Nisbett and Ross outline a theory of "knowledge structures" (roughly analogous to the concept of "world view" employed here) and relate those structures to how people perceive and understand the world. They especially focus on the power of established cognitive schemes to affect what is observed and how it is explained.

Popper, K.
   1989   *Conjectures and Refutations: The Growth of Scientific Knowledge.* 4th edition. London: Routledge.

   This is an influential statement on the practice of science that was taken to heart by many archaeologists. Popper particularly stressed the importance of refuting theories as a way of understanding the world.

Theory, Middle-Range and Analogy

Rabb, L., and A. Goodyear
   1984   Middle Range Theory in Archaeology: A Critical Review of Origins and Applications. *American Antiquity* 49:255–268.

   Rabb and Goodyear consider how middle-range theory figures in archaeological interpretations. Their essay appeared at a point when these issues were being much debated by researchers in the field.

Schiffer, M.
   1976   *Behavioral Archaeology.* New York: Academic Press
   1987   *Formation Processes of the Archaeological Record.* Albuquerque: University of New Mexico Press.

   In these two volumes, Schiffer lays out a detailed consideration of the various human- and natural-caused processes that shape the material patterning observed at archaeological sites. This work in middle-level theory was designed to help translate what was found archaeologically into statements about ancient behavior.

CHAPTER 2

THEORIES, PERCEPTIONS, AND EXPLANATIONS IN THE SOCIAL SCIENCES

Introduction

I N THIS CHAPTER , WE CONSIDER THE NATURE OF THEORIES within the social sciences in general, and in archaeology in particular. Special attention is paid to the relationship between theory and data, especially how variables are defined and hypotheses tested under non-laboratory situations. This discussion leads to a consideration of why archaeologists cannot seem to agree on one overarching theory to guide our work. The answer lies, we argue, not only in difficulties experienced in evaluating any conceptual scheme, but in the very nature of the phenomena we study, that is, human behavior in all its variety. The chapter ends with an extended discussion of how much theory determines what we observe or whether we can perceive data that run counter to our theoretically generated expectations. This last issue is central to assessing the value of theory as a research tool. If all we ever see is what our conceptual frameworks condition us to find, then our knowledge of the past is predetermined by the conceptual structure we bring to the study.

Hard Theories, Soft Sciences

Archaeologists, like everybody else, need conceptual tools to reduce all that can be seen to a relatively few observations that may be described and understood. Casting around for means to this end, we are leery of the dangers and limitations inherent in world views. Science offers a far more attractive model for creating knowledge that is rigorously tested. But herein lies a dilemma: we deal with human behavior, a far more complex phenomenon than bean plants or falling bodies. Can we use science as our model for constructing theories of human action?

There are two problems that we encounter right from the start in answering this question: how to define our **variables** and how to test our interpretations. This is hardly a difficulty unique to archaeology, as it affects all the social sciences.

Consider, for example, the question of what factors contribute to an individual's intelligence. We cannot directly see "intelligence" but have to assess this important, abstract capacity indirectly using a surrogate measure. This often assumes the form of scores on IQ tests. Are these measures accurate estimates of how bright someone is? Maybe, but what is really being measured in IQ tests? Is it the test-taker's familiarity with standardized exams? Are there cultural assumptions built into the test that systematically favor those who grew up accepting those ideas? We are a long way from Sir Isaac Newton's Second Law of Motion, so clearly expressed in force = mass × acceleration, which elegantly describes the variables at work on an object. We will travel quite a bit further from that model of theoretical elegance by the time we are done.

Let us assume for the moment that IQ exams really do provide a reliable measure of the intelligence of each person who takes them. What factors possibly affect the outcomes of these exams? Among the variables that might influence someone's score are nutrition, family environment, inherited characteristics, health status, and socioeconomic class. Even if we successfully ignore the clear interrelations among some of these elements and treat each as a discrete variable, how would you define these factors and measure them? What does family environment mean? What elements are important in defining this variable? Would you check to see if both parents are present? Is it significant if other relatives also live with the family? What about relations among family members: are they hostile, friendly, neutral?

Do you see the problem? To measure any one of these factors, you would have to create an argument that links aspects of that variable to intelligence. Next you would have to come up with ways to measure those aspects, which, often as not, can only be seen indirectly. Both of these steps are generally subsumed within middle-level theory, as they involve linking the abstract concepts and relations of high theory (what causes intelligence?) to patterns that are directly observed (variations in IQ scores among individuals). In deciding among variables to study, you will, therefore, be guided by high-level theory. High-level theory will also help you to define those elements that make up such variables as nutrition or socioeconomic class and help you to develop measures for them. High-level theory, in short, is an integral part of your study from the beginning.

Now, having settled on a variable and measured it, how will you test its importance in affecting the results of IQ tests? Say your hypothesis states that family environment plays the largest role in determining an individual's intelligence. You could, we suppose, begin by whisking off sets of identical twin infants (thereby controlling for genetics), having members of each pair subjected to the same nutritional regime, given identical schooling, raised within the same social class, and monitored regularly for disease. A member of every set, however, would be raised in one type of family environment while the other would develop under contrasting familial circumstances (we are assuming, for simplicity's sake, that there are only two relevant family settings). Intelligence tests would then be administered to the subjects on a regular basis and the scores compared. Any divergence in results would be due to variations in family environment.

Clearly, such an experiment is morally unacceptable. No possible gain in knowledge could make up for the misery suffered by the children and their birth parents. There are serious reasons, however, for questioning whether such a study would even be feasible. Could you create identical educational settings, ensure that each participant had the same health, and so on? If not, how could you be sure that any divergences in IQ scores within each pair of twins were due solely to family setting? And even if you could overcome these obstacles, there would still be the nagging problem of what your IQ tests actually measured and how relevant your definitions of family environment were to questions of intelligence.

Now consider the kinds of situations with which archaeologists deal. Take, for example, the hypothesis that the shift from hunting and gathering to the raising of plants and animals was caused by increased population pressure; that is, humans had increased in number to the point that foraging for food could no longer support the population. Domestication—making choices that altered the genetic structures of plants and animals, and producing these altered plants and animals outside of their natural ranges—was a way of producing more food to feed more people. This transition occurred at various points in prehistory but always so far back in time as to be beyond our ability to see it directly and manipulate the relevant variables. You could go back to the same hospital where you retrieved the twins for the IQ test, collect some more infants, divide them into Groups A, B, and C, and raise them all as hunters and gatherers in some untouched environment. Group A could be the control, its population changing only due to natural processes of birth and death. Group B, however, would be subjected to a higher rate of population growth when members of Group C are introduced to their society. You could then watch and determine if, and at what point, the folks in Group B started domesticating flora and fauna to feed their ever-expanding number of hungry mouths. The obvious moral problems with this study aside, it is very doubtful that the results would constitute a legitimate test of the original hypothesis. The sheer logistical difficulty of establishing the three groups under identical conditions and defining the relevant variables precisely would be enough to bring the study to a crashing halt, not to mention the problems that would be experienced in trying to replicate the findings. Archaeologists, in short, can rarely measure their variables directly or evaluate their high-level theories by testing hypotheses under laboratory conditions.

This is not to say that testing hypotheses and their underlying theories is impossible in the social sciences in general and archaeology in particular. We can, and do, try to match our theories to data through hypotheses, a process we will see repeated numerous times in our discussion of the Naco Valley Archaeological Project. But how does such testing proceed if we cannot control the conditions under which comparisons of theoretically generated expectations and observations occur? As **Alison Wylie** (see sidebar) indicates, hypotheses in archaeology are assessed by bringing as many different lines of evidence to bear on our accounts as possible. Ideally, these lines of evidence should be independent of one another and based on established understandings about how the aspects of the world in question work. Independence is an especially important consideration. If two or more lines of evidence are *independent*, if the results from one are not conditioned by results produced by the other, then their support for a particular interpretation strengthens our confidence in the accuracy of the theory on which it is based.

This sort of testing procedure is commonplace today in situations where conclusions drawn about past events have very serious and immediate consequences. Forensic scientists, for example, use multiple lines of evidence, from fingerprints to analyses of all manner of material traces such as blood spatter patterns and DNA, to infer how a crime was committed and by whom. In order for these data to stand up in a court of law, not only must the evidence be independent, but the procedures for trans-

---

Alison Wylie

Alison Wylie, with her MA in archaeology and PhD in philosophy, is uniquely suited to address questions of reasoning and explanation in archaeology. Her work in this field has focused on how archaeologists make claims about past social and cultural forms based on very fragmentary data that are only indirectly related to the behaviors we seek to reconstruct. Wylie has played a central role in discussing the place of analogic reasoning, the use of multiple lines of evidence, and the importance of background knowledge in formulating and evaluating statements about the human past.

---

forming bits of fiber and hair into meaningful information about the case must be based on widely accepted, well-understood principles.

How does this process work out in archaeology? Stop for a moment and think back to the argument about domestication's causes cited earlier. Again, keeping it simple, say we are trying to evaluate the hypothesis that rising population drove people to start planting crops and herding animals. Try to come up with the various lines of evidence you would need to tell whether expanding numbers of people led to experiments that converted wild plants to cultivated ones. As you proceed with this exercise, list out what you would need to know to test this proposition *and* how you could recognize that evidence archaeologically . What you are engaged in here is **operationalizing** your hypothesis, that is, moving from the abstract realm of ideas to how those ideas might look in the real world of archaeological data. This crucial process is conducted in the realm of middle-level theory. As you go along, ask yourself:

1. How independent is each line of evidence?

2. What assumptions do you have to make to measure such variables as population pressure archaeologically?

3. How much faith do you have in these different lines of evidence?

One line of approach could involve examining the actual fragments of plants and animals recovered from excavations at sites in the area under study. These would likely be turned over to specialists in the analysis of floral and faunal remains who would use their expertise to distinguish domesticates from their wild forms. We would also give some of this material to labs where they could be assigned a temporal placement by such methods as **carbon-14 dating**, based on the regular decay of naturally occurring isotopes in organic samples. In both cases, the techniques used are well established, and their results are independent of each other and of the hypothesis under study. Deciding that a particular seed is from a domesticated plant—say, corn—is based on principles well rooted in biology. It has nothing to do with whether you believe in the population pressure argument. Similarly, the carbon-14 procedures used to date that piece of vegetation depend on established premises of physics. These are unrelated to both the question of the plant's domesticated status and the issue of whether rising numbers of people drove the process of cultivation and animal keeping. As a result, if these procedures confirm our expectations about relations among domestication, time, and population densities, we can justifiably argue that agreement among such different approaches is unlikely unless our hypothesis is correct.

So much for the easy part. We still have to reconstruct population sizes and densities at different points in an area's history from the archaeological remains at our disposal. Here it gets trickier, because now we have to specify relations between what we observe (archaeological remains) and what we want to know (population numbers) using principles that are poorly understood and upon which there is no general agreement. For example, we could use site size as a measure of population numbers: the bigger the site, the more people lived in it. This makes sense if you can fashion a convincing argument that there is a direct relationship between these variables. What if large sites are occupied by relatively few people who like a lot of space between their residences, while smaller sites supported more individuals who were tightly packed together? Well, you could address that problem by excavating portions of the sites you found and determining how many residences there were at each. That is a good approach, but how do you distinguish a place where people actually lived from structures that served as kitchens or storehouses? If non-residential buildings are used to calculate population sizes, then you are going to overestimate the number of people present at any point in time at any one site. So, now you have to construct a set of arguments about ancient activity patterns that allow you to identify buildings used as residences and separate them from those that served other purposes. These arguments will be based on their own sets of assumptions about what the material remains of kitchens, warehouses, and sleeping or working spaces look like after they have been abandoned for several millennia. These arguments and assumptions are also probably going to be open to debate in ways that the principles and assumptions used in carbon-14 dating or the recognition of domesticates are not. This is because reconstructing ancient activities from material debris is an open-ended, uncertain affair.

You are not done yet. Once you estimate how many residences were occupied at one site in one period, you have to convert that figure into the number of people who lived there. How many individuals inhabited each building defined as a "house"? Here you will need to construct arguments linking the sizes and arrangements of living spaces to numbers of inhabitants. This requires another, rather long, frequently argued about set of interrelated inferences and assumptions that tie residential space to population figures.

In reconstructing the functions of ancient buildings and specifying population-to-residential area ratios, you will probably rely on some kind of reasoning by analogy. This means that you will look at living populations, or those recorded in historic documents, and use their material and behavior patterns to infer what was going on in the past. You might review, for example, *ethnographic* (descriptions of cultural behaviors written by anthropologists) or historical accounts of residences occupied by people who lived similar lives under similar conditions to those of the social groups you are studying. If your reference population consists of the living descendants of the ancient people you are examining, all the better. Such historical ties increase the probability that relations among material patterns and behaviors (such as building forms and their functions) are accurately perceived: the ancient and modern people are participants within the same, but changing, cultural tradition. However the connections between the sources and subjects of analogies are established, it is common practice to reason from the present to the past, identifying ancient houses by comparing their sizes, forms, and associated artifacts with those recorded from more recent periods. We often use a similar train of reasoning to infer how many people lived in residences of different sizes, moving out from what we can document directly (residential space) to what we cannot (population figures).

These arguments by analogy are sometimes subsumed within **middle-range theory**. Middle-range theory refers to processes of reasoning and the procedures used to identify links between specific behaviors and their material outcomes. Middle-range theory can include *ethnographic analogy* (searching the anthropological literature for discussions of specific actions and their distinctive material correlates); **ethnoarchaeology** (directly observing particular material patterns that result from specific behaviors performed by people in the course of their daily lives); and *experimental* *archaeology* (sometimes called *replication studies*, these involve the researcher in performing actions designed to reproduce patterns observed in the archaeological record). This reasoning from the present to the past can be included within **middle-level theory** in that it represents a special means for bridging the gap between high-level theory and empirical observation. Middle-range theory, however, is not tightly tethered to specific high-level theories, in that its explanations are not dependent on principles derived from those abstract formulations. Arguing that a particular configuration of bones, stone tools, and fire hearths is the result of (and explained by) meat processing at a particular place and point in time is based on a set of observations that are relatively free of assumptions specific to any high-level theory. Middle-range theory may not be unique to archaeology, but it is highly developed here because it provides a crucial link between what we find (spatial relations among objects) and what all of us, regardless of our theoretical orientations, want to know (what human behaviors caused those material patterns). It is patterns in those behaviors that we ultimately want to explain through applications of high-level theory.

In reasoning by analogy, we are not looking for exact matches between present and past actions and their material markers. Instead, documented actions and their concrete results are used to narrow the range of ancient behaviors that might have been performed at a particular place and time. These sorts of arguments are crucial to producing an important line of evidence needed to evaluate relations between *demography* (population) and *domestication* (the process of developing human control over plants and animals). They are, however, advanced with a good deal less certainty than, say, claims based on faunal and floral analyses. You could easily find yourself in the position, therefore, of being able to say with some certainty when domestication began and what was cultivated in a given area. But you might not be able to establish to everyone's satisfaction that population increases actually drove this momentous event. Because we do not directly witness the actions we want to study or the variables that affected them, archaeologists end up explaining what probably occurred by what likely happened. The results are almost invariably ambiguous (unclear) and contested (arguable, and argued about). No one should ever be convicted of a crime based on this sort of evidence. (See Chapter 8 for a detailed example of this reasoning process in the context of our research in the Naco Valley.)

Evaluating hypotheses in archaeology is certainly difficult, but it is essential to any investigation. Research must be structured, and hypothesis testing is one of the primary ways that archaeologists organize and direct their studies. We learn about the past by assessing the utility of a theory through testing hypotheses based on it. The very attempt to assign functions to buildings and numbers of people to residences, for example, leads us to explore such topics as how domestic spaces were organized and how household life was structured. Investigating such matters can illuminate aspects of ancient cultures that were previously unknown. Ultimately, it may be that we cannot say whether population numbers rose prior to domestication in a particular area or, if they did, whether such growth alone caused people to cultivate plants and/or herd animals. By striving to evaluate this hypothesis using all the lines of evidence available to us, however, we will come to understand a great deal.

At any point in time, therefore, we may not be sure that the hypothesis we propose to explain the behaviors that generated the material patterns we observe is "true." At best, we may be able to say that one particular hypothesis accounts for the data in hand better than any other hypotheses known to us. What "better than" means usually involves some estimation of whether a hypothesis can explain in greater detail and depth what is observed than can alternative propositions and whether it can do so in ways that involve the fewest unproven assumptions. This **inference to the best explanation** in archaeology means that interpretations of the past are always tentative; they are always works in progress. Any hypothesis may be replaced as new data not accounted for in it come to light. Alternatively, new hypotheses, possibly derived from novel theories, might offer explanations of the existing data that more successfully account for what is observed and predict more accurately what is yet to be found than earlier hypotheses. We will see this process repeated many times in the research we conducted in the Naco Valley (Chapters 7–9). Any hypothesis about the past should therefore be understood as the best available interpretation of a set of observations that exists at a particular moment in time.

Coexisting Theories in Archaeology

Deciding which inference to the best explanation should be adopted is made difficult in part by problems of measuring variables (like population numbers) and testing expectations about their relations outside laboratory conditions. As a result, we often have multiple, plausible theories and their hypotheses designed to explain the same phenomenon. Unable to disprove definitively one and establish the truth of the other, we have no way to declare the absolute validity of a single perspective. **Thomas Kuhn** (see sidebar) forcefully argued this position in his discussion of **paradigms** within the sciences. Paradigms comprise the overarching concepts and assumptions that guide work within a specific scientific discipline, such as chemistry, along with the methods and criteria of evaluation employed in pursuing and assessing the results of these investigations. Kuhn noted that whereas each field in the physical sciences now has its own distinctive paradigm, social science disciplines are each characterized by a variety of competing paradigms. Difficulty in testing definitively specific high-level theories through clearly stated and evaluated hypotheses is one cause of this difference between the physical and social sciences.

There is another reason, however, for the persistence of competing theories in archaeology, in particular, and the social sciences, generally. Social scientists of all stripes study patterned human behaviors, what

Thomas Kuhn

Thomas Kuhn received his PhD in physics but went on to make his major contributions to knowledge as a historian and philosopher of science. In his best-known work, *The Structure of Scientific Revolutions* (1962), Kuhn argued that knowledge about the physical world does not accumulate in a gradual and continuous process as a result of the rigorous application of scientific procedures. Instead, all research, in the physical sciences at least, is conducted within a sequence of temporally sequential, mutually incompatible paradigms. Paradigms consist of those bodies of theory, associated methods, and criteria for evaluating research results that all practitioners of a field (such as physics) share. While pursuing investigations within such a shared paradigm, scientists make great progress in answering open-ended questions posed by the generally accepted theory, employing widely used methods, and assessing the quality of their work against a set of universally acknowledged criteria. During these periods of "normal science," observations that do not match the theory's expectations gradually accumulate. Ignored at first, such anomalous findings eventually become so numerous that they have to be acknowledged. At this point, the guiding paradigm is seen as deeply flawed, and a period of "revolutionary" science ensues, during which a novel theoretical structure is formulated. Once established, this conceptual framework guides a new phase of normal science which will eventually generate the observations needed to overturn it. Some philosophers of science claim that Kuhn is refuting the objectivity of scientific knowledge. To them, if truths do not exist apart from the paradigms in which they are created, there is no basis for stating with any certainty which understandings of the world are valid and which are wrong. Kuhn denies that this was the message he intended to convey.

Emile Durkheim

Emile Durkheim rose to prominence in his native France during the late 19th and early 20th centuries. He went on to train most of the first French sociologists and to found courses of study in this discipline at some of the country's most prestigious universities. Tragically, many of his students did not survive the First World War, and he died in 1917 before the end of that conflagration. Durkheim is often identified as the "father of sociology," not only because of his role as an educator, but also for the part he played in establishing the study of society as a field distinct from other disciplines, especially psychology. There was, at the turn of the 20th century, a strong tendency to see the actions of people in groups as shaped by the desires and goals of the individuals comprising those groups. Durkheim argued that recurring patterns of collective behaviors, what he called "social facts," were not reducible to individual dispositions, but were governed by forces operating at the level of society. It was these forces that shaped individual beliefs and actions, not the other way around. Explaining why people behaved in certain ways when interacting with one another, therefore, required a science of society (sociology) distinct from a science of the individual (psychology). The explanations Durkheim offered changed throughout his career. Initially he relied on functional accounts, explaining regularities in group behaviors by demonstrating their roles in promoting social cohesion. Later he broadened the scope of his inquiry, attending to the complex ways in which people's understandings of themselves and the world around them were expressed in widely held symbols ("collective representations") that were shaped by, and helped shape, the society in which they lived. The latter approach is most clearly expressed in his book *The Elementary Forms of Religious Life* (1912). Understanding social form and continuity thus, in Durkheim's view, came to require (1) describing interpersonal interactions; and (2) grasping the ways in which these mundane dealings were imbued with emotional power through the manipulation of cultural symbols.

Emile Durkheim (see sidebar) called **social facts**. Social facts consist of actions that exhibit predictable forms, forms shaped by shared cultural expectations. They may include the ways people attend religious celebrations, cooperate in preparing fields for planting, participate in political campaigns, or start domestication. The problem for social scientists is that explaining these patterned and recurring actions requires taking account of a wide range of factors. Explanations of observed patterns in human behavior, in short, can rarely be reduced to cause-and-effect relations among a small range of variables. It is not the case that only one or another factor among genetics, nutrition, health, family structure, educational experience, and social class determines an individual's intelligence score. All of them together, combined in complex ways, have some impact on that measure. Similarly, population pressure alone most likely did not motivate people to start domesticating wild species; this variable may have been part of a more extensive suite of forces that led to the observed outcome. Social scientists, therefore, are faced with a challenging puzzle. We must use theories to narrow our focus so we can successfully study the operation of a few factors and their effects. The very behaviors we examine, however, derive from a wider range of forces than could be included in one theory.

Simplification or Distortion in Archaeological Theories

Theories successfully advance research to the extent that they provide simplified views of reality. But do theories simplify or distort reality? There is no easy answer to this. Some would argue that particular theories can identify *the most important* variables and their relations that go into shaping the events and processes being investigated. A researcher might claim, for example, that nutrition is *the* most significant of the many factors conditioning intelligence scores; or someone might say that population pressure is *the* crucial force behind domestication. Such assertions return us to the problem of deciding which claims are correct. Alternatively, we can acknowledge the complexity of human behavior, seeing different theories as complementary, non-competitive tools. Using these concepts, we can specify which *aspects* of that reality can be observed, described, and explained by using specific theories. In this view, the proliferation of theories in archaeology is not an unfortunate by-product of problems encountered in testing claims. Instead, it is an essential feature of any discipline whose members seek to understand human actions. No one theory provides a complete and adequate description or explanation of the processes being investigated: all research is inherently and inescapably incomplete. Every viable theory thus provides valuable insights from which we can all benefit.

Researchers, in this view, choose among established theories, or create new ones, as they address specific questions. Different theories, then, are variably useful in solving an assortment of problems. This is not surprising when you consider that people originally developed the concepts and relations making up any theory in an effort to answer a particular question that had not been considered significant earlier on. If, for example, everyone working on the issue of human intelligence followed a theory that stressed the causative importance of socioeconomic class, there would be a great many concepts and relations available that encouraged us to imagine how this variable affected the results of IQ tests. As valuable as such formulations might be in grasping a particular aspect of the problem, they would be virtually useless in addressing the question of how a person's nutritional status influences his or her intelligence score. If you, as an innovative researcher, wanted to deal with nutrition's impact, your first step would be to specify a new set of concepts and relations among them that were appropriate to the task. Then you would make an argument for how you think they relate to intelligence. In other words, you would have to create a novel theory to answer this question. Because human behavior is so complex, affected by so many variables, the questions we can advance about any important aspect of it, like intelligence, are numerous. Consequently, the number of social science theories designed to answer those questions will remain large, each one geared to investigating a significant but limited aspect of our field of study.

In general, therefore, researchers need intellectual tools that allow them to concentrate on certain aspects of what they study, to pinpoint variables of interest, specify their relations, and then evaluate the validity of the supposed connections. Theories provide these conceptual structures. Social scientists, including archaeologists, deploy theories for many of the same reasons their colleagues in the physical sciences, such as chemistry and biology, do. Social scientists, however, face much greater problems defining their variables and testing causal relations among them than do practitioners of the physical sciences. These difficulties result in large part from:

1. the complex interplay of factors that influence any variable we choose to study (such as IQ scores, or the domestication of plants and animals);

2. the need to measure many of these factors indirectly (such as family structure or population size);

3. our inability to isolate relations among variables in laboratory settings (although some kinds of laboratory work can shed light on aspects of both problem examples).

As a consequence, archaeologists, like social scientists generally, draw on as many different independent lines of evidence as possible in evaluating hypotheses based on their theories. We try to be as explicit as possible in describing how variables and their relations are measured. Still, we are often left with inferences to the best explanation that are subject to revision. What constitutes a "best explanation" changes as new data become available and new theories are developed to account for those findings.

Disproving theories by definitively refuting their associated hypotheses is therefore very difficult in archaeology. Researchers can easily, and in good faith, disagree about what recovered data mean and how this information relates to the question under consideration. Such uncertainty contributes to the elaboration of numerous theories in archaeology, each with its own set of adherents. Even if we could all agree on which hypotheses are right and which are wrong, however, there is reason to believe that our discipline would still entertain multiple ways of viewing the past. As noted above, the behaviors we study are products of complexly interconnected variables. Insofar as theory succeeds by focusing attention on specific aspects of reality, then no one theory could effectively take account of all the factors needed to describe and explain fully any situation. Theories, therefore, may well help us achieve insights concerning human behavior, but those insights are always partial and incomplete. The more conceptual tools we use to study the past, the more interesting and useful vantage points we have for understanding what people were doing and why they were doing it. No one of them is completely right; neither is any utterly wrong.

Theories: Fulfilling Their Promises or Self-Fulfilling Prophecies?

Up to this point, we have been circling around a very important issue. We argued that theories provide the basic concepts and relations that we use to observe. They give us the categories into which we organize data, and the basic principles by which that organization is accomplished. Attempting to explain variations in intelligence scores by differences in nutrition requires that you see the world in terms of calories, vitamins, and the composition of diets, as well as mental functions and problem-solving abilities. This is a very different world from the one perceived by someone employing a theory of socioeconomic class, which categorizes people according to income levels, what they own, and the company they keep. Such divisions are no surprise, nor need they cause alarm. Each theory is being used to cast some light on a particular feature of a complicated phenomenon.

The primary cause for concern involves the relationship between data and theory. A theory structures how data are collected, categorized, and interpreted. Those data, in turn, are used to evaluate hypotheses through which the validity of a theory is tested. If your theory conditions you to expect that nutrition plays a major role in determining intelligence, and leads you to collect information relevant to describing this link, are you predisposed from the beginning to accept this view? If you do not recognize the significance of data that support other theories because your theory does not provide concepts appropriate for identifying such variables, how can you be sure that what you see is not just what you expected to see? Is theory testing one long, drawn-out example of the self-fulfilling prophecy in which what we want to find is the only thing we ever locate?

This problem is all the more serious because it suggests that the primary advantage of theories—their ability to focus our attention by highlighting some variables and their relations while ignoring others—is also their principal drawback. Using theories in archaeology demands that we confront this problem, if only to make ourselves aware of the limits of our conceptual tools.

There are reasons for believing that the situation is not as bleak as it sounds. One way to imagine a solution to this dilemma is to think about language. Language is like a theory: it contains concepts (words) and principles specifying how those concepts are related (grammar). Early 21st-century English, for example, includes ideas about time that arrange this continuum into discrete units (seconds, minutes, hours, and so forth) and organize them into a linear, non-repeating sequence (captured in a verb structure that emphasizes distinctions among past, present, and future tenses). Now, imagine time as an ever-repeating cycle in which what happens today has occurred in the past and is fated to recur in the future. Concepts like past, present, and future are less significant in this context. Verb tenses geared to this view of time might reflect distinctions among, say, the purposes of an action rather than when in a sequence of events a particular action took place.

The point is, can you imagine time as cyclical and not linear? We guess that you have a much easier time picturing this scenario in your mind than expressing it in words. Our language is largely opposed to such a cyclical model, though something of this perspective is captured in our references to the seasons. Lacking the vocabulary and grammar to convey these relations in any detail, we find it difficult to grasp a cyclical temporal framework and harder still to talk about it. *But*, it is still possible to overcome the limits of language and imagine things and relations for which we have no words. If this is the case for language, it is all the more so for theory. Concepts and relations in theory, like words and grammar in language, facilitate perceiving some things but not others, and discussing particular connections but not others. Nevertheless, theory's control is not so absolute that it excludes making observations that do not fit existing categories. We can recognize data that defy our expectations. It is not easy to do so, and, initially, we may be at a loss for words to express just what it is we saw, but it is possible.

Copernicus may not have expected to encounter evidence that the earth orbited the sun; he may have resisted the implications of his observations for awhile but ultimately had to acknowledge that something was going on that did not match what his theory told him should be the case. On a more everyday level, people can learn languages with vocabularies and grammars that diverge markedly from those of their native tongue, geared to expressing very different views of the world and its workings. The process may be difficult, but it is realizable. Language and theory channel speech and thought, making it easier to talk about and imagine the world in certain ways, but they do not prevent us from pursuing other modes of perceiving, thinking, and talking.

Theories engage data through their hypotheses, and examples of hypothesis rejection abound in archaeology. To take but one case, most mid-20th-century researchers accepted the hypothesis that major lowland Maya centers, such as Tikal (Guatemala), Copan (Honduras), and Palenque (Mexico), were, at their peak (AD 600–900), ceremonial centers without significant numbers of permanent residents. Supporting populations, it was argued, were dispersed around these massive sites in small hamlets. Major centers were, it was believed, home only to priest-kings and their entourages and functioned as well as sites for the performance of large-scale rituals. All members of lowland Maya societies were fed by peasants who, like their descendants in the 20th century, practiced low-yield, land-intensive forms of agriculture called **swidden** or *slash-and-burn*.

This theory discouraged archaeological research into the lives of commoners and their agricultural practices. Farming and the role of peasants in food production were addressed primarily through ethnographic investigations among Maya farmers living in the lowlands of Mexico, Belize, and Guatemala. In part, this view was founded on the assumption embedded in the theory underlying the Ceremonial Center hypothesis—namely, that not much had changed in the lives of lowland Maya agriculturalists since well before the 7th century AD. Questions concerning ancient subsistence and domestic practices were best dealt with by studying contemporary "survivors" of the Maya past. Archaeology had little to add to the consideration of these topics.

What research among modern peoples could not reveal was how low-land Maya rulers orchestrated major rituals. These activities were seen as the bases of elite power and the means for tying together the natural and super-natural realms. Maya lords were driven from office during the Spanish Conquest in the 16th century, and little was known about their beliefs and practices. Archaeology was the primary means by which this lost aspect of the past could be reconstructed. Investigators, therefore, focused their attention on studying the imposing buildings and monuments that dominate major sites. Most of these buildings and artworks played important roles in elite religious cults; some constructions served as residences for high-ranking nobles.

Research guided by these ideas was fruitful, yielding many new insights into the nature of lowland Maya life, especially as practiced by the aristocracy from AD 600 to 900. Ironically, these investigations also undermined the very hypothesis that shaped them. As work at lowland Maya centers intensified, it became harder and harder to avoid noticing the large number of residences packed around the monumental buildings that were the focus of archaeological attention. Small constructions were initially ignored because they did not fit the prevailing empty-ceremonial-center hypothesis, but eventually investigators started mapping all buildings at a site, regardless of their size. Although archaeologists continued to debate exactly how many people lived in these smaller buildings, there was no denying that the numbers were considerable. Such dense population concentrations were certainly not predicted by the Ceremonial Center hypothesis. They also lacked modern analogues in the tropical Central American lowlands, where cities and towns are rare. Contemporary agricultural practices that sustain widely spread-out modern Maya populations would not have produced enough food to support the numerous densely occupied centers of AD 600–900. Assumptions of unchanging cultural and economic practices lasting a thousand years or more were now called into question. As a result, archaeologists ushered in a new wave of projects specifically designed to reconstruct prehistoric agricultural practices and the lifestyles of the humble and, up to now, anonymous commoners. Rejection of the Ceremonial Center hypothesis required construction of new middle-level theories to direct research. This process is still very much ongoing.

The demise of the Ceremonial Center hypothesis, slow in coming as it was, is a good example of how inferences to the best explanation change. Some researchers had begun questioning this view back in the 1930s, but these pioneers were largely ignored because their evidence for large ancient populations was not strong enough to overcome the established precepts of so powerful a perspective. Still, that interpretive structure was eventually toppled by the gradual accumulation of observations that highlighted flaws in what was then considered the "best explanation" of observed findings. These observations were made while doing work guided by the conceptual framework they questioned. More striking still, the observations were made even though the prevailing hypothesis did not have concepts appropriate for describing and explaining the recently found dense concentrations of commoner residences.

If theory, operating through hypotheses, controlled perception absolutely, theory would never change to account for anomalous—that is, unexpected or contradictory—findings. Observations that did not make sense in the context of a theory simply would be explained away or ignored. The above example leads us to question such a simplistic view of the relationship between theory and data. The concepts and relations that guide our work do exert powerful influences on what we see and what we think is going on. In a field like archaeology, where measuring relevant variables and testing their relations usually yields ambiguous results, these influences are particularly strong and hard to overturn. Early doubters of the Ceremonial Center hypothesis could not conduct experiments to test its validity. All they could do was point to what evidence existed for commoner settlement at major sites. Initially, this material could be understood in several different ways; those researchers who did not doubt the ceremonial center perspective selected interpretations that matched the positions of the dominant viewpoint. Arguments could, and did, come about, but as long as the data did not definitively contradict accepted understandings, the Ceremonial Center hypothesis was safe. As the example illustrates, however, uncertainty concerning the significance of a few pieces of data may be resolved by a larger body of observations. The central point is that, hard and protracted as the process may be, hypotheses, and the theories that give rise to them, are ultimately refutable. This is the case even if the data used to challenge a hypothesis are collected by the very researchers who subscribe to the perspective under evaluation.

Summary

Where have we arrived after this brief review of observation, description, and explanation? At the least, we should be able to acknowledge that these processes, which we take so much for granted in daily life, are actually very complex. Further, a world that bombards us constantly with a wide array of sensory inputs would be impossible to navigate without filtering all that can be seen into a manageable number of observations. The conceptual framework that screens input also organizes those observations into an intelligible, predictable structure. World views serve this invaluable purpose for all of us. The unexamined nature of their rules and ideas and our willingness to accept their validity on faith make these pervasive models unsuitable—not for daily life, but for systematic studies of processes and relations that operate in various times and portions of the globe (and beyond, as in the case of astronomy). Doing systematic research requires substituting theories for world views. Theories perform many of the same services as their everyday cousins but provide a sounder foundation for knowledge. A theory provides concepts and principles that are clearly and openly stated, and we are required to assess a theory's validity.

The last point means that theories must be repeatedly tested against data to see how well they describe and explain what really happens. Acceptance comes only after the evaluation process has been going on for a long time, after many hypotheses have been assessed, and even then questions about any theory's validity should linger. Archaeological theories, like all conceptual schemes in the social sciences, are difficult to test in ways that yield results accepted by the majority of researchers in the field. This problem, coupled with the complexity of the phenomena we study (human behavior as it occurred in many times and places), contributes to a proliferation of theories, each describing and explaining aspects of the material being examined. We can choose to bemoan such "conceptual anarchy." Alternatively, and more productively, we can acknowledge that different theories provide complementary ways to study human behavior. Each theory is a tool suited to making sense of a specific aspect of a very complex reality. As with any implement, you choose one to perform a task for which it is appropriate. When excavating a burial, you would be well advised to put away the shovel and get out the dental picks, spoons, and brushes. There is no point questioning the need for shovels or brushes; they each have their uses. Similarly, theories are developed to help answer particular sorts of questions. By their very nature, they can only direct our attention to limited aspects of reality. Consequently, when choosing theories, as in selecting tools, we must be aware of what purposes they serve.

But we must still insist that theories be answerable to data. By using multiple lines of evidence, we can gradually restrict the number of plausible interpretations of any past set of events. Some of the data we use to evaluate theories will be admirably reliable and independent of the theory being assessed (such as carbon-14 dating). Some, perhaps most, will be problematic in nature, their relevance and independence being uncertain and open to debate. The more lines of evidence that are brought to bear on a hypothesis derived from a theory, however, the clearer will be our sense of that theory's utility. Ironically, when we use all the evidence at our disposal to reject our guiding theory, we will have the greatest confidence that we are doing our jobs right and gaining a more reliable understanding of the past. Each time we accomplish this feat, we assert that, hard as they can be to interpret, archaeological data do effectively constrain our understanding of how our predecessors lived.

But how are high-level theories constructed in archaeology? What goes into making these conceptual schemes and how are they applied in studying ancient human behavior? We turn to these considerations in the next two chapters.

Further Reading

Mesoamerica, General Discussions

Becker, M.
1979   Priests, Peasants and Ceremonial Centers: The Intellectual History of a Model. In *Maya Archaeology and Ethnohistory*, ed. N. Hammond and G. Willey, pp. 3–20. Austin: University of Texas Press.

Becker summarizes here the history of the Ceremonial Center hypothesis that we referred to in this chapter.

Morley, S. G.
1946   *The Ancient Maya*. Stanford, CA: Stanford University Press.

This volume will give you a good idea of how archaeologists viewed lowland Maya prehistory at the middle of the 20th century. It has the advantage of having been updated over the years, major revisions being written by George Brainerd (1983) and Robert Sharer (beginning in 1994), all titled *The Ancient Maya* and published by Stanford University Press. Skimming these different versions will give you a good sense of how views of lowland Maya prehistory, including the Ceremonial Center hypothesis, have changed.

Theory, General Discussions

Dark, K.
1995   *Theoretical Archaeology*. Ithaca, NY: Cornell University Press.

Dark offers another perspective on theory in archaeology.

Durkheim, E.
  2008   *The Elementary Forms of Religious Life*. Oxford: Oxford University Press (originally published in 1912).
          In this book, Durkheim examines how religious sentiments and symbols function to infuse social norms and values with emotional power, thereby enhancing people's commitment to rules that might otherwise seem restrictive and burdensome. Society, in this view, is transformed through religion from a collection of people into a moral community willing to subordinate individual interest in the name of the common good.

Hansen, M., and J. Kelley
  1989   Inference to the Best Explanation in Archaeology. In *Critical Traditions in Contemporary Archaeology*, ed. V. Pinsky and A. Wylie., pp. 14–17. Cambridge: Cambridge University Press.
          This article recounts how the concept of inference to the best explanation can be applied in archaeological settings.

Kehoe, A.
  2008   *Controversies in Archaeology*. Walnut Creek, CA: Left Coast Press, Inc.
          The concept of inference to the best explanation used here was drawn from this review of how archaeologists evaluate claims about the past.

Kuhn, T.
  1962   *The Structure of Scientific Revolutions*. Chicago: University of Chicago Press.
          Kuhn's discussion of paradigms in this book was widely influential in considerations of theory within and beyond the physical sciences. His contention that observations are strongly conditioned by the theory the investigator espouses challenged Positivist accounts that saw scientific knowledge as accumulating gradually and continuously through objective applications of the scientific method.

Praetzellis, A.
  2000   *Death by Theory: A Tale of Mystery and Archaeological Theory*. Walnut Creek, CA: AltaMira Press.
          Praetzellis provides another overview of archaeological theory, this time written in the form of a mystery.

Salmon, M.
  1982   *Philosophy and Archaeology*. New York: Academic Press.
          Salmon outlines a systematic approach to the structure of theory in archaeology, focusing on the nature of the conceptual frameworks used in the field (especially those related to Processual archaeology) and the means of evaluating hypotheses based on those theories.

Wylie, A.
  2002   *Thinking with Things: Essays in the Philosophy of Archaeology*. Berkeley: University of California Press.

  This collection brings together essays written by one of the pre-eminent philosophers of science working in archaeology. She provides an overview of the major debates in archaeological theory along with suggestions as to how they might be resolved. Chapters 11–16, in particular, deal with questions of archaeological explanation, while Chapter 9 summarizes arguments concerning analogic reasoning in archaeology.

Theory, Middle-Range and Analogy

Binford, L.
  1981   *Bones: Ancient Men and Modern Myths*. New York: Academic Press.

  This book, which reviews aspects of middle-range theory, was written by the scholar who played a major role in introducing the concept.

Rabb, L., and A. Goodyear
  1984   Middle Range Theory in Archaeology: A Critical Review of Origins and Applications. *American Antiquity* 49:255–268.

  Rabb and Goodyear consider how middle-range theory figures in archaeological interpretations. Their essay appeared at a point when these issues were being much debated by researchers in the field.

Schiffer, M.
  1976   *Behavioral Archaeology*. New York: Academic Press
  1987   *Formation Processes of the Archaeological Record*. Albuquerque: University of New Mexico Press.

  In these two volumes, Schiffer lays out a detailed consideration of the various human- and natural-caused processes that shape the material patterning observed at archaeological sites. This work in middle-level theory was designed to help translate what was found archaeologically into statements about ancient behavior.

Yellen, J.
  1977   *Archaeological Approaches to the Present*. New York: Academic Press.

  Yellen considers the different uses of analogy in interpreting the remains of past behaviors.

Theory, Processual

Watson, P. J., S. LeBlanc, and C. Redman
  1984   *Archaeological Explanation: The Scientific Method in Archaeology*. New York: Columbia University Press.

  Watson and her colleagues provide here a clear and highly influential call for practicing archaeology as a science.

CHAPTER 3

DIMENSIONS OF THEORY IN ARCHAEOLOGY

Introduction

I N THIS CHAPTER , WE ADVANCE THE ARGUMENT that how archaeologists craft their high-level theories depends in large part on the answers they give to three questions:

1. What causes human behavior?

2. How much free will do people exercise in determining their actions?

3. Are the events and developments observed in one area at a particular moment conditioned by the action of general principles, or are they the product of historical processes unique to that society and time period?

There is no one correct response to these queries, nor do the answers fit easily within discrete categories. Rather, views on causation, free will, and general principles tend to fall out along continuums of variation whose end points are defined by extreme positions. For the purposes of this discussion, however, we review some of the more common selections archaeologists have made from these continuums. Table 3.1 summarizes these much-used approaches to issues of causation, free will, and the applicability of general behavioral principles. How the choices are combined into coherent theories is taken up in Chapter 4.

Table 3.1. Summary of the major approaches to answering the general questions addressed in the construction of archaeological theory

QUESTIONS OF:	SUMMARY ANSWERS IN TERMS OF:
Causation	**Materialism**: The physical conditions of life play the primary roles in determining all individual behavior. **Symbolic**: People's actions are motivated by their understandings of the world and their place in it; these understandings arise from individuals' regular interactions with culturally determined structures of meaning. **Political**: Human behavior is everywhere is driven by contests over material resources that are essential to success in power struggles waged among factions within a society.
Free will	**Structural determinism**: Individual actions are determined by factors operating beyond direct human control and, often, even beyond human understanding. **Agency**: People engage in a recursive relation with structure, employing, and sometimes changing, its principles in the course of these dealings.
General principles	**Generalizing approaches**: Human behavior results from the actions of forces that have similar effects in all times and places. **Particularizing approaches**: Human behavior is determined by factors that are unique to specific cultures at particular moments in their histories.

Making a Theory

Archaeologists are active participants in broad social science debates. As such, many of our theories are inspired by the work of our colleagues in other fields. There is nothing unusual about this interdisciplinary borrowing. We are all involved in trying to understand human behavior in its full variety, and we do well to pay attention to what our associates in related disciplines have to say. How we answer the questions listed above, therefore, is strongly related to how other social scientists have dealt with the same issues. The scholars from whom we have borrowed the most often are cultural anthropologists. The overlap in interests between cultural anthropology and archaeology is considerable. Practitioners of both fields deal with patterned human behavior, usually among non-Western peoples, though the time scales involved and the methods used are very different. In addition, cultural anthropologists and archaeologists are frequently members of the same anthropology departments in the United States (although this is not the case in other parts of the world), giving them ample chances to talk with each other. The discussion of theory formation that follows, therefore, treads in that venerable tradition of borrowing examples and inspiration from cultural anthropology.

Causation

Issues of causation deal with the question, Why do people behave as they do? The answers tend to stress material, symbolic, or political factors of causation. Materialists, as their name implies, contend that the tangible, physical conditions of life play the *major* roles in determining how we act at any given moment and why those patterns of behavior change in specific ways through time. Archaeological interpretations commonly stress the material characteristics of the physical environment, such as climate, soil fertility, and rainfall. They might also take account of features of our genetic structure, with behaviors in this case determined by the need to promote the passage of our genes into future generations (see the references grouped under "Theory, Evolutionary Archaeology" for examples of this approach).

We need not be consciously aware of the impact these conditions have on our lives; they are influential regardless of whether we acknowledge them or not. This disconnect between consciousness and causation is explained by the argument that we are not aware of the real reasons for why we do what we do: we are too close to our actions, and our world views fail to provide the analytical distance needed to grasp the real reasons for our actions. Outside observers, operating with concepts and theories refined over many hundreds of hours of observing us and others, have the perspective and specialized knowledge to make sense of our behaviors. We definitely have reasons for what we do, but the explicit explanations that we rattle off do not get to the heart of the matter: they are stories we tell ourselves to make our lives seem logical. Our conscious motivations and desires, therefore, do not necessarily drive our actions in a direct way. The outside observer listens to our tales critically, explaining our actions in ways that make sense to her or him, using terms that may well have no counterparts in our language. This is the **etic** point of view, in which the observer sees us more clearly than we see ourselves.

Materialist perspectives also tend to be utilitarian. That is, a behavior can be explained when it is shown to meet a need related to life's material conditions. For example, **Roy Rappaport** (see sidebar) conducted an ingenious, elegant materialist analysis of the relations among pigs, ritual, and war in the late 20th-century New Guinea highlands. Here, among populations of Tsembaga Maring, Rappaport found that warfare between neighboring groups was triggered, in part, by growth in the number of pigs they were raising. When the pig numbers reached the point where they could no longer be easily sustained by the environment, tensions arose. Pigs were now rooting around in peoples' gardens, eating food intended for family members. This led to hostilities among people in different settlements. Rituals associated with war involved the slaughter of pigs: those preparing to fight would eat the meat. These rites fulfilled the double function of reducing the number of pigs destroying gardens while also providing a high-quality source of protein to those who needed it most—that is, the warriors who required the energy to carry them through the struggle ahead. Peace-making ceremonies also required killing numerous pigs to be eaten in large-scale feasts. By the end of this war-and-ritual cycle, pig populations would have dropped to such a low level that they no longer threatened the environment. When people did not have to deal with rogue, rampaging pigs, they could relax and the situation would calm down. The cycle was ready to begin again.

Roy Rappaport

Roy Rappaport came late to anthropology at the age of 37. Beginning in 1963 with his dissertation research among the Tsembaga Maring of highland New Guinea, Rappaport devoted much of his career to studying the role of ritual in regulating people's relations with one another and with their natural environments. Ritual, the stylized expression and acting out of sacred propositions, had previously been largely ignored by materialist anthropologists. Seen as pertaining to the realm of ideas, religion and the activities associated with it were usually viewed as secondary to more causally important relations among technology, demography, and those aspects of the physical setting to which a population was adapting. Rappaport countered that it was through ritual that energy flows crucial to a group's survival could be monitored and controlled by the society as a whole. Far from being peripheral to the crucial (from a materialist perspective) business of adapting to the physical environment, ritual could be central to that project. Rappaport went on to theorize more generally about how rituals acted to preserve the integrity of cultural systems. In this work, he extended his analysis of ritual's functions in promoting adaptation to include consideration of how religious observances might encourage cultural continuity by reducing the ambiguity introduced into human relations by the advent of language. Rappaport argued that the flexibility and versatility of language make lying possible, thereby threatening the feelings of mutual trust on which all social relations are based. Ritual, with its invariant sets of actions and prayers, codifies certain basic truths as sacred and unchanging. These shared premises comprise a set of basic assumptions on which people can rely in their dealings with one another. Such trust helps make life predictable and comprehensible, thus ensuring a degree of cultural continuity and equilibrium.

Notice what Rappaport has done. He has framed a hypothesis, informed by materialist principles, which links seemingly unrelated forces and events—pig population growth, warfare, and rituals—into a coherent adaptive system through which Tsembaga Maring populations successfully adjusted to their environment. They fought and participated in rituals *because of* the adaptive consequences of these actions. If asked, the Tsembaga Maring would probably laugh at the suggestion that their sacred ceremonies had anything to do with keeping pig numbers at environmentally safe levels. They have their own explanations for what they do. In the etic perspective, however, the observer has the last word.

As the Tsembaga Maring case suggests, materialists also tend to stress action over thought in explaining human behavior. If we do not know the real reasons underlying our actions, if we behave in ways that fulfill functions of which we are largely unaware, then observing what we *do* is more important for research than finding out what we *think* about it. It is the observable consequences of an action that are of prime importance. Rituals kill pigs that are becoming too numerous. Participants may imagine that these pig sacrifices appease ancestors, but the fact is that they reduce pig numbers. Materialists, therefore, lean toward quantitative approaches. Significant patterns in human action are identified by counting and correlating. If you want to know whether killing pigs during rituals reduces nutritional stresses, then you need to know how many pigs are killed, when they are dispatched, who eats them, how much is consumed by different members of the population, and what is the nutritional value of the pigs. Answering these questions requires the use of numbers.

By contrast, those championing a symbolic approach argue for the causal primacy of motivation: people do what they do *not* because they are driven by unseen forces, but because they feel it is in their best interests to pursue specific courses of action. Motivation derives from the sense people make of the world and their place in it. This perception comes from the meaning we attribute to all aspects of our surroundings, physical and artificial. Life is therefore a dense network, or web, of **symbols**—things to which we attribute significance. Everything around us is a symbol, so everything is meaningful. These symbols, in various combinations in various settings, bring about certain feelings and dispositions that, in turn, encourage specific actions and discourage others.

When entering a house of worship—say, a synagogue, mosque, or church—you know what sorts of behaviors are expected and which are considered inappropriate, based on the symbols you see all around you.

How we act, therefore, is determined by the structure of our symbolic environment. Participants in the same culture share similar principles for perceiving and understanding that symbolic system. They therefore tend to behave in comparable ways when confronted with the same symbolic cues.

Symbolism turns materialism on its head. The material conditions of life exercise authority over human behavior not through forces separate from human consciousness, but precisely because we attribute significance to them: we make them symbols. An event is explained when we identify two things:

1. its place within the complex suite of meaningful symbols;

2. the distinctive logic of the world view that structures those symbols.

This is sometimes called an **emic** perspective—that is, the view from within a culture. People do not eat pigs because they need an infusion of protein. That may be an unintended effect of their rituals, but it is not their cause; it does not explain why they do it. Rather, people eat pigs because they assign significance to those animals. Among groups of Tsembaga Maring who occupied the New Guinea highlands in the mid- to late 20th century, the meanings attributed to pigs were reinforced by the wide array of other symbols that accompanied their ritual slaughter and consumption.

In symbolist approaches, thought is privileged over action; what people think is at least as important, if not more so, than what they do. Consequently, qualitative data are often more important in symbolic perspectives than quantitative information. If explanation depends on getting at meaning, then you have to build up a picture of what symbols people use and how they perceive them.

Those favoring political explanations of human behavior argue that contests over **power**—the ability to direct the actions of others or to resist such efforts—are root causes of human behavior. We do what we do because we are either seeking advantage for ourselves and our associates, or because we are contesting the efforts of others who are pursuing such gain. Life is a struggle in which material and ideological factors are not so much causes of action as they are the weapons of choice.

Power operates at several levels, from the ability of individual actors to define and accomplish their goals to the broader economic, political, and ideological structures in which those decisions are made and aspirations take shape. Archaeologists, like social scientists generally, have tended to be interested primarily in the structural aspects of power, those overarching frameworks that encourage some actions while discouraging others. This is because we are mostly concerned with patterning in human actions. Understanding why a great many people seem to be making, or to have made, similar choices requires looking at the factors that constrain and enable those decisions. Going to college is an expression of power; you are taking steps to achieve an objective (e.g., to further your education). That you are not alone in making the same decision suggests that there are potent structural forces at work that encourage continuing studies after high school. The fact that most higher-paying jobs in our capitalist-based economy require a college degree may be but one factor in the constellation of structural variables that condition so many to enroll in colleges and universities. Social scientists would want to know how those structural factors combine to encourage so many people to exercise the power to choose college. They would also be interested in the associated variables that discourage many others from making the same decision. (See Chapter 9 for a discussion of how Practice theory reverses this top-down emphasis by considering the ways in which individual power and structural power are related.)

Much research on questions of power is inspired by quite diverse Marxist writings. In general, Marxist political theories hold that all societies are divided among factions. Members of these groups unite in common cause to secure the physical resources needed for survival by organizing themselves to employ existing technology effectively. Just owning a big plot of land on which you can grow crops is of little benefit if you cannot get others to cooperate with you on a regular and predictable basis in planting, weeding, and harvesting. You need to manipulate both the physical resources and the social means of acquiring those assets.

But other members of your society also seek to achieve the same ends; at the very least, they want some of that land and would prefer that you work for them rather than the other way around. So, life is a continuing contest in which people scheme to capture material assets, to organize the labor to convert them into usable forms, such as food and tools, and to institutionalize these arrangements. In many cases, these contests result in a structure in which power, and the resources needed to achieve it, are widely dispersed. In some instances, enterprising competitors manage to monopolize some set of generally needed materials. With this monopoly, they can forge relations that effectively funnel those goods to them and not to others. Under such circumstances, hierarchical structures take shape, not because they meet a basic need or because they are embedded within symbolically meaningful environments, but because they are advantageous to some.

The materialist cast in most political theories is balanced by an emphasis on **ideology**. Variably defined, ideology generally refers to beliefs shared by members of a society that explain the world and the positions of people within it. In symbolic perspectives, such world views are important sources of action and its interpretation; but to political theorists, they are often another means people use to achieve or question domination. This is because ideologies have political content. As expressed through various tangible and intangible symbols, they can be used to hide existing inequalities. This is accomplished by denying the existence of inequities or legitimizing such distinctions by making them appear to be fair, inevitable, and/or blessed by the supernatural: monarchs rule by divine right; the rich earned their privileges by dint of hard work; the poor will always be with us; seek not riches in this life, but look for great rewards in the next. In this sense, ideologies and the symbols that make them physically visible are used by those in power to create structures that preserve the status quo and, not incidentally, the privileges of those who benefit most from current arrangements. Symbols can also be used in revolutionary movements to change the structure by questioning and, possibly, overthrowing those in power. In either case, political theorists argue that what people do and believe is strongly conditioned by the power relations that affect their existence. Those realities, which constitute a society's political structure, are always characterized by competition, inequality, and their associated tensions. When looking at that pig feast in the New Guinea highlands, the primary question to political theorists is not what physical needs are being met, or what pigs mean to those involved, but who benefits from this ritual and who loses? How are pigs, as food and symbols, being manipulated to the advantage of some and the disadvantage of others? Answer that question and, according to political theorists, you will have identified the salient features of a political structure that explains this rite.

There is a utilitarian strain to political arguments: events happen to accomplish purposes. They are explained when those purposes, and how the events function to achieve them, are revealed. But the objectives are political and not dictated solely by the material conditions of life. There is also a concern with meaning, though symbols and world views are shaped by power struggles. Quantitative and qualitative data, therefore, are often relevant to political theories because what people do and what they believe are both important in competitions for power. Etic and emic viewpoints can thus be combined in political theories, though the power differentials and contests shaping people's lives exist largely beyond the awareness of those involved. Ultimately, the outside observer is the arbiter of what is causally significant and what is not.

Free Will vs. Overpowering Force

Running independently of the materialist/symbolist/political triad is an approach that contrasts theories stressing **structural** forces of causation with those that emphasize the relatively free action of individuals and groups. We have already discussed how studies of power in the social sciences have tended to emphasize structural forces in explaining individual decisions and actions. Adaptation to the environment or the pervasive influence of dominant world views are also structural processes cited as important by different theorists in shaping human action. Proponents of such approaches need not agree on what drives history, but they do concur that people are more made by, than make, that history. We act within constraints that, in extreme examples of this view, make free will an illusion.

Structural theories tended to dominate early anthropological and archaeological thought and are still common today. Much of the theoretical debate in these fields throughout the 20th century, in fact, was over what factors dominate the structures channeling human behavior. The power of these structures was not in doubt. Roy Rappaport's study of the Tsembaga Maring exemplifies a hypothesis based on a structural theory: people do what is necessary to maintain a balance among pig numbers and environmental variables and have relatively little choice in the matter.

Agency is described in various ways, but most definitions specify that it is the potential that people have to define and achieve their goals. Agency theorists acknowledge that individuals act within structures that are not of their creation. Where they diverge from structural theorists is in the importance they attribute to the innovative ways "agents"—or people making (conscious or unconscious) choices—work within these constraints to secure objectives. It is by manipulating the system to obtain short-term gains that relations within the world of ideas, power, and materials are constructed. This manipulation can also lead to structural change through small differences carried forward through time. Transformations resulting from such actions often have surprising consequences, in part because no agent is ever fully aware of how his or her behaviors relate to a diversity of structural factors, ranging from features of the physical environment to economic, social, and political processes operating over various spatial scales. Actions taken in specific places may well initiate changes that cascade out in multiple and unexpected directions. Life can be seen as one long, unfolding accident taking place within a set of constraints called *structure*.

For example, Protestant leaders in Scotland beginning in the late 17th century strongly promoted literacy so that people of all ranks could read the Bible. They were very successful in their efforts, and soon a great many men and women could read. So many potential readers created a market for books, spurring the appearance of publishing houses. Not surprisingly, these booksellers did not just print Bibles. Instead, they sold a variety of secular as well as sacred texts; many of the secular works actually questioned the literal interpretation of the Bible put forward by the ministers who initiated the literacy crusade. Seeking to create a society founded on careful reading of the Scriptures, these religious leaders inadvertently helped to lay the seeds for the Scottish Enlightenment in the 18th century. Leading lights of this movement, such as David Hume and Adam Smith, did much to undermine a view of the world founded on religion, replacing it with a secular approach to knowledge. Life does not always work out as planned.

Agency theory does not signal a return to the "Great Person" approach to understanding human behavior. Larger-than-life individuals such as Napoleon and Julius Caesar are not looked upon as shapers of human destiny. Instead, it is the actions of people of all ranks, many of whom remain largely anonymous, that determine the course of culture change. When Agency theorists refer to individual actions, the people they talk about are often generic representations of men and women, young and old, rulers and followers, rich and poor. We may not always be able to identify their specific actions but can, we hope, see the accumulated effects of what these people did.

Those who adopt the principles of Agency theory have another question to answer: which people are most influential in shaping history? Early Agency theories privileged the actions of elites in causing social, cultural, and political change. In the last decade or so, theories have appeared that stress the power of the supposedly disenfranchised to create their history. There is no reason to think, however, that *either* lords *or* commoners play the largest role in culture change. As in the case cited above, religious elites (who also exercised considerable secular power at the time) drove culture change in 17th-century Scotland by mandating the teaching of reading and writing to a much broader range of the population than had been given this opportunity in earlier centuries. It was what their subordinates did with that knowledge, however, that changed the course of Scottish history. In the process, elites and commoners, together, if not in complete agreement, created a new, increasingly secular political, economic, and symbolic structure that none of them imagined at the start of the process. This structure, in turn, provided new conditions for the expression of individual agency. (See the discussion of Practice theory in Chapter 9 for another take on relations between structure and agency.)

It may all come down to a question of emphasis. Structural theories stress the power of overwhelming forces to direct human action. People kill pigs in the New Guinea highlands because they need to reduce the number of these animals and get some high-quality protein—end of story. Agency theories look at how people, operating within a structure of pig overpopulation in a tropical highland environment, create strategies to cope with that problem, strategies that involve warfare and certain kinds of rituals.

Generalizing vs. Particularizing Approaches

Archaeologists who emphasize a generalizing approach to studying the past seek to identify principles of human behavior that are not restricted to specific times and places. The underlying assumption here is that people tend to react to similar stimuli in similar ways. In addition, under specifiable conditions, certain predictable results are likely, if not inevitable. People, unlike gas particles, are cantankerous and willful, not to mention self-reflective, and so are never completely predictable. We can therefore state that certain actions or developments are more probable than others under certain conditions, even if we cannot claim that they must occur.

Human behavior in this approach is knowable, operates within certain broad restrictions, and, hence, follows specifiable channels that repeat in historically unrelated sequences. Such approaches gained prominence in the Enlightenment from the 17th century onward and underpin much work done in archaeology. The materialist explanation of Tsembaga Maring behavior cited earlier assumes that people act in ways that guarantee their survival. Adaptation to the environment is thus a general precept that can be used to explain human behavior in all times and places. The Tsembaga Maring cycle of pig demographics, conflict, and ritual is but a specific acting out of this overarching principle.

Those opposed to this view argue that each culture is sufficiently different, its historical circumstances sufficiently distinctive, that generalization is, at best, futile, and at worst, misleading. Any similarities in the appearances or developments of particular cultures and societies are superficial, obscuring the true differences that lurk beneath. Such particularism is frequently based on the previously mentioned emic position that people act for reasons that they understand, and those reasons are invariably culturally and historically specific. This is because meaning is highly variable, members of no two cultures defining the world, its contents, and processes, in the same ways. Hence, what people think and do will be driven by complex, symbolically rich sets of cues that are unique to their particular cultures at specific points in time. What motivations drive a 21st-century banker to build a mansion and an 8th-century Maya lord to erect a palace are therefore very different urges that might be misleadingly characterized as the same Edifice Complex.

Summary

Theories, therefore, are shaped by concepts and relations drawn from these three continuums. As you build a theory, you decide what factors exercise the greatest influence on human behavior (material, symbolic, or political), how much freedom people enjoy in shaping their culture, and whether you can draw on, and are looking for, general principles of human action or are insisting that specific sets of behaviors be understood in their own unique terms. It is from such elements that broad theoretical traditions are built. The next chapter outlines several of those influential approaches.

Further Reading

Case Studies Cited in the Text (Non-Archaeological)

Herman, A.
2001   *How the Scots Invented the World*. New York: Three Rivers Press.
        The example of how the literacy program initiated by Presbyterian ministers inadvertently contributed to the advent of the Scottish Enlightenment is drawn from this book.

Rappaport, R.
1968   *Pigs for the Ancestors: Ritual in the Ecology of a New Guinea People*. New Haven, CT: Yale University Press.
        This is the source for the example of the Tsembaga Maring's complex relations with their pigs. It is an elegant exposition of materialist principles in practice.

Theory, Evolutionary Archaeology

Barton, C., and G. Clark

1997 Evolutionary Theory in Archaeological Explanation. In *Rediscovering Darwin: Evolutionary Theory and Archaeological Explanation*, ed. C. Barton and G. Clark, pp. 3–15. Arlington, VA: Archaeological Papers of the American Anthropological Association, No. 7.

This essay summarizes the basic premises of Evolutionary archaeology, an approach that draws heavily and directly on processes specified in the synthetic theory of biological evolution. We do not address Evolutionary archaeology here, as it does not figure prominently in the case studies. Yet this school constitutes an important approach to the past, and you could productively start here for an examination of the topic.

Dunnell, R.

1982 Evolutionary Theory and Archaeology. In *Advances in Archaeological Method and Theory: Selections from Volumes 1–4*, ed. M. Schiffer, pp. 35–99. New York: Academic Press.

This is one of the seminal statements of Evolutionary archaeology by a scholar who was central to the perspective's creation.

Theory, General Discussions

Flannery, K., ed.

1986 *Guila Naquitz: Archaic Foraging and Early Agriculture in Oaxaca, Mexico*. New York: Academic Press.

There is no doubt that it is difficult to discern the theory underlying this detailed discussion of the evidence for early domestication in the valley of Oaxaca. For our purposes, we suggest skipping to the concluding chapter, written by Flannery. Here he discusses the general nature of theory in archaeology in a clear and engaging manner.

Geertz, C.

1973 *The Interpretation of Culture: Selected Essays by Clifford Geertz*. New York: Basic Books, Inc.

These essays are seminal statements by an anthropologist who was among the leaders in articulating the relations among symbols, culture, and human action. See especially the article "Thick Description: Toward an Interpretive Theory of Culture" for a synopsis of Geertz' s views.

Robb, C.

1998 The Archaeology of Symbols. *Annual Review of Anthropology* 27: 329–346.

This is a comprehensive account of different archaeological approaches to the study of symbols.

Wolf, E.

1982   *Europe and the People without History*. Berkeley: University of California Press.

Wolf considers here capitalism's impact on cultures around the world, highlighting the various spatial and temporal scales over which power operates and influences cultural development. Though inspired by Marxist principles, the book might be read as an alternative to Immanuel Wallerstein's World Systems theory.

1990   Facing Power—Old Insights, New Questions. *American Anthropologist* 92:586–596.

This essay summarizes the different levels of power to which anthropologists and archaeologists might fruitfully pay attention.

Theory, Interpretivist

Hodder, I.

1992   *Theory and Practice in Archaeology*. New York: Routledge.

The essays in this collection, all by the editor, outline the relation between data and theory understood as a "hermeneutic spiral." Hodder's argument is founded on an Interpretivist approach to understanding prehistory, and he contrasts this with the hypothesis-testing model usually associated with Processualism. Hodder's Chapter 15 presents a particularly clear example of his approach.

Hodder, I., ed.

1982   *Symbolic and Structural Archaeology*. Cambridge: Cambridge University Press.

These essays translate the ethnographic concern with symbols, and their importance in guiding human behavior, to archaeological contexts.

Hodder, I., and S. Hutson

2003   *Reading the Past: Current Approaches to Interpretation in Archaeology*. 3rd edition. Cambridge: Cambridge University Press.

This review of archaeological theory stresses the importance of agency and meaning in understanding the past as well as the distinctiveness of each culture.

Theory, Marxist

Kohl, P.

1981   Materialist Approaches in Prehistory. *Annual Review of Anthropology* 10:89–118.

Kohl reviews the different forms materialism has taken in archaeology, with an emphasis on Marxist-inspired approaches to studying the past.

McGuire, R.
  1992   *A Marxist Archaeology*. New York: Academic Press.
         McGuire provides a comprehensive look at the use of Marxist principles in archaeological interpretation.

O'Laughlin, B.
  1975   Marxist Approaches in Anthropology. *Annual Review of Anthropology* 4:341–370.
         O'Laughlin's strong statement of Marxist interpretive principles was published when this perspective was finding increasing acceptance among anthropologists in the United States.

Patterson, T.
  2003   *Marx's Ghost: Conversations with Archaeologists*. Oxford: Berg.
         This broad-ranging consideration of Marx's influences on archaeology is written by a scholar well versed in Marxist scholarship.

Theory, Practice

Dobres, M., and J. Robb, eds.
  2000   *Agency in Archaeology* Routledge: London.
         Reading this collection of essays will give you a good sense of how agency has been incorporated in archaeological research.

Dornan, J.
  2002   Agency and Archaeology: Past, Present, and Future Directions. *Journal of Archaeological Method and Theory* 9:303–329.
         Dornan provides a helpful review of how Agency theory was applied in archaeology at the turn of the 21st century.

Ortner, S.
  1984   Theory in Anthropology since the Sixties. *Comparative Studies in Society and History* 26:126–166.
         This overview of changes in anthropological thought appeared during a crucial interval in theory development; the essay also provides a clear introduction to Practice theory.

CHAPTER 4

PUTTING THEORIES TOGETHER: ARCHAEOLOGICAL SCHOOLS

Introduction

OUR FIRST EXPOSURE TO ARCHAEOLOGICAL THEORY in courses and texts is often organized around **schools of thought**. Schools of thought are broad conceptual structures that comprise more or less coherent approaches to understanding human behavior combining specific choices made along the continuums outlined in Chapter 3, together with methods of data gathering appropriate to these approaches. There may well be arguments among researchers operating within a school about how best to combine and interpret that perspective's precepts. As a result, any one school gives rise to multiple high-level theories that nonetheless share the basic premises of the overarching conceptual framework from which they derive. Four of the major schools that developed in archaeology over the past century are Culture History, Processual archaeology, Marxist archaeology, and Interpretivist (or Postprocessual) archaeology. We highlight these perspectives because of their importance in our own work and that of archaeologists generally (their positions are briefly summarized in Table 4.1).

These schools can be seen as paradigms in the sense that Thomas Kuhn uses that term: distinct perspectives, founded on very different fundamental premises, from which to investigate the world. Though Kuhn tends to view paradigms in the natural sciences as mutually exclusive, we will see in Chapters 5–9 that the high-level theories inspired by different archaeological schools, and even the schools themselves, have permeable boundaries. Data

67

Table 4.1. Schematic rendering of the basic precepts that characterize the four schools of archaeological thought

THEORETICAL SCHOOL	CAUSATION	AGENCY	GENERALIZATION	ASSOCIATED METHODS
Culture History	Cultural processes, **especially diffusion** and migration, shape cultural forms that determine human behavior.	People are constrained to act in certain ways that are dictated by the precepts and values of their cultures.	Each culture is a unique configuration of traits and underlying principles, the outcome of its own unique history.	Fieldwork focuses on identifying the spatial distribution of material traits used to **define cultures and on** discerning changes in them over time.
Processualism	Adaptation to aspects of the physical environment, primarily through applications of technology, shapes all aspects of a culture.	Individual behavior is determined by the need to promote **effective adaptations** to the physical environment.	As there are limited ways people can adapt **to the world's finite** array of environments, there are recurring patterns of cultural forms explicable by general adaptive processes.	Fieldwork now includes gathering data to permit reconstruction of human–environment interactions occurring within a wide array of settlements.
Marxism	Human behavior arises from human–environment interactions mediated through social relations in which **power differences are strongly** implicated.	Tension exists between the power of political structures to shape action and the ability of agents to change these structures. Such tensions can be a potent basis for culture change.	Because people seek the same political goals by manipulating material resources derived from a limited range of potential environments, there are recurring patterns of cultural forms and processes of culture change.	The need to understand human–environment relations encourages the use of many data-gathering strategies developed by Processualists. Interest in the political roles of ideology results in studies of the cultural meanings of material symbols.
Interpretivism	Human action is motivated by decisions **informed by a reflexive** relation between people and their symbolically rich environments.	There is a recursive relation between cultural structure and individual agency in that all behavior enacts structural principles, principles that can be changed as they are performed in people's daily lives.	Each culture's symbolic framework is variably experienced and understood by its members and is a product of its unique history.	Research shifts to understanding the multiple ancient meanings instantiated in materials through detailed analyses of recurring patterns in their contexts of recovery.

and methods generated in one are often used by practitioners of the others. Still, like paradigms, Culture History, Processual, Marxist, and Interpretivist archaeologies strongly condition how researchers view the same data, often in different ways, and frequently talk past one another. They, like the high-level theories derived from them, are also highly resistant to being proven false. Hence, though the schools of thought outlined here appeared at different times, all of them persist, in some form, to this day.

In the pages that follow, we describe the basic premises of the four schools, relate them to one another, and highlight their similarities and differences in reference to issues of causation, agency, and the possibility of making general statements about human behavior. Special attention is directed to how members of each school view the central archaeological concerns of culture, history, and the significance of recovered materials in understanding both. Differences in the ways in which these essential issues are addressed help cast light on the distinctive premises of each school.

We devote relatively little attention to tracing the sources of archaeological ideas in broader debates and trends in social theory (see Trigger 2006 for a detailed consideration of these connections). Nevertheless, it is helpful to recall that the arguments agitating the surface of archaeological discourse at any time are extensions of more general discussions engaged in by people from within and beyond academia. We therefore point to relations among the schools of thought discussed here and three wide-ranging movements in social theory: Romanticism, Modernism, and Post-modernism. Though not definitive, this review should give you some idea of how archaeological theory is tied into broader traditions of intellectual discourse.

Culture History

Culture History, the oldest of the schools discussed here, dominated the field from the early through the middle 20th century (Figure 4.1). Culture historians during this period were faced with the daunting task of organizing the rapidly accumulating collection of archaeological materials from various parts of the world into chronological and spatial units.

Central to the above research was the idea of an **archaeological culture**. Following on the pioneering work of such researchers as **V. Gordon Childe** (see sidebar), these entities were seen as analogous to the living cultures studied by ethnographers. Scholars like Childe believed that within an archaeological culture, people shared the same core beliefs and

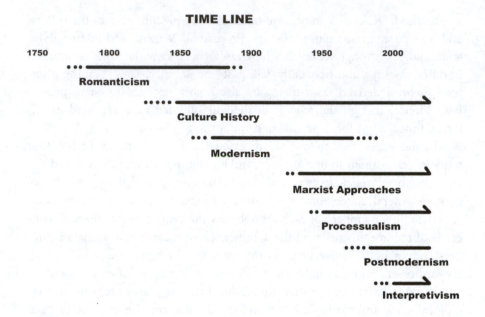

FIGURE **4.1** A schematic time line showing the temporal relations among the major schools of archaeological thought discussed in the text and the broader intellectual traditions out of which they arose.

values, which in turn gave rise to similar patterned behaviors employing comparable artifacts. As archaeologists do not excavate people in action (fortunately), we have to infer the existence and borders of ancient cultures from material remains. The "stuff" of archeology results from behaviors generated by those presumed shared beliefs and values. This led Culture Historians to define archaeological cultures as spatially bounded, recurring groups of distinctive **traits**. Traits were treated as discrete units of behavior and the material remains resulting from those actions. A particular style of pottery decoration might be a trait, as could a specific form of architecture or a kind of stone tool. These features were thought to have accumulated in a generally continuous manner over the years, each culture shaping its characteristic suite of traits according to its own core principles. But where did those traits come from? Trait adoption, according to Culture Historians, usually resulted from one of two processes: **diffusion**, the spread of ideas and/or goods without the permanent movement of people; and, **migration**, in which people come along with the goods and ideas.

V. Gordon Childe

V. Gordon Childe is one of archaeology's most original theorists. The principles he elaborated in his numerous studies of European prehistory were, and remain, widely influential. Early in Childe's career, he played a leading role in outlining crucial features of the Culture History school. Though Childe remained committed to diffusion as a major cultural process, his later work innovatively incorporated concepts derived from Marxist thought into explanations of long-term culture change. For example, Childe argued that while metallurgy may have originally diffused to Europe from the Near East, its historical significance was largely determined by how it was involved in the different relations of production that characterized these areas. Copper and bronze working in 4th-millennium BC southern Mesopotamia was, he claimed, rigorously controlled by monarchs who used monopolies over metal tools and weapons to sustain their exclusive rights to paramount power. Consequently, innovations in metallurgy that could have led to increased efficiency in, and decreased costs of, production were stymied by elites who were uninterested in any changes that might make copper and bronze implements more generally available. Europe's more egalitarian social structures, in contrast, encouraged innovations in metalworking, as itinerant smiths sought to increase production to meet the growing needs of numerous clients. Social relations, therefore, could frustrate or encourage technological changes, those transformations then affecting a culture's history. Hence, Childe contended that southern Mesopotamian societies continued to stagnate as oppressive regimes blocked technological innovations. European societies, in contrast, flourished, spurred by free competition within relatively open markets. Childe's original formulation is no longer widely accepted. Nonetheless, his attempts to explain the past by paying attention to relations among social and economic processes continue to inspire investigations within and outside Europe to this day.

Archaeological cultures were grouped into **culture areas**, continuous stretches of terrain characterized by relatively homogeneous environments and occupied by cultures that shared similar trait inventories. The material and behavioral commonalities that defined culture areas resulted from the spread of traits more or less uniformly from an innovating center. Trait distributions were broadly limited by environmental factors; examples from one zone would not easily diffuse to neighboring territories with markedly different physical settings.

The above approach to describing ancient cultures stressed the action of **sui generis** cultural processes, those operating solely within the cultural realm. Diffusion, the primary source of culture change, was purely a result of human interactions free of any significant input from non-cultural factors. The closest that most Culture Historians came to incorporating extra-cultural variables into their accounts of past human behavior was their reference to the physical environment's power to limit the spread of certain cultural features. The environment, however, was considered more of an inert stage on which the human drama unfolded than an active contributor to those developments; it provided resources that members of a culture might exploit or ignore, but it did not significantly encourage the appearance of some traits.

A culture's history was reconstructed through shifts in material **styles**, those aspects of an object not strictly determined by functional or technological constraints. The shape of a ceramic vessel might be largely dictated by its uses, whereas the temperature at which it was fired was strongly conditioned by the available technology. How that pot was decorated, however, was relatively independent of these functional and technological features and changed more rapidly than either of them. Materials were grouped into categories, or *taxa* (plural; the singular is *taxon*), based on shared stylistic **attributes**, or identifiable features. Deposits at a site that contained the same stylistically defined taxa in approximately the same proportions were deemed to be roughly contemporary and comprised a **component** in the site's occupation. Settlements occupied for only one period were single-component sites, while those used for longer periods had multiple components. All components within a given area in which the same stylistically defined categories were found in approximately the same percentages belonged to the same **phase**. Each phase was equivalent to a distinct period in a culture's history.

The chronological order of components and phases was reconstructed using principles of **stratigraphy** and **seriation**. Studies of stratigraphy, the vertical arrangement of the strata or layers revealed in an archaeological excavation, specified the course of stylistic change based on the relative depths of items bearing certain styles within undisturbed archaeological deposits; the older the style, the deeper under ground the materials on which it was found would be (Figure 4.2). Where such deep, well-preserved deposits were lacking, components could be placed in a time sequence using seriation. This method is based on differences in the proportions of the stylistically defined categories found within deposits. Applications of seriation proceed from the premise that stylistic change is gradual. A style within any material class (such as pottery) increases in popularity over time to a maximum point before dwindling to obscurity as it is replaced by other styles on the rise. Different components within a region will therefore be characterized by differing proportions of the stylistically defined taxa pertaining to specific material classes such as pottery or stone tools. Ordering components in ways that conform to seriation's assumptions creates a chronological sequence; but unlike with stratigraphy, it is impossible to tell which end of that continuum is the earliest and which is the latest without additional information.

Culture, history, and material objects take on specific meanings in this framework. Culture can be imagined as a receptacle into which history, operating primarily through diffusion and migration, poured objects and their associated behaviors, or traits. People then shaped these features into unique trait configurations distinctive of particular cultures according to their shared ideas and rules. Individual behavior was determined by these patterned wholes, all participants sharing equally in the beliefs and practices of the cultures to which they belonged. In this sense, culture was treated as **normative**, people's actions being narrowly channeled by cultural rules, or norms.

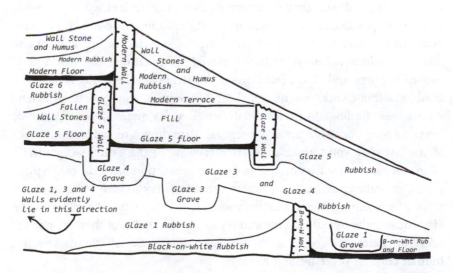

FIGURE 4.2 Rendering of an early section from the southwestern U.S. illustrating how architectural and cultural sequences are combined, in this case to distinguish different archaeological phases. Note how each of the major stratigraphic units is linked to a phase defined with respect to a distinct set of ceramics (different classes of glazed wares and black-on-white decorated pottery). Drawn after Figure 6.6 in Trigger 2006.

History, in turn, was generally, though not invariably, viewed as a continuous process by which traits gradually accumulated and changed within a culture. Because it was not possible to predict which traits might appear in any particular culture at any specific moment, history was not thought to be governed by general laws. Variations in the forms and styles of material remains were used to define cultures and distinguish phases in their histories.

The lowland Maya Ceremonial Center hypothesis discussed in Chapter 2 derives from a Culture History framework. The very idea of "lowland Maya culture" was the outcome of culture historical research over the first four decades of the 20th century. This early work defined the traits used to characterize this culture and specify its boundaries (discussed further in Chapter 7). Assumptions of cultural continuity that allowed researchers to see modern Maya farmers as cultivating their fields in much the same ways as did their 7th-century antecedents fit well with this school's premises. And belief in such persistent cultural continuity was based on the notion that the tradition of beliefs and practices that distinguished the lowland Maya from all other cultures was strikingly resistant to change in its core values.

Culture Historians, therefore, were primarily concerned with determining temporal and spatial patterning for as wide a range of different cultures as possible; this is called, in short, defining **time-space systematics**. In this way, they imposed order on the ever-increasing and diverse array of archaeological materials retrieved from around the world. The named cultures and time periods used to categorize these objects crystallized into frameworks within which archaeologists continue to work and report their findings to professional as well as lay audiences. To get some sense of how pervasive these conceptual structures are today, think back to the last time you toured a museum. How were the exhibits organized? Were they structured according to culture areas, time periods, other principles, or some combination of these variables? Try to imagine alternative ways of presenting the materials you saw. We tend to take the Culture Historical units of culture area and phase for granted, but they are not the only, or naturally given, ways of organizing materials to understand human cultural diversity and history.

Culture History, Romanticism, and Anthropology

The version of Culture History described above developed most strongly in the United States within the broader field of anthropology, which was, in turn, strongly influenced in the early 20th century by **Romanticism**. This broad intellectual tradition developed in Europe by the late 18th century in strong reaction against scientific approaches to knowledge espoused by Enlightenment scholars. Writers in the Romantic tradition covered a wide range of fields, though they especially dealt with the arts and literature. There are several aspects of this general approach that were particularly relevant to the early development of U.S. anthropology. Romantics cast Enlightenment science, exemplified in the work of such figures as Sir Isaac Newton, as overly concerned with breaking natural phenomena down into their constituent elements and modeling their relations as governed by general laws (recall $F = ma$ from Chapter 1). Such an approach to human behavior was judged by Romantics to be inadequate, in part because the cultures in which those behaviors occurred were not organic phenomena but human creations. Those creations, in turn, were characterized by distinct configurations of beliefs and values unified by a shared "genius" that was unique to particular groups of people. Understanding why people acted as they did, therefore, required paying close attention to the enduring principles that distinguished each culture and made the lives of its members coherent.

Romanticism thus encouraged anthropologists to treat each society as an aggregate of people united by shared cultural precepts that shaped individual beliefs and actions and arose from that group's unique history. This perspective contributed to, and drew inspiration from, nationalistic movements that defined nation-states as coherent entities whose members were supposedly joined by bonds of tradition, language, and custom. These bonds were thought to infuse all their actions with a shared spiritual and emotional essence distinctive of a particular people.

Anthropologists such as **Franz Boas** (see sidebar) in the United States and archaeologists such as V. Gordon Childe in Britain translated these broad precepts into action within museums and universities in the first half of the 20th century. They did so in reaction against what they took to be an overly analytical and generalizing approach to human behavior espoused by their predecessors in the field. The latter, sometimes called **evolutionists**, dominated U.S. and European anthropology during the late 19th and early 20th centuries. In general, evolutionists argued that each culture could be understood as a collection of behaviors that represented a stage in the overall development of human culture. Explaining any action was not dependent on placing it within the context of the beliefs and values that characterized a particular culture. Instead, observed human behaviors were accounted for by setting them within the supposed evolutionary sequence through which all cultures passed en route to what were taken to be more rational, moral, and complex forms of living. If 19th-century Western Europe and the United States represented the current apex of this trend, then it was possible to argue, for example, that polygyny (one husband with several wives) represented an earlier form of marriage than the monogamy (one wife, one husband) found in Western Europe and the United States. As for why polygyny was practiced in some places, the evolutionists' answer was that the people engaging in these unions were enacting an earlier stage in the development of marriage. All behaviors could be arranged in this supposedly ascending order, and all could be explained by reference to the same universal laws of evolution.

Led by Boas and Childe, many U.S. and British anthropologists and archaeologists rejected this analytical and comparative approach and its premise that the operation of universal laws and universal criteria could be used for cultural ranking. Rather, they argued for the notion that each culture must be understood in its own terms by reference to:

1. its distinctive set of traits;

2. the unique configurations those traits comprised;

3. the incomparable history that formed both.

Documenting these unique human cultures became a major goal to which archaeologists working with the Culture History tradition could contribute.

Childe, Boas, and their intellectual allies also argued strongly against racial theories of human behavior that were prominent in the late 19th through middle 20th centuries. These views generally stressed the notion that each culture's unity was based on its members' shared biology and not on learned ways of thinking and acting. Culture was, in short, an expression of underlying physical features, passed on by biological inheritance. Such racial understandings of culture encouraged a relatively static view of human behavior: what people thought and did was limited by the biology with which they were born. Going along with this view was the strong tendency to rank cultures based on supposed differences in the biologically based intelligence and rationality of their members.

Childe, in particular, attacked racially based arguments for lack of cultural coherence in archaeology. By stressing the importance of such processes as diffusion in shaping culture histories, he challenged the biolog-

Franz Boas

Franz Boas was trained in the natural sciences in his native Germany before migrating to the United States in 1887. By the time of his arrival, he had gravitated to the new field of anthropology, after having conducted research among the Inuit of Baffin Island in the Arctic and initiated studies with the Kwakiutl of Northwest North America. Boas was perhaps the most influential anthropologist in the United States through the middle of the 20th century, training the vast majority of the professionals who would go on to found anthropology departments across the country. In essence, Boas argued strongly against evolutionary and racial theories of human behavior, insisting instead that (1) each culture is unique, cannot be ranked, and is the product of its own distinct history; (2) human behavior is largely determined by the norms and values that characterize each culture; (3) these norms and values are passed down across the generations by learning and not inherited biologically; (4) culture change, therefore, happens as people learn new ways of living; (5) there are no biological limits, such as those thought to be imposed by race, on what people can learn and the cultures they can create; and (6) the serious study of human cultures requires adopting methodological relativism, in which the researcher does not allow his or her value judgments to interfere with describing and explaining the culture under study. Though anthropology in the United States and elsewhere has changed quite a bit from Boas's day, these basic premises still underlie a great deal of the research conducted in the field.

ical determinism of those working within the racial paradigm. If people could adopt new ways of acting and thinking from other cultures, then it was clear that learning, rather than biology, determined the current forms of all cultures and the histories out of which those configurations of values, practices, and artifacts emerged. Childe's questioning of racial interpretations had political as well as intellectual implications. German archaeology in the early 20th century was largely dedicated to writing a history of Europe that emphasized the overall biological and cultural superiority of a supposed Germani (later called "Aryan") race and the widespread distribution of its associated culture. Casting "Aryans" as the ancestors of "true Germans" at least implicitly supported Nazi claims to German racial superiority and to a "greater Germany" coterminous with the maximum distribution of putative Aryan settlements. Childe's vigorous rejection of such assertions, therefore, was a strong challenge to an intellectual tradition and a political ideology.

Summary of Culture Historical Premises

Culture Historians focused on defining cultural boundaries and histories, relying primarily on the cultural forces of diffusion and migration. Each culture was treated as a unique outcome of these unpredictable historical processes, processes that were reconstructed through the study of material forms and styles in diverse media.

Culture History remains a potent force in archaeology. Basic dating procedures and definitions of culture areas developed in this school are so deeply embedded in all archaeological practices as to be nearly invisible. Nevertheless, simplistic assumptions about the utility of reducing cultures to trait lists and accounting for their histories primarily through diffusion and migration have been generally superseded by more sophisticated interpretations. In some senses, all archaeologists are Culture Historians because all of us must describe the temporal sequences that exist in the areas we study. Insofar as researchers insist that these sequences are shaped by unique circumstances particular to a specific place, and the experiences of those who lived there, they are continuing the Culture History tradition.

Processualism

By the 1950s, Processual archaeologists, led by scholars such as **Lewis Binford** in the United States and **David Clarke** in Britain (see sidebars), were roundly criticizing the descriptive approach of their Culture History colleagues who saw cultural development as particularistic, or unique to a group. The novelty of the Processualist perspective (sometimes called *New Archaeology*) lay in its rigorous approach to building theory with the goal of explaining why events occurred as they did. This overt concern with developing theory significantly changed the course of archaeological research.

Though Processual archaeology was, and is, a fairly big tent, its basic premises are materialist, etic, and generalizing, and include an emphasis on structure over agency. Essentially, according to this view, human behavior in all times and places is driven by the need for physical survival. This need is clear to the outside observer, though it might not have been fully evident to the people studied. Survival is ensured by members of a culture adapting effectively to their physical environment. Adaptation occurs by managing relations among technology, demography (population numbers, densities, and distribution), and a host of physical factors such

Lewis Binford

Lewis Binford was one of the founding figures in Processualism. Beginning in 1962, he wrote a number of highly influential articles and books that helped define the basic premises of what came to be called the "New Archaeology." This approach stressed an explicit concern with theory, rigorous testing of ideas about the past, and the search for general principles of human behavior. Binford went on to play a major role in developing and refining methods in ethno-archaeology. He eventually conducted fieldwork in Alaska, Australia, and Africa among living hunters-and-gatherers to gain a better sense of the relations among certain behaviors and the material patterns that resulted from them. This research in middle-range theory was designed to facilitate the systematic testing of hypotheses about past actions, especially those engaged in by our earliest ancestors. Overall, Lewis Binford certainly deserves the tribute bestowed on him in the journal *Scientific American* as "quite possibly the most influential archaeologist of his generation."

as soil fertility, the habits, seasonality, and productivity of local flora and fauna, and rainfall. Which of these and other ecological variables are important to a culture's survival depends to a great degree on the technologies deployed by members of that group. The same swamp that is a source of valuable nutrients to hunters and collectors might be an obstacle to development for an industrialized society. In this view, social relations are structured to ensure that technology is used advantageously to promote adaptation. The beliefs held by people are, in turn, largely determined by these same adaptive processes. People, in short, do and think what is adaptive for them to do and think.

All aspects of culture form and change, therefore, are shaped by how people adjust to those aspects of their physical environments that have a direct impact on their lives. Since there are a limited number of environments, and only so many ways people can adapt to them, Processualists would expect there to be general similarities in the forms cultures take and in the adaptive processes by which those forms are achieved. Identifying and explaining such broad patterns are the ultimate goals of a Processual archaeology; thus, Processualism is viewed very much as a generalizing science.

Initially there was a strong evolutionary component to Processual archaeology. It was thought that cultures tended, in general, to change in the direction of growing population sizes and levels of complexity. The

David Clarke

British archaeologist David Clarke was among the most theoretically sophisti-cated of the Processual archaeologists working in the 1960s and 1970s. His vol-ume *Analytical Archaeology* (1968) is perhaps the most thoroughgoing review of archaeological theory ever produced by a member of that school. In this and sub-sequent writings, Clarke synthesized insights from Systems theory, with calls for rigorous hypothesis testing through the application of quantitative methods and for a scientific, or generalizing, approach to the study of the past. Part of what distinguished Clarke from some of his most prominent contemporaries was his flexible approach to the structure of archaeological explanation. By the early 1970s, he had rejected then-popular efforts to model archaeological theory-building on formats derived from the natural sciences, favoring instead attempts better suited to dealing with the uncertainties of archaeological data. Especially important in this regard, he argued, is our reliance on samples of material re-mains, the representativeness of which is uncertain, to infer the behaviors that generated the patterns observed among recovered artifacts and features. His ar-ticle "Archaeology: The Loss of Innocence" (1973), written near the end of his trag-ically short life, conveys Clarke's appreciation for the unique challenges archaeol-ogists confront in attempting to describe and explain past events and processes. The levels of archaeological theory he presciently identified in this work are still foci of attention in archaeology theory construction today.

variable "complexity" was measured, first, by an ever-increasing number of cultural institutions, and second, by the arrangement of people into ever-clearer hierarchies. This trend was codified in several influential *typologies* (categorizations) that grouped cultures based on their supposed stage of evolutionary development. For example, foragers and hunters liv-ing in small, egalitarian mobile groups, regardless of their geographic lo-cation or time period, were classed together. They were thought to rep-resent a form of organization that predated sedentary, hierarchically ranked societies whose economies were founded on domestication of plants and animals. Though the shift from small to large, simple to com-plex, was not seen as inevitable, or as "better," it was treated as a pervasive pattern in human history, driven, like all aspects of culture, by processes of adaptation. Evolutionary strains are still variably evident in the work of Processualists.

Related to Processual archaeology is **Systems theory**, the perspective that all parts of a culture are so strongly interrelated that changes in one aspect of behavior, or subsystem, lead to shifts in all other parts (Figure 4.3). Most Processualists saw these connections as a one-way street; that is, changes in relations among demography, technology, and the environment caused social modifications that, in turn, led to transformations in beliefs and values. As some Systems theorists such as **Kent Flannery** (see sidebar) pointed out, such unidirectional causality does not always hold true. In general, however, a systemic view of culture insists that no aspect of human behavior can be understood in isolation from everything to which it is related. This contextual viewpoint implies that *a culture is the basic unit of adaptation*, as people survive by participating in the interrelated behaviors that make up a cultural system.

The population-pressure hypothesis for domestication outlined in Chapter 2 is based on Processual principles. In this case, a technological innovation (domestication) is explained by arguing that it developed to promote the continued survival of growing populations within a physical setting where natural resources could not keep pace with the

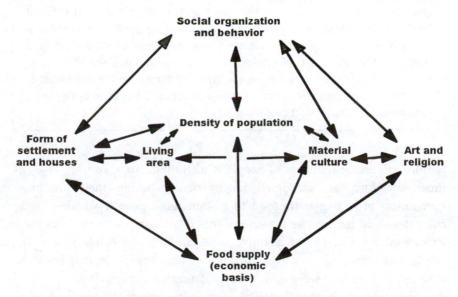

FIGURE 4.3 An example of how culture can be represented as a system of interrelated subsystems. In this drawing by Graham Clark, the double-headed arrows indicate that all aspects of a culture, such as food supply, social organization, and density of population, influence and shape one another. Processualist views of Systems theory tended to emphasize unidirectional causation, with technological/demographic variables determining the form of social relations and basic beliefs. Drawn after Figure 7.3 in Trigger 2006.

Kent Flannery

Kent Flannery was in the vanguard of those researchers who established the foundations of Processualism. He was always distinguished, however, by his healthy skepticism of the claims made by some Processualists that archaeology's primary goal was to identify general laws by which specific past events could be explained. Instead, Flannery pioneered the application of Systems theory precepts to the study of the past. In several highly influential papers, he argued that causality rarely travels in a straight, untroubled line from one set of processes (such as adaptation to the environment) to others (such as the organization of society). Rather, each culture is composed of subsystems, such as economics, politics, and religion. These components, in turn, are connected to and influence one another. Hence, a shift in, say, political relations can feed back on, and lead to changes in, such aspects of behavior as farming techniques and ritual practices. These transformations might, under certain conditions, encourage other shifts throughout a culture and the physical environment to which its members are adapting. Understanding any example of culture change, therefore, requires gathering data that would allow the investigator to reconstruct this series of feedback loops. Flannery's research prescription had the positive effect of pushing archaeologists to gather data relating to a wide range of variables in their studies, to take all aspects of a culture seriously, and not to write off some as causally insignificant. The system perspective also encouraged us to be alert to the complexity of past cultures and the danger of explaining them by reference to simplistic chains of direct causation.

---

rapidly increasing numbers of people. Cultivating crops and herding animals, therefore, are accounted for by demonstrating their presumed function of providing more food to sustain more people, whether those cultivators and herders were aware of this relationship or not. As in most Processual hypotheses, the adaptive consequences of a behavior are crucial in understanding its cause; what those who engage in that behavior may think about it is secondary to formulating an explanation.

The need to adapt is thus part of the structure that controls human actions, channeling behavior in ways that promote physical survival. Explanation is achieved by identifying how an artifact or behavior functions in promoting adaptation to the environment. Culture changes happen when major shifts occur in technology, population numbers and densities, and/or the environments to which people are adapting, requiring transformations in social forms, political arrangements, and beliefs.

Culture, to Processualists, is no longer a product of unintentional historical processes, but a package of tightly integrated behaviors shaped by adaptive necessity. The form of each cultural element, whether it is a method of farming or a means of organizing kinship relations, is shaped by all other aspects of the cultural system. No one piece can be understood in isolation from the greater whole of which it is a part. Further, that "greater whole" is molded by adaptive processes. The most innovative and crucial elements of adaptive processes are the mutually reinforcing aspects of technology, demography, and the features of the physical environment to which they are related. Unlike Culture Historians, Processualists bring the environment firmly within the cultural realm and give it an active role in shaping culture. In doing so, they adopt a **reductionist** view of culture, one in which explanations of human behavior focus on the interplay of cultural and non-cultural factors. This is not environmental determinism. Instead, it is the creative interaction among technology, demography, and features of the local ecology that changes both culture and environment.

Some traces of a normative view of culture persist in this viewpoint: everyone cooperates in the common effort to survive. This does not mean that all members of a culture engage in the same activities or experience life in identical ways. People often have different roles to play in adapting their societies to the environment, roles enacted in different places spread across the landscape. Consequently, research has to be conducted at a variety of different locales, from major political capitals to the humblest hamlets, to capture the diverse ways people in the past interacted with one another and with their environments in the process of adaptation. This concern with capturing the range of behavioral variation within cultures gave rise to studies of **settlement patterns**. In these, archaeologists set out to describe, through systematic survey and excavation, the full array of adaptive activities pursued at different sites within a specific area occupied, or at least used, by members of a culture.

Recognition of behavioral variation within and across sites also helped focus attention on issues of **sampling**. In particular, how could you be certain that your settlement studies had captured the complete range of activities conducted by members of a culture scattered over multiple sites? Archaeologists had always used samples of sites, excavated materials, and the like to make statements about life within a specific culture at a particular time. Processualists were, and are, concerned to make the rationales for such statements explicit. They delved into the sampling literature in such fields as statistics to ensure that claims made about antiquity were based on proper samples. These samples needed to capture as much of the range of ancient behavioral variation as possible. Such an interest in sampling came about because archaeologists recognized that behavioral diversity exists in any culture. Noticing and working with diversity marks a major shift from the strong normative position of many Culture Historians.

History is also seen in a new light. Processualists do not believe that cultures change due to unpredictable events. Instead, a culture's history is characterized by the gradual unfolding of adaptive processes which follow a logic and set of principles that are both knowable and widely applicable across different world areas and time periods. For this reason, making generalizations about patterns of culture change is not only possible, but one of the central goals of scientific archaeology.

Material culture tends to be understood by Processualists from a utilitarian perspective. If adaptation is the principal causative process operating to shape cultural forms and histories, then it is especially important to understand how recovered artifacts and features were used to promote survival. Processualists do not ignore stylistic variation. Such features are still crucial to at least writing chronologies and defining the boundaries of archaeological cultures, which remain basic units of analysis. Now, however, specifying the functions of recovered finds is seen as central to understanding how these items were employed in adaptive processes.

Modernism

Processualism hardly arose out of thin air. It is, in many ways, an expression of a broad approach to knowledge called **Modernism**, which was rooted in the 19th century and developed in opposition to Romanticism. Modernists, in general, were seeking to understand basic truths about humans as biological and social beings as well as about the world we occupy. That information was to be used to create rational and fair societies. In the Modernist view, earlier efforts to define such truths based on religious dogma and the political principles of monarchy had failed to yield verifiable knowledge and just societies. Modernists argued that the findings and procedures of science offered the greatest hope of understanding the world *and* liberating all people from want, disease, and the tyranny of unquestioned, outmoded assumptions and practices. Great accomplishments in technology and medicine, along with the identification of general principles in mathematics, physics, chemistry, and biology that accounted for a wide array of natural processes, seemed to confirm the power of science to achieve these goals.

There is no one Modernist stance, nor was it a static position that continued unchanged during the period in question. From our perspective, the most important, widely shared points uniting adherents of this view are the notions that:

1. any phenomenon in the world can be understood through judicious, rigorous observations made under a guiding scientific theory;

2. scientific theories are largely free of political, social, and emotional content, thus providing objective lenses on reality unbiased by personal and cultural factors;

3. all phenomena are ultimately shaped by the operation of universal principles, with study directed to identifying those principles;

4. identifying these precepts would lead to explanations of what is being examined;

5. the knowledge gained through such investigations can be used to reform society on more rational and efficient bases, so that the prejudices, poverty, and ailments (social and physical) plaguing all nations and communities can be eradicated; further, science is a way of discovering the Truth about life and nature, and on such Truth further knowledge and enlightened social policy can be founded.

This very optimistic view of science and its implications infused Processualism. Archaeologists could contribute to the Modernist agenda by identifying long-term and widely applicable processes of culture change. Knowledge of these processes could help predict the futures of current societies, enabling policy makers to define procedures for lessening the negative impacts of upcoming transformations.

Summary of Processualist Principles

Like Modernists in general, Processualists reject studies of local particularities in favor of broad generalizations concerning human behavior. Each culture's history is different to some extent, but all are shaped by overarching processes operating everywhere in similar fashions. Like

Culture Historians, Processualists believe that human behavior now and in the past is driven by forces beyond the understanding and control of most individuals. These causative variables, however, are not the products of purely cultural forces, such as diffusion, but arise from the creative interplay among technology, demography, and the physical environment in the process of adaptation. These materialistic principles are still constraining and directing human behavior today. By studying their operation in the past, we can understand modern adaptive dilemmas better and make informed decisions about how to solve such problems. In this way, knowledge derived from archaeology can contribute to a safer and saner future for all humanity.

Whatever critiques might be leveled against Processualists, at the very least they made theory development and testing explicit concerns. They also alerted us to the creative relations between culture and environment as well as to behavioral variation within cultures. From these concerns, Processualists developed very valuable methods for measuring behavioral and environmental variables, including settlement survey and various techniques for recovering data relevant to reconstructing ancient environments and diets. Processualists continue to refine their theory and methods today, and their field techniques are widely used by members of diverse schools.

Marxist Archaeology

If Processualism is a big tent, Marxist archaeology is a civic arena. Researchers inspired by **Karl Marx**'s writings (see sidebar) have taken his ideas in various directions, some stressing the importance of material conditions in driving human history, others focusing more on the role of ideas in culture change. In part, these differences reflect the varied ways that concepts originally developed to describe and explain capitalist political and economic relations can be reinterpreted to understand the actions of people who lived well before the dawn of that system.

Marxist-inspired scholars do agree on some things. They are generally committed to the study of *structural power*—that is, the constellation of variables, largely operating outside human awareness, that limit or expand individuals' abilities to define goals and act to achieve them. In pursuing their investigations, individuals using Marxist approaches also tend to agree that Processualist efforts to identify the material structures conditioning human thought and action are "vulgar." This has nothing to do with manners and everything to do with questions of causation. Marxists see the Processualist emphasis on the causative primacy of technological/ demographic/environmental relations as overly simplified and, hence, vulgar. Instead, Marxists contend that ensuring physical survival is a social, not purely technological, process. The populace secures vital energy from environments by organizing individuals by whatever means possible (kinship, contracts, and so forth) in regularly recurring groups to use technology. The social and technological are therefore inextricably bound together with each other and with the environment in creating a structure

Karl Marx

Karl Marx delved below the surface of capitalist economic relations in an effort to reveal the basic mechanisms by which they operated in the 19th century and how they arose from organizationally simpler forms. His goal was to reform society by exposing to all the exploitive processes on which capitalism was based. Debate continues to rage about how Marx's texts should be read and how their insights into the operation of capitalism translate into interpretations of human societies generally. Despite these arguments, Marx's work is important to social scientists in large part because of the importance he placed on social heterogeneity. Briefly, Marx stressed that people encounter reality and their culture differentially, based on the positions they occupy within a society. These positions are largely defined, in Marx's view, by a person's socioeconomic class. Each class is distinguished by the relations its members have to the forces and relations of production. Simply put, the first factor refers to the knowledge and technology people bring to bear in extracting energy from the natural environment, a process that always involves mobilizing the enduring social connections through which skills and techniques are put in play. The latter interactions are the relations of production. Classes exist in antagonistic relations, their dealings usually characterized by some form of exploitation. This exploitation often involves the extraction of labor and its products from those with poor access to the forces and relations of production by those who have privileged control over them. Wealth thus flows up the hierarchy to a very few and is based on the systematic impoverishment of the majority. Various researchers have questioned whether class, even in modern industrial economies, is the primary determinant of how people engage with the forces and relations of production. Factors such as gender, ethnicity, and age, alone and in conjunction with class, have been put forward as equally important in shaping social positions. Nevertheless, Marx's original insights continue to inspire much social science research into political and economic processes as well as the varied ways contests over power fragment societies.

that determines human behavior. Survival is still of central importance, as it is in any materialist theory, but that goal is achieved primarily through social manipulation of technology.

Further, Processualists often presuppose that cultures seek *equilibrium*, a state in which the environment and the people occupying it are in balance. This balance can be upset, leading to major cultural and ecological transformations. The normal state of the system, however, is equilibrium. Marxists view this proposition as functional "hunky-doryism," in that everything works out well for everyone in the long run. Marxists counter that this view of life conveniently misses what is to them an obvious point: in most cases, some people benefit more than others from cultural patterns. In the course of organizing social and technological relations to secure energy, a few enterprising souls gain privileged control over one or both of these processes, thereby creating a structure that promotes society's continued existence *and* their own agendas. The outcome is not equilibrium, but a standoff among factions whose members are prepared to protect or challenge the status quo.

People, however, find it difficult to live under such constant high anxiety, and the use of force alone to guarantee one faction's dominance is both alienating and ineffective. Here is where **ideology** comes in. Rather than seeing belief systems as promoting and encouraging adaptive behavior, as Processualists do, Marxists argue that symbolic structures mask or rationalize existing inequalities. Such ideologies, therefore, are tools used by those in power to dupe, and gain the support of, those outside the charmed circle. It is in this sense that religion, like all systems of values and beliefs, is the opiate of the people. It dulls the senses of the masses, obscuring the inequalities that pervade a society, and inducing in the majority an illusion of well-being. Achieving significant culture change in favor of the majority requires that they see through this conceptual smoke-and-mirrors to the real oppressions exercised over them by a privileged few.

Consequently, Marxist thinkers opt for political explanations in which, to a great extent, change is driven by the actions of agents working to advance or undermine, explain or question, exploitive power relations. The resulting political structures powerfully condition the actions of those working within them. Still, there is more room for individual agency in shaping those structures than tends to be the case in most Processualist theory. Insofar as people seek the same political goals within a limited range of available physical environments, a restricted array of political structures will tend to reappear across multiple cultures and time periods. To Marxist scholars, there are just so many ways that the physical environment, technology, social relations, and ideology can be combined in the service of political advancement; and one of archaeology's goals is to identify those regularities.

Allowing for the diversity of thought represented by Marxist researchers, it is still fair to say that most of them fall out toward the political, structural, and generalizing ends of the continuums discussed in Chapter 3. The primacy of ideology in the work of at least some Marxist archaeologists means that they have an interest in the symbolic realm that is not always matched by Processualists. If ideology is employed to deceive the masses, then the investigator must understand what its component symbols mean to those who use them. Marxists may well, therefore, combine emic and etic approaches in their studies of past societies. Still, it is the etic reality of political structures born of power struggles over material resources that shape the emic understandings expressed in ideology. Etics trump emics when it comes to explaining human behavior in this perspective.

Adopting a Marxist perspective encourages a view of culture, history, and materiality that diverges from those described for Culture History and Processualism. Culture, for Marxists, is still a system of interconnected parts, no one of which can be understood in isolation. Consequently, these parts are functions of one another, and function to achieve certain goals. Explaining actions requires linking them to one another and to their political objectives. These systems, however, bear little resemblance to their Processualist analogues. For one thing, culture in Marxist thought is not normative or oriented toward attaining equilibrium. Rather than being composed of people engaged in the cooperative enterprise of promoting group survival, any culture is seen as divided by factional strife. All are seeking advantages for themselves and their immediate group of relatives and associates, often at the expense of others. These contests center on efforts to control crucial cultural features:

■ the technology used to secure essential energy from the environment;

■ the social relations needed to put that technology to use; and/or

■ the beliefs, values, and symbols by which understandings of the world are generated and expressed.

Any human behavior is explained when its role in these competitions is demonstrated. Culture, here, as was the case for Processualists, is understood in materialist and reductionist terms; that is, cultures are seen largely as mechanisms for securing energy from their physical settings. The quest for survival, in Marxist views, however, generates real winners and losers.

As in Processualism, artifacts and features tend to be understood primarily in relation to their functions. This is generally the case in schools that stress the overriding importance of certain goals in guiding behavior. Whereas in Processualism the behavioral goal is thought to be adaptation, in Marxism the concept of "function" is broadened to include the ways in which aspects of material culture are used in political contests: How are objects employed strategically to create structures in which the dominion of a few over the many is imposed and rationalized? Artifacts and features are thus examined to infer how they served to secure resources from the environment, and how those assets were turned to political gain and ultimately legitimized the resulting inequalities through appeals to systems of beliefs and values.

History is transformed in Marxist perspectives as well. Rather than a gradual unfolding of local or broad-level processes, cultural shifts develop primarily out of contests among factions for both the material and social means of securing power, and out of the ideologies needed to rationalize that acquisition. There is some freedom here for individual action, as people and their allies maneuver, negotiate, and occasionally fight for political preeminence. These agents may not be able to shape history to their own desires completely; they still have to contend with the structural (primarily material) forces that ultimately guide all human desires and actions. Nevertheless, people are not seen as history's pawns to the extent evident in Processualism and Culture History. However much the latter two schools may differ, they both converge on the notion that individuals are more created by, than creators of, history.

Marxism, like Processualism, is rooted in Modernist thought. Proponents of both sets of views contend that the rigorous study of archaeological remains will yield real, verifiable insights into the general principles guiding human behavior. Marxists are somewhat less confident about the value-free nature of theory than are Processualists. Many conceptual schemes, Marxists argue, reinforce unequal power relations within current societies. Shoring up inequality contributes to ideologies that promote the status quo rather than revealing the relations of exploitation and oppression inherent in these political systems. From a Marxist perspective, Processualist thought, with its emphases on the general benefits of cooperating in adaptive processes, serves to obscure real inequalities by recasting them as means to promote group survival. Marxist theorists, however, believe they can escape this "trap" because their conceptual schemes not only illuminate past actions but reveal the roots of modern inequities. This knowledge can then be used to question current pervasive, undesirable distinctions, thus contributing to the creation of more just and fair societies. Marxist takes on Modernism are therefore not as buoyant and hopeful as are those of Processualists; human societies do not naturally trend toward liberty, equality, and fraternity, though they can be forced in this direction when political action is based on scientifically acquired knowledge.

Summary of Marxist Principles

Marxist archaeologists are inspired by a Modernist commitment to apply scientific procedures to the study of human behavior. Their search for generalizations focuses on repetitive patterns in the ways in which cultures are shaped by power contests waged among factions seeking to control the material conditions of life through technology, social relations, and/ or ideology. History is a predictable outcome of these political competitions, in which artifacts and features are fashioned and used to gain advantage over others or challenge such pretensions. The result in any one case is a tense and unstable political structure in which different factions are alert to opportunities to shift the balance of power.

As with Processual research, such investigations are not merely ends in and of themselves. Rather, the identification of general principles guiding human action in all times and places will contribute to a clearer understanding of modern conditions. It is on the basis of such knowledge that actions designed to encourage greater human freedom and happiness can be taken. Inequality, exploitation, and oppression are everywhere, and everywhere hidden, by potent ideologies. Creating fair societies requires seeing past these illusions of equity, recognizing injustice for what it is, and acting to reform social and political relations for the benefit of all. Marxist theory, according to its practitioners, leads in this direction, stressing the capacity of informed agents to reshape their societies. People may be duped by ideology and constrained by material conditions embodied in connections among technology, social ties, and the environment. And yet they are never simply victims of such interactions, but are capable of initiating cultural change.

Interpretivism

Pursuing the previous metaphor, Interpretivism (also known as *Postprocessual archaeology*) is less a tent or an arena than a housing development with loose zoning laws. Scholars in this school pursue diverse research agendas and entertain very different ideas about how much, if any, of the past is knowable, and how it is to be understood. It is safe to say that whatever differences separate them, Interpretivists take issue with the generalizing, etic, structuralist, and materialist strains of Processualism as well as most expressions of Marxism. On the other hand, they have at least some interests in common with Culture Historians.

Postmodernism in the Social Sciences

Like all archaeological schools, Interpretivism developed out of broader strains of thought, in this case a body of theory generally glossed as **Postmodernism**. Originating in the humanities, especially literary criticism, Postmodernism questions the existence of single, authoritative readings of texts. Members of the school challenge the idea that it is possible to decide exactly what a writer was trying to convey in his or her work, going so far as to argue that the real meaning of a text is created through the dynamic interplay between the reader and the written word. At Postmodernism's base is the notion that language, in its vocabulary and grammar, does not convey meaning precisely and unambiguously. Rather, texts, despite the best efforts of authors, are always capable of multiple interpretations; their meanings are indeterminate. As there is no definitive account of a book's meaning, readers have no choice but to make their own, equally valid interpretations of what is being said, based on their unique perspectives born of their distinct personal histories. Meaning, therefore, is always **relative** and never absolute; it depends on who is doing the reading and the context in which that reading occurs. As a result, generalizations about a text's significance offered by such "authorities" as literary critics or the authors themselves are untenable.

The spread of Postmodernist approaches into the social sciences from the mid-20th century onward relied, in part, on seeing all human behavior as a text. Like a written work, what people do conveys meanings that observers who have local knowledge can decode to some extent. As is the case with written words, there is no straightforward relationship between actions and their significance. Just as texts are susceptible to multiple readings, all human behavior can be understood in different ways, even by people living in the same community. Once again, meaning is relative, shaped by the background, preferences, and life history of the interpreter. Since no two people are identical, no two people view the world and make sense of it in exactly the same ways. Knowledge of all sorts, therefore, is subjective, because all meanings derive not from the objective content of an action (such as writing a word or shaking someone's hand), but from the subjective impression that a specific individual has of that act's significance. It goes without saying that the interpretations of people's behavior offered by trained "experts," such as anthropologists, are no better than the views put forward by others.

How these insights have been elaborated by different scholars has given rise to a wide array of perspectives whose defenders often have disagreed, and still disagree, forcefully. The diversity of viewpoints emerging from such arguments is partially due to the goals embraced by Postmodernists. Rather than seeking to create a coherent body of theory, Postmodernists are intent on critiquing existing intellectual frameworks, especially generalizing approaches derived from Modernism. This aim is itself conditioned by Postmodernist views that theory, like all aspects of life, is intricately bound up with power relations. In this sense, Postmodernists carry forward the Marxist notion that theory is rarely value-free and may consciously or unconsciously promote exploitation. Unlike Marxists, however, Postmodernists contend that no theory exposes the unvarnished realities of culture and nature. Since all theory is political, the best a scholar can do is to reveal, or **deconstruct**, the subtle ways in which conceptual schemes of every stripe contribute to rationalizing and obscuring the structures of inequality that pervade modern life. Once these implicit political meanings are revealed, people can see clearly the ideological web of oppression in which they are trapped, and then act to free themselves from it.

Postmodernists have other reasons for rejecting Modernist, scientific approaches to the study of human behavior. According to many Postmodernists, theories that encourage generalizing perspectives on human action and thought diminish appreciation for cultural diversity and human agency. Scientific perspectives, such as Marxism and Processualism, see people as subject to forces (political or adaptive) beyond their control, even as they submerge differences among cultures in a search for similarities of process and development. Seeking to diminish diversity and agency might be justified if the broad principles that Processualists and Marxists seek can be identified. To many Postmodernists, this is impossible.

On the one hand, according to Postmodernists, the operation of such overarching forces as adaptation and power struggles cannot be specified in the absence of a theory that gives them pride of place. The validity of that theory cannot be established in the absence of supporting data. Yet, any findings marshaled in support of a theory are already predetermined by that conceptual scheme and do not constitute an independent test of its validity. We reviewed this notion in Chapter 2 when we discussed the relationship between theory and data. At that time, we took a "weak" view of the connection, saying that our conceptual frameworks condition us to make some observations but not others. Nevertheless, the power of theory over our imagination and vision is not so great as to prevent recognizing information that contradicts the basic principles of our guiding theory. Some Postmodernists take a much "stronger" stance concerning this relationship, arguing that theory colors data so thoroughly that the data are created in the image *of* the theory. If such is the case, then the search for general principles is hopeless. We can never be sure if what we are seeing is just a reflection of what our theory conditions us to recognize.

In addition, Postmodernists contend that the complex interconnections among human behaviors render invisible to us the operation of any broad principles of human action that might exist. This notion is called **intertextuality**. In essence, intertextuality means that there are multiple links among various aspects of human actions and beliefs. The connections operate simultaneously on several spatial scales over varying lengths of time. As a result, in essence everything determines, and is determined by, everything else. Identifying causation within this maze is impossible; the best one can hope to do is to describe the phenomenon under study as expressively and completely as possible. The appearance of domestication may indeed be conditioned by demographic shifts and political calculations. But these are only two threads within a much more complicated web of political, economic, social, and ideological factors that together created, and were reflexively created by, domestication. Specifying which of those threads was more significant in promoting cultivation and herding is, to Postmodernists, impossible without some guiding theory. As we have already seen, however, all theory is suspect because of the way it skews observation and conveys political biases.

At the heart of Postmodernists' profound dislike of generalizing, scientific theory is their view that Modernist theories are politically dangerous: they contribute to the creation of **totalizing narratives** of the sorts used to undergird authoritarian states. In this view, Nazis and totalitarian Communists, for example, are united in that their regimes were based on generalizing accounts of human history and behavior. Their visions differed from each other but were both founded on supposedly scientific premises that provided blueprints for regimented, highly centralized, and bureaucratic regimes. In these systems, the freedom to dissent was but one of many casualties. Unlike Modernists, Postmodernists see science not as a means of liberation, but of exploitation. By denying the utility of science in all fields, but especially in the social sciences, Postmodernists aim to undermine the rationales of would-be despots.

The Postmodernist world, therefore, is a complex, unpredictable place in which reality does not exist independently of those who experience it. Unwilling to make sweeping generalizations, Postmodernists do not focus on what is for them the impossible search for Truth. Instead, they seek to describe specific situations as these play out over particular moments in time and are experienced by certain people with distinct backgrounds. In this view, sweeping narratives of human history and behavior are challenged by the complexity of individual cases; and each case is shaped by countless historical forces.

In this way, Postmodernism resembles Romanticism as it was translated into action by U.S. anthropologists in the early to middle 20th century. Proponents of both viewpoints argue against what they have characterized as the misapplication of scientific approaches to the study of human behavior. Stressing instead the uniqueness of specific instances of action and belief, they deny that these cases could be included within a general account of human action. While Culture Historians still talk about internally homogeneous cultures, Postmodernists question whether such bounded, internally undifferentiated entities exist. The unit of analysis in all three of the schools discussed thus far—namely, the spatially delimited culture—is very much an open question in Postmodernist studies. For some, it consists of social groups whose fluid borders constantly shift and reshape themselves; people move with variable ease within and across social formations. For others, the focus is on the individual.

Postmodernism in Archaeology

Postmodernism is manifest in archaeology through Interpretivism, also known as Postprocessualism. Taking hold by the late 1980s, Interpretivist archaeology now constitutes a significant school of thought. It encompasses a diverse array of perspectives for much the same reasons that

Postmodernism gives rise to so many different ways of understanding the world. Some Interpretivists stake out extreme positions, denying the possibility of ever being able to make reliable statements about the past. Truth, to them, is a mirage that only the naive believe exists. Archaeologists are unable to see the world objectively, so the best they can do is present accounts of the past that might be persuasive, elegant, and evocative, but not necessarily, or likely, correct. Our remarks below are limited to a brief review of moderate Interpretivist stances which argue that aspects of the past can be successfully understood and conveyed to wider audiences.

Moderate Interpretivists, such as **Ian Hodder** (see sidebar), do not demonstrate the profound distrust of theory that some Postmodernists express. Rather, many explicitly develop conceptual structures from which to describe and interpret past behaviors. While we do not deny the rich variety of these schemes, we think they share:

1. an emphasis on the emic meaning of archaeological remains and the behaviors that patterned them;

2. attention to the diversity of behaviors and beliefs within what had traditionally been seen as unitary archaeological cultures;

3. a focus on the agency of people, acting alone or more commonly in groups, in shaping those diverse cultural patterns.

The unit of analysis is no longer a given; instead, it is to be discovered among the varied ways people differentiate themselves as individuals (where it is possible to see them archaeologically) and as members of larger entities of varying time durations and spatial scales.

Drawing from the symbolic end of the causal continuum, Interpretivists argue that determining what objects and behaviors meant to those who made, used, or enacted them is more significant in understanding the past than is identifying their adaptive and/or political functions. If you want to comprehend why people built a house of a certain form or decorated their pottery in a particular way, you have to place that behavior within the symbolic context that guided and informed the actions of those you are studying. In keeping with emic explanations in general, this approach asserts that people do things for reasons that make sense to them, and are not driven by unperceived forces. In large part, those reasons emerge from the symbolic environments in which people live, settings comprised to a great extent of meaningfully charged objects.

Ian Hodder

Ian Hodder helped pioneer the Interpretivist stance in archaeology and remains one of its most prominent and influential proponents. He began his career within the Processualist tradition. Some of his earliest writings in the 1970s promoted the application of general principles drawn from economic geography to explain the patterned distribution of ancient settlements across the landscape. Hodder shifted toward Interpretivism in the early 1980s, championing the notion that human behavior is not the product of universal laws, but an outcome of historical processes that shape the meaningful structure of each culture. He further questioned the Processualist premise that the cultural significance of artifacts and features could be reduced to their roles in certain basic tasks, such as securing sustenance and shelter from the natural environment. Instead, Hodder contended that the things archaeologists find were integral parts of the symbolic environments of those who made and used them. The emic meanings of these objects, as well as their prosaic functions, must be understood if we are to describe and explain the behaviors in which archaeological materials were used. Hodder conducted ethnoarchaeological research in Africa. His goal was not to identify universal relations between behaviors and their material correlates. Rather, Hodder used studies of living social groups to illustrate the complex ways in which artifacts and features are deployed strategically by people to accomplish objectives within systems of meaning unique to their culture. Hodder's ongoing work at the Turkish site of Çatalhöyük illustrates his evolving understanding and application of Interpretivist principles.

How people interpret these symbolic settings is conditioned by such factors as their age, gender, ethnicity, political affiliation, and class. For example, your view of the symbolically charged world is affected by whether you are an adult, African-American, heterosexual male of an upper class, or a Hmong female teenager from a lower class who is still sorting out her gender and sexuality. The categories formed by the intersection of these complexly related factors are, themselves, culturally created and understood. For these reasons, people in any one culture do not interpret the world the same way, but approach life and its meanings from diverse perspectives. Frames of reference are frequently at odds, with differences expressed along a continuum, from overt arguments to unspoken acknowledgment and acceptance of variation. In any event, explaining behavior requires paying attention simultaneously to the symbols people manipulate and the divergent ways they approach those structures of meaning.

Symbolic structures are not simply inherited but are created in the course of their use. Culture Historians saw any culture as a structure made up of widely shared rules determined by tradition. In contrast, Interpretivists view cultures as consisting of variably shared understandings of the world actively shaped and transformed through their application in daily interactions. Certainly, people operate within structures of meaning that they do not create. Those frameworks, however, are not static. In the course of using culture strategically to achieve aims, aspects of the existing structure are reinforced while others may be challenged and transformed.

For example, every time you show up to class and complete your assignments on time, you employ and reinforce concepts of responsibility, respect, and punctuality that are valued ideals within early 21st-century, middle-class U.S. culture. You are not compelled to conform to these standards by some political force, nor are you incapable of imagining a life in which tardiness is a virtue. Rather, you choose to engage in behaviors that express these values in part because of the positive rewards their performance yields. You could decide to skip class and put off handing in papers, thereby challenging basic cultural precepts. If enough individuals followed suit, then there would be a significant change in at least this aspect of culture; if you alone rebelled, you would find yourself in a difficult situation. The point is that culture is less a predetermined script than a negotiated conversation in which all participants contribute, influencing its production and reproduction through all that they do and say. This **recursive**, or mutually inter-influencing, relationship between structure (those overarching cultural frameworks) and agency (the actions people take using concepts and other resources provided by those structures) is a major source of culture change and a focal point of Interpretivist studies.

Since the world is viewed, understood, and manipulated from diverse standpoints, there are many ways of entering the study of ancient behavior. You could, for example, examine how artisans working within a specific industry, such as pottery making, used their craft to secure economic rewards, political gain, and/or the capacity to define their place within the conceptual realm. **Gender** has been a particularly fruitful avenue of investigation. Deriving considerable inspiration from feminist theories, archaeologists working within Interpretivist modes have sought to understand the past by highlighting the multitude of ways in which people's sexual identities were defined by and affected their life experiences. Age, ethnicity, and class are other factors that commonly define the different vantage points from which people engage with symbols and meaning.

Like Marxist archaeologists, Interpretivists see all societies as internally divided. Members of both schools also attribute at least some causal weight to individual agency. People create and change their cultures throughout their lives. But they are variably aware of the structures of the social, political, cultural, and economic relations that constrain them, or of their effects on those constructs. Interpretivists also carry forward the Marxist notion that cultural patterns are often structured by power relations, but deny that power struggles everywhere condition behavior in predictable ways. Because the symbolic frameworks and cultural categories people use in their interactions are historically constructed, and each culture's history is unique, it is not possible to make statements about relations between meaning and behavior that apply to more than one place or time period. Human behavior, therefore, is **historically contingent**—that is, understandable primarily as the outcome of specific developments occurring in distinct places over particular time spans. From an Interpretivist stance, there is no way, going back to our domestication example, to link population shifts and increasing human control of plants and animals in a straightforward, cross-culturally valid way. Each case of rising populations and cultivating crops is different and must be explained with reference to local histories and meaning structures.

Summary of Interpretivist Principles

Interpretivists look for the causes of human behavior within the structured relations of symbols by means of which we understand and interact with the larger world and make statements about our place within it. Each culture is a distinct conceptual framework shaped by its own unique history. That history, in turn, is largely formed by patterned but unpredictable interactions among people who draw on concepts, categories, and values from established cultural storehouses to achieve their basic objectives. Material items, whether pots or temples, make manifest (or **instantiate**) concepts, categories, and values that enable certain behaviors while discouraging others. In the course of acting within meaningful environments partially shaped by material symbols, much of a culture's basic structure is reinforced. On the other hand, some aspects are changed as individuals consciously or unthinkingly reinterpret established structures of meaning.

Material remains, then, are examined to determine their meanings to those who made and used them. Since we do not have informants and so are unable to see these symbols in action, archaeologists infer an object's emic significance from how it was employed to instantiate social relations and cultural values. Such patterns of use are inferred from regularly recurring relations among objects in specific contexts. Thus, in a very simplified case, if adult females are consistently buried with goat mandibles in a particular area and period, while men are accompanied to the afterlife by rabbit femurs, we might infer that, in this particular cultural logic, maleness could be expressed by rabbits and femaleness by goats, at least in burial settings.

If causation arises from locally understood motivations, and if those motivations are spurred by symbolic contexts, then it is crucial to understand how material culture figured in shaping the settings from which meaningful actions arose. Just as no two cultures are the same, all individuals have distinct personal histories, leading to their unique approaches to life and understandings of it. There are various factors that go into the construction of any specific person's view of the world, some of which are exclusive to that person and usually not recoverable from archaeology's mute remains. There are, however, certain vectors, such as gender, age, class, occupation, and ethnic affiliation, which regularly, if not predictably, contribute to the varied ways people understand the culture in which they live and the enthusiasm with which they subscribe to its precepts. Not all of these dimensions are equally significant for every culture; nor is any culture's set equally important to everyone in that group. Generalizations about meaning and how it gives rise to certain behaviors cannot, therefore, be made within and between cultures.

Interpretivist archaeology, therefore, is more a humanity than a science, more concerned with describing the variety of life experiences of past people than with perceiving the operation of general principles that supposedly shaped those lives. The emphasis on the unique histories of individual cultures links this perspective with Culture History, though Interpretivists perceive a great deal more variety within each culture than Culture Historians tended to acknowledge.

The Permeability of Archaeological Schools

It might be comforting to think that archaeologists sign up for the school that best fits them, dutifully following its principles throughout their careers. Some certainly do. In general, however, most archaeologists borrow from these different perspectives, changing their stances on issues of causality, generalization, and agency throughout their professional lives. Why this is the case, we think, has a lot to do with the nature of theory and its role in archaeological interpretation. No one perspective is an adequate guide to raising and answering all interesting questions about the past, because, by its nature, theory, even at this broad level of generalization, focuses our attention on some aspects of reality while encouraging us to ignore others. As our interests, and what we find, change, so do the theories we employ.

But why should our interests change? In part, this is because of the complexity of our subject matter. There is probably nothing more complicated than human behavior, unless it is human behavior playing out over vast spans of time. We may start out studying one aspect of the past—say, how pottery is made—and later find ourselves investigating the symbolic significance of the decoration on pots in a particular place and time. It is not that archaeologists are fickle but that the many and often surprising ways behaviors are related in all societies frequently lead us in unexpected directions. Following those unanticipated paths requires shifts in the theories we use as guides. It is not surprising, therefore, to find so many schools in archaeology. Each perspective offers a different lens for viewing what we find. Over time, you are likely going to have to fashion your theories in different ways as unanticipated results and new interpretive possibilities arise.

Theory and Particular Cases of Practice

This last point is exemplified in the three case studies considered in this book. The greatest attention is focused on the 10 field seasons we devoted to research in the Naco Valley of Honduras (Chapters 7–9). Each of these chapters describes:

- the theories guiding work during specific field seasons;

- the hypotheses derived from these conceptual structures that we evaluated against data collected during those seasons;

- how key variables were measured;

- the ways in which theory changed throughout this process.

The final sections of Chapters 7–9 summarize what we inferred life in the Naco Valley was like at the end of each research period. Comparing these reconstructions gives a sense of how much shifts in theory can affect our understandings of past people and their cultures.

Chapters 5 and 6 address these same issues with respect to two well-known, extended research efforts devoted to understanding the rise of social complexity in southern Mesopotamia (Chapter 5) and the cultural and social significance of Stonehenge in southern Britain (Chapter 6).

Here we explore how investigators from different theoretical schools have approached the study of ever-present issues that challenge our capacity to explain the past. Some conclusions about the recursive relations among theory and data are offered in Chapter 10.

Further Reading

Archaeology, Histories

Stocking, G.

  1968 Franz Boas and the Culture Concept in Historical Perspective. In *Race, Culture, and Evolution: Essays in the History of Anthropology*, ed. G. Stocking, pp. 195–233. New York: The Free Press.

      This article remains one of the clearest reviews of Boas's contributions to the development of U.S. anthropology.

Trigger, B.

  1980 *Gordon Childe: Revolutions in Prehistory*. London: Thames and Hudson.

      Trigger's biography highlights Childe's major contributions to archaeology while reviewing the broader intellectual context in which these concepts took shape and had their impacts.

  2006 *A History of Archaeological Thought*. Cambridge: Cambridge University Press.

      This volume provides a comprehensive review of theory development in archaeology through the early 21st century.

Willey, G., and J. Sabloff

  1993 *A History of American Archaeology*. 3rd ed. San Francisco: W. H. Freeman.

      Willey and Sabloff describe changes in the theories adopted by North American archaeologists into the 1990s. The book is especially strong in outlining the nature of the Culture History perspective.

Archaeology, Methods

Brainerd, G.

  1951 The Place of Chronological Ordering in Archaeological Analysis. *American Antiquity* 16:301–313.

      Brainerd's essay is a classic early statement of seriation principles.

Harris, E.

  1975 The Stratigraphic Sequence: A Question of Time. *World Archaeology* 7:109–121.

      Harris provides a detailed consideration of how stratigraphic principles are used in archaeological dating, with some suggestions for improving their applications.

Mueller, J., ed.

1979 *Sampling in Archaeology*. Tucson: University of Arizona Press.

This collection of essays summarizes some of the arguments for incorporating systematic approaches to sampling in archaeological research.

Wintle, A.

1996 Archaeologically Relevant Dating Techniques for the Next Century. *Journal of Archaeological Science* 23:123–138.

Though focused on methods of dating our hominid ancestors, this article presents an overview of some of the basic procedures used to create archaeological chronologies in general.

Archaeology, Settlement Survey

Fish, S., and S. Kowalewski, eds.

1991 *The Archaeology of Regions: The Case for Full-Coverage Survey*. Washington, DC: Smithsonian Institution Press.

This collection of essays conveys some sense of the debates in the arena of settlement survey, especially those dealing with sampling problems, as these played out in the late 20th century.

Willey, G.

1953 *Prehistoric Settlement Patterns in the Viru Valley, Peru*. Bureau of American Ethnology Bulletin 155. Washington, DC: Smithsonian Institution.

This is a fundamental, early statement of the advantages of settlement survey as written by one of the masters of the field.

Theory, Culture History

Childe, V. G.

1925 *The Dawn of European Civilization*. London: Keagan, Paul.

In this, one of his earliest published works, Childe lays out some of the basic precepts that guided his studies of European culture history.

Kroeber, A.

1939 *Cultural and Natural Areas of Native North America*. Berkeley: University of California Press.

Kroeber offers here a classic statement and application of the Culture Historical approach in anthropology.

1940 Stimulus Diffusion. *American Anthropologist* 32:1–20.

This essay is a clear and concise exposition of one of Culture History's basic processes of culture change.

Lyman, R., and M. O'Brien

2006 *Measuring Time with Artifacts: A History of Methods in American Archaeology*. Lincoln: University of Nebraska Press.

Lyman and O'Brien's account relates the development of such basic Culture Historical techniques as stratigraphic analysis and seriation to trends in archaeological theory. As with the following book, the perspective adopted here is avowedly that of Evolutionary archaeology.

Lyman, R., M. O'Brien, and R. Dunnell
  1997 *The Rise and Fall of Culture History.* New York: Plenum Press.
      In this book, the authors offer a review of the strengths and weaknesses of the Culture History school. Lyman, O'Brien, and Dunnell are major figures in Evolutionary archaeology.

Willey, G., and D. Lathrap, eds.
  1956 An Archaeological Classification of Culture Contact Situations. In *Seminars in Archaeology 1955*, ed. R. Wauchope, pp. 3–30. Salt Lake City: Society for American Archaeology.
      This essay gives you a sense of how researchers were trying to systematize archaeological treatments of diffusion and other related Culture Historical processes.

Willey, G., and P. Phillips
  1958 *Method and Theory in American Archaeology.* Chicago: University of Chicago Press.
      Willey and Phillips offer a classic expression of the Culture Historical approach.

Theory, Evolutionary Archaeology

Barton, C., and G. Clark
  1997 Evolutionary Theory in Archaeological Explanation. In *Rediscovering Darwin: Evolutionary Theory and Archaeological Explanation*, ed. C. Barton and G. Clark, pp. 3–15. Arlington, VA: Archaeological Papers of the American Anthropological Association, No. 7.
      This essay summarizes the basic premises of Evolutionary archaeology, an approach to explanation that draws heavily and directly on processes specified in the synthetic theory of biological evolution. We do not address Evolutionary archaeology here, as it does not figure prominently in the case studies. Nevertheless, this school constitutes an important approach to the past, and you could productively start here for an examination of the topic.

Dunnell, R.
  1982 Evolutionary Theory and Archaeology. In *Advances in Archaeological Method and Theory: Selections from Volumes 1–4*, ed. M. Schiffer, pp. 35–99. New York: Academic Press.

This is one of the seminal statements of Evolutionary archaeology by a scholar who was central to the perspective's creation.

Theory, Feminist

Conkey, M., and J. Gero
1997   Programme to Practice: Gender and Feminism in Archaeology. *Annual Review of Anthropology* 26: 411–437.

  This article reviews the varied ways gender issues impinge on archaeology and archaeologists and how the topic is approached by researchers.

Geller, P., and M. Stockett, eds.
2006   *Feminist Anthropology: Past, Present, and Future*. Philadelphia: University of Pennsylvania Press.

  Authors in this collection deal with applications of feminist perspectives on research and current academic practices.

Hays-Gilpin, K.
2000   Feminist Scholarship in Archaeology. *Annals of the American Academy of Political and Social Science* 571:89–106.

  Hays-Gilpin summarizes here feminist approaches in archaeology as of the end of the 20th century. Much of the current discussion of social identities in archaeology is inspired by feminist studies, and this is a good source to consult as you try to understand relations between gender and social affiliation.

Joyce, R.
1993   Women's Work: Images of Production and Reproduction in Pre-Hispanic Southern Central America. *Current Anthropology* 34:255–274.

  Joyce's article is a study of gender as revealed in the archaeological record of southeast and southern Mesoamerica.

Nelson, S.
1997   *Gender in Archaeology*. Walnut Creek, CA: AltaMira Press.

  Nelson offers another take on gender issues in archaeology. Though originally raised in Interpretivist circles, gender is increasingly a topic pursued by members of most archaeological schools.

Theory, General

Brumfiel, E.
1992   Distinguished Lecture in Archaeology: Breaking and Entering the Ecosystem—Gender , Class, and Faction Steal the Show. *American Anthropologist* 94:551–567.

  Brumfiel criticizes aspects of Processual archaeology, stressing the importance of agency and conflict in interpretations of the past.

Cohen, M.
  1977   *The Food Crisis in Prehistory*. New Haven, CT: Yale University Press.
         This book provides a good example of arguments that link popu-
         lation growth to the advent of domestication.

Hegmon, M.
  2003   Setting Theoretical Egos Aside: Issues and Theory in North Ameri-
         can Archaeology. *American Antiquity* 68:213–243.
         This is a review of general issues in archaeological theory couched in
         a discussion of how these concerns play out in the study of North Amer-
         ican prehistory. Hegmon's discussion of "processual-plus" highlights
         processes of cross-fertilization among different schools of thought.

Theory, Interpretivist

Hodder, I.
  1990   *The Domestication of Europe*. Oxford: Blackwell.
         This book provides a classic account, from an Interpretivist view-
         point, of plant and animal domestication in Neolithic Europe.

  2006   *The Leopard's Tale: Revealing the Mysteries of Çatalhöyük*. New York:
         Thames and Hudson.
         This engagingly written account summarizes the interpretations
         of Hodder and his team concerning life within the Neolithic commu-
         nity of Çatalhöyük. The volume provides a good sense of how Inter-
         pretivist principles can be applied to the study of the prehistoric past.

Hodder, I., ed.
  2001   *Archaeological Theory Today*. Cambridge: Cambridge Polity Press.
         The essays in this compendium outline different perspectives on
         archaeological theory; the book is especially strong on Interpretivist
         approaches.

Hodder, I., M. Shanks, A. Alexandri, V. Buchli, J. Carman, J. Last, and G.
Lucas, eds.
  1995   *Interpreting Archaeology: Finding Meaning in the Past*. London: Routledge.
         This collection of essays provides a good sense of the varied ways
         Interpretivists go about understanding the past.

Joyce, R.
  2002   *The Languages of Archaeology: Dialogue, Narrative, and Writing*. Oxford: Blackwell.
         Joyce deals here, from an Interpretivist perspective, with the complex
         ways in which theory, data, and the reporting of both are interrelated.

Preucel, R.
  1995   The Postprocessual Condition. *Journal of Archaeological Research* 3:147–175.
         Preucel's essay is a much-cited synopsis of Interpretivist archaeology.

Preucel, R., ed.

1991 *Processual and Postprocessual Archaeologies: Multiple Ways of Knowing the Past*. Center for Archaeological Investigations, Occasional Papers No. 10. Carbondale: Southern Illinois University Press.

Essays in this volume capture the Processual/Interpretivist debate when it was at its most vibrant. The contribution by Ian Hodder (Chapter 3) summarizes the latter stance.

Roseneau, P.

1992 *Post-Modernism and the Social Sciences: Insights, Inroads, and Intrusions*. Princeton, NJ: Princeton University Press.

Roseneau reviews Postmodernist theory and discusses its application to the social sciences generally.

Shanks, M., and C. Tilley

1987 *Re-Constructing Archaeology*. Cambridge: Cambridge University Press.

The authors present an overview of Interpretivist archaeology and a critique of Processual approaches to the past.

Tilley, C., ed.

1993 *Interpretive Archaeology*. Oxford: Berg.

These essays examine such Postmodernist themes as the material record as a text, and apply Interpretivist perspectives to the study of the European Neolithic.

Whitley, D. S., ed.

1998 *Reader in Archaeological Theory: Postprocessual and Cognitive Approaches*. London: Routledge.

This is a compendium of essays written in the 1980s and 1990s dealing with developments in archaeological theory, especially Interpretivist approaches to understanding the past.

Theory, Marxist

Childe, V. G.

1951 *Social Evolution*. New York: Schuman.

This book, written near the end of his career, provides a good example of Childe's application of Marxist principles to the study of prehistory.

Kohl, P.

1981 Materialist Approaches in Prehistory. *Annual Review of Anthropology* 10:89–118.

Kohl reviews the different forms materialism has taken in archaeology, with an emphasis on Marxist-inspired approaches to studying the past.

McGuire, R.
  1992   *A Marxist Archaeology*. New York: Academic Press.
         McGuire provides a comprehensive look at the use of Marxist
         principles in archaeological interpretation.
McGuire, R., and R. Paynter, eds.
  1991   *The Archaeology of Inequality*. Oxford: Blackwell.
         The articles included here convey how Marxist principles can be
         applied in archaeological interpretations.
O'Laughlin, B.
  1975   Marxist Approaches in Anthropology. *Annual Review of Anthropology*
         4:341–370.
         O'Laughlin's strong statement of Marxist interpretive principles
         was published when this perspective was finding increasing accept-
         ance among anthropologists in the United States.
Patterson, T.
  2003   *Marx's Ghost: Conversations with Archaeologists*. Oxford: Berg.
         This broad-ranging consideration of Marx's influences on archae-
         ology is written by a scholar well versed in Marxist scholarship.

Theory, Processual

Binford, L., and S. Binford, eds.
  1968   *New Perspectives in Archaeology*. Chicago: Aldine.
         Essays included in this seminal volume convey Processual archae-
         ology in full flower. See especially L. Binford's introductory chapter
         entitled "Archaeological Perspectives" for an overview of the ap-
         proach. J. Hill's article, "Broken K Pueblo: Patterns of Form and
         Function," is a classic exposition of the methods of hypothesis testing
         espoused by Processual archaeologists.
Clarke, D.
  1968   *Analytical Archaeology*. London: Methuen.
         Clarke's text was a highly influential effort to address the structure
         of archaeological research and interpretation from a Systems theory
         approach.
  1972   Models and Paradigms in Contemporary Archaeology. In *Models in
         Archaeology*, ed. D. Clarke, pp. 1–60. London: Methuen.
         This essay provides an overview of relations among theories, mod-
         els, hypotheses, and data as outlined by one of the leading figures in
         Processual archaeology.
  1973   Archaeology: The Loss of Innocence. *Antiquity* 47:6–18.

In this short essay, Clarke reviews developments in archaeological theory and methods, emphasizing some of the problems with the Culture History school and with the efforts of Processual (or New) archaeologists to come up with novel approaches to explanation and description. Clarke's outline of levels of theory in archaeology is particularly prescient.

Flannery, K.

1968   Archaeological Systems Theory and Early Mesoamerica. In *Anthropological Archaeology in the Americas*, ed. B. Meggers, pp. 67–87. Washington, DC: Anthropological Society of Washington.

This statement of the principles underlying Systems theory and its application to the study of domestication was widely read and cited.

1972   The Cultural Evolution of Civilizations. *Annual Review of Ecology and Systematics* 3:399–426.

This is a classic statement of how Systems theory principles might be applied to studying ancient states. Though Flannery was critical of many aspects of Processualism, his essay was and remains widely cited by those analyzing state formation processes from the Processualist perspective in southern Mesopotamia and elsewhere.

1973   Archaeology with a Capital "S". In *Research and Theory in Current Archaeology*, ed. C. Redman, pp. 47–53. New York: Wiley.

Flannery offers here an early criticism of the search for general laws in Processual archaeology.

LeBlanc, S.

1973   Two Points of Logic Concerning Data, Hypotheses, General Laws, and Systems. In *Research and Theory in Current Archaeology*, ed. C. Redman, pp. 199–214. New York: Wiley.

This is a clear statement of the basic principles of hypothesis testing as they were employed by Processual archaeologists.

Longacre, W.

1970   *Archaeology as Anthropology: A Case Study*. Tucson: University of Arizona Press.

This application of Processual principles to an archaeological example was widely influential.

CHAPTER 5

TAKING ON THE STATE IN SOUTHERN MESOPOTAMIA

Introduction

THE LAND BOUNDED BY THE TIGRIS AND EUPHRATES rivers, encompassing large swaths of Iraq and southwestern Iran, has been the subject of archaeological attention for roughly two centuries. Researchers from Europe and the United States, in particular, were and are drawn to the area in large part because it has been consistently seen as a, perhaps *the*, crucible in which the basics of modern society were forged. Investigators in southern Mesopotamia, therefore, have grappled with events perceived as shaping world history.

It is no surprise that representatives of all the schools of thought outlined in Chapter 4 have applied their perspectives to reconstructing, and divining the significance of, what occurred between the Tigris and Euphrates. To the extent that these rivers embody the grand stage on which humanity took major steps toward creating how we live today, archaeologists of all theoretical persuasions have tried to describe and explain these developments. We examine aspects of southern Mesopotamia's research history as examples, on a general level, of how the theories discussed thus far in the abstract were put into practice by various investigators. This discussion is not exhaustive. Nor do we highlight these specific approaches to Mesopotamia's past because we think they are right, but because they exemplify aspects of the theories discussed particularly well. Further, you should not mistake what follows as a summary of Mesopotamian prehistory. Rather, we are selectively drawing on a voluminous body of research, not to see what it can tell us about an area's history, but for what it reveals about the role of theory in understanding that past.

We begin with a brief review of southern Mesopotamia's physical form and history, before moving on to consider the ways in which theory and data were, and are, being related through the work of researchers operating within different schools of thought. In each case, we are looking at:

- the particular forms taken by theories;

- the methods used to gather data relevant to these interpretive structures;

- how those finds were viewed in relation to the central issues identified in Chapter 4 of culture, history, and the significance of material remains.

Southern Mesopotamia

Southern Mesopotamia covers approximately 15,000 km^2 (5,800 square miles) bordered by the Persian Gulf and the Tigris and Euphrates rivers (Figure 5.1). The environment is characterized by variation, especially in essential water supplies, over space and time. Fluctuations in rainfall, both in southern Mesopotamia and in the headwaters of the Tigris and Euphrates, can produce severe droughts and destructive floods, depending on the year. Similarly, although the Tigris-Euphrates delta, formed at their confluence with the Persian Gulf, is a swamp, other tracts farther upstream vary from well-watered fertile floodplains to dry grasslands. Complicating matters is the general scarcity here of certain basic natural resources, especially metal ores and stones suitable for making tools, weapons, and status-defining ornaments. Surviving in this environment required developing means to even out access to water, and the crops and animals dependent on it, over space and time as well as to acquire goods not immediately available.

Given the challenges posed by this environment, it is perhaps no surprise that southern Mesopotamia was not occupied until relatively late in Near Eastern prehistory. The earliest known settlers here were apparently migrants from northern Mesopotamia (Syria, southeastern Turkey, and northern Iraq), who brought with them (by about 5900 BC) a fully developed agricultural and herding complex, along with established trade connections throughout the Near East. Around 1,900 years later, population had risen considerably, and signs of political hierarchies are evident in the

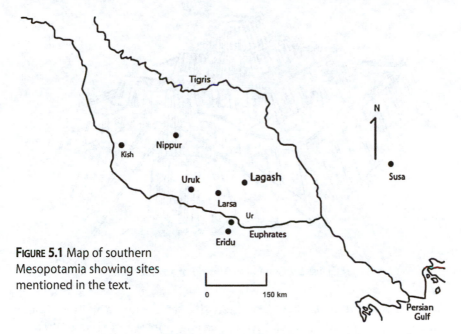

FIGURE 5.1 Map of southern Mesopotamia showing sites mentioned in the text.

form of monumental, mostly religious, constructions and in some distinctions in the size and degree of elaboration of residences and burials. Most of these markers of social distinction are found in the few towns that served as capitals of small political units (or *polities*). The leaders of these diminutive polities were closely tied to religious institutions devoted to worshiping deities. Temples were raised atop massive mud-brick platforms, or *ziggurats*, which physically dominated settlements and the landscape generally (Figure 5.2). "Priest-leaders" were apparently supported by tribute, in the form of food surpluses and labor, paid by town residents and the inhabitants of the smaller villages loyal to a capital.

In approximately 3200 BC, there was a major political shift. Fully 13 to 15 towns now blossomed into cities, each containing several thousand people. Urban growth seems to have been fueled primarily by migration from the villages within each capital's hinterland. Drawing in part on the labor of these city-dwellers, leaders of ever more powerful bureaucracies commissioned monumental buildings of unparalleled scale, once again primarily devoted to propitiating the supernatural. In addition, they supervised construction of irrigation canals which brought increasing tracts of land under cultivation, and collected large quantities of food paid out in tribute. Much of this growing power was apparently still vested in the hands of priest-rulers who controlled land, water, foodstuffs, and labor in

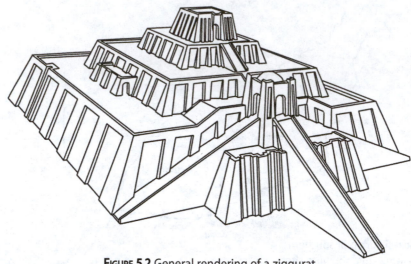

FIGURE 5.2 General rendering of a ziggurat.

the names of the gods they served. At the same time, a writing system called *cuneiform* came into use. An increasing number of texts written on clay tablets chronicle ever more complex economic and political relations among a wide array of powerful actors, including representatives of governing councils and holders of private estates.

From about 2900 to 2200 BC, contests between these small states, and among factions within each of them, resulted in the increasing emergence of secular leaders and more dramatic hierarchical distinctions separating a wealthy, powerful minority from an ever more impoverished majority. Commoners were steadily losing land to religious and secular institutions. It is the period from 3200 to 2200 BC that has attracted most of the attention of archaeologists interested in when, how, and why the centralized, hierarchically structured political forms familiar throughout the world today first emerged. It is these issues that most of the theories discussed below were devoted to illuminating.

Objects of Biblical Significance

The first multi-year excavations conducted in the area were carried out in the 19th century, sponsored by the French and English governments and their national museums. This work was designed to secure spectacular objects associated with societies (primarily the Assyrians, at first), personages, and events described in the Bible. An example of the sort of finds excavated and put on display in Europe includes the friezes from the site of Nineveh, which are now in the British Museum. These remarkable sculptures date to the 9th through 7th centuries BC and depict in great detail aspects of daily life as well as the often militaristic accomplishments of the center's Assyrian monarchs.

Advances in the decipherment of cuneiform—the written language that appears in the texts and inscriptions found throughout such early foci of investigation as the sites of Nineveh, Nimrud, and Larsa—greatly accelerated interest in Near Eastern antiquities. Beginning in 1837, the ability to read these ancient accounts allowed researchers to link rulers celebrated in monuments to biblical events and people. These translations also revealed early versions of the flood story, which provided yet another connection to happenings familiar to most European Jews and Christians from their readings about Noah. There was a strong impetus, therefore, to unearth and display materials that provided dramatic physical links to what were widely understood to be the roots of Europe's Judeo-Christian heritage. Their display in the British Museum and Louvre, in London and Paris, respectively, also bolstered political assertions of control over a valued past by nations seeking international dominance in the present.

It follows from these goals that digging in 19th-century Mesopotamia favored objects over **context**. Context refers to the horizontal and vertical associations among materials, including the soils in which they are embedded, as revealed during archaeological research. It makes a big difference whether the sheep bone, pot, and stone mallet recovered from a site are found next to one another near a hearth, separated within distinct soil levels, or grouped together in a pit with a human skeleton. That difference is context. It is only by recording these associations among dirt, artifacts, and features that we can tell the relative ages of materials and how those found together might have been used in preparing food, honoring the dead, or some other activities. It is this paramount concern with context that sets professional archaeologists apart from looters, who seek individual objects prized for their beauty and connections to aspects of a valued past. Consequently, insofar as excavations conducted throughout most of the 19th century in Mesopotamia were designed to find spectacular, exotic remains of mysterious ancient civilizations, they resembled modern looting more than the practices of professional archaeology. That said, it is unfair to criticize these early researchers for failing to live up to the standards of a profession that did not yet exist. What is important for our purposes is not to assign blame, but to recognize that the conduct of archaeology in Mesopotamia during the 19th century was strongly conditioned by a pervasive conceptual structure that saw the area's history as known through biblical accounts. The methods employed thus favored the retrieval of objects tied to that recorded past rather than the testing of hypotheses through close attention to context.

The conceptual framework that channeled excavations in Mesopotamia throughout most of the 19th century treated material culture as a set of distinct objects. Their primary value lay in their capacity to evoke events, people, and places known from the Bible. The concept of "culture" has no obvious role to play in this approach, save for the notion that Europe's shared Judeo-Christian heritage arose in, and spread out from, Mesopotamia. The primary goal of these early studies was to illustrate, not to reconstruct and explain, that heritage; hence, the methods employed emphasized recovering objects rather than recording context.

Culture History and the Sumerians

The limitations of the biblical perspective were accidentally revealed while archaeologists worked under its guiding principles. Researchers in Mesopotamia gradually became aware that the people they knew from the Bible were late manifestations of earlier civilizations. The impetus toward this dawning realization was the recovery of ancient texts, copied and maintained by Assyrian scribes, which pointed to the existence of people who were ancestral to later, better-known societies. Understanding the nature and history of Mesopotamian civilization would require reaching back to populations, called the Sumerians, who lived in time periods not recorded in the Bible.

Work was then devoted to discovering people, places, and events for which there was scant, or no, textual documentation. New principles and methods were needed to pursue this study into uncharted territory. Those premises and techniques brought context to the fore in order to:

■ define prehistoric southern Mesopotamian cultures;

■ identify the phases that made up their histories;

■ put those intervals in chronological order;

■ explain the shifts that occurred over the reconstructed time spans.

These steps, as discussed in Chapter 4, are essential features of the Culture History approach.

Cultures and phases were defined by distinctive collections of material styles, especially in ceramics and architecture. These units, in turn, were ordered chronologically, based on the results of deep stratigraphic excavations dug within the massive, physically dominant architectural complexes found in ancient Mesopotamian cities. The earliest research foci were temples and their associated constructions. These large edifices often reached their final dimensions through a long process of building new temples atop older ones: each temple platform encased its predecessor like a set of nested dolls. The resulting sequence of distinct building efforts yielded a convenient means for identifying changes in material styles over time, since every phase was bracketed by distinct construction episodes. In order to construct these chronologies, researchers expanded the range of artifacts they collected. Mundane objects such as pottery sherds, previously discarded as uninteresting, now were studied for changes in their styles and used to define the phases ordered temporally through stratigraphy. Phases defined by stylistic traits in artifacts and architecture were also treated as the remains of distinct cultures along the lines outlined in Chapter 4. Each phase was seen as pertaining to a particular, relatively homogeneous cultural unit. Changes in temporally diagnostic material styles were thought to have been introduced to a site by diffusion or migration.

Research teams were therefore no longer primarily concerned with finding items that spectacularly illustrated a known past. This is not to say that dramatic discoveries were not being made. Excavations conducted from 1922 to 1936 of 1,800 burials at the city of Ur revealed 16 very elaborately outfitted tombs thought to have been the final resting places of the city's leaders. Dating to the 3rd millennium BC, these so-called royal tombs contained not only items of extraordinary craftsmanship, but also the remains of attendants sacrificed to serve their masters and mistresses after death. Such lavish displays of wealth and power captured the world's attention and strongly suggested that these early monarchs enjoyed a preeminence that might have matched the opulence exhibited by their Assyrian successors. Still, Culture Historians were primarily engaged in the project of defining phases, tracing the distribution of their diagnostic styles across the landscape, and searching for ever older predecessors of known cultures discovered in ever deeper excavations. As noted above, almost all of this work called for digging in ancient cities with large edifices whose extensive construction histories provided relatively clear temporal divisions linked to the rebuilding of architectural monuments.

By the beginning of the 20th century, the goals of exploring Mesopotamian sites had changed from anchoring biblical accounts in physical remains to describing the roots of civilizations recorded in that text. The search was on for the Sumerians, seen as the creators of a pan-Mesopotamian civilization carried forward by Assyrians, Babylonians, and, ultimately, 20th-century Europeans and Americans. Since the Bible does not describe these original inhabitants, their history had to be written through the study of material remains. Accomplishing that ambitious task required putting a variety of recovered objects in context, both vertically within stratigraphic sequences, and horizontally, as styles diagnostic of phases were used to trace cultural boundaries across multiple sites. Cultures, defined as associations of distinctive material traits, were crucial components of this new conceptual scheme. Their locations on the landscape and changes over time defined a history characterized, it was thought, primarily by migration and diffusion. Mesopotamia's past in this scheme was important because the westward spread of its essential traits, particularly forms of government and writing, to Europe via Greece was thought to have formed the basis of European civilization.

Basic Culture Historical principles and practices, such as the definition and temporal ordering of phases by such techniques as stratigraphy, remain central to all field research in southern Mesopotamia. After World War II, however, new questions were asked about this area's past. It was still presumed that southern Mesopotamia played an important role in creating the modern world, but now that role was less closely and exclusively tied to the forging of European civilization. Instead, it dealt with the emergence of a political form believed to have first appeared between the Tigris and Euphrates that had come to dominate the globe.

Processualism and the Rise of the State

The political form in question is the **state**. When Processual archaeologists refer to the "state," they generally are talking about a mode of social and political organization characterized by:

1. political centralization, with power concentrated in a few hands and backed with coercive force monopolized by the power holders;

2. hierarchies, in which all members of a society are ranked within one overarching system by virtue of their differential access to power and wealth;

3. social differentiation, referring to variations in the activities pursued by, as well as the composition of, social groups making up the state.

States differ considerably in their outward forms; each has its own religion, language, customs, and laws, for example. Nonetheless, many argue that the above three elements constitute a core of functionally interconnected parts that evolve in a predictable manner. Processual archaeologists argue that even within different, historically unrelated world areas, the state resulted from of a sequence of earlier, simpler sociopolitical forms. These "universal" evolutionary processes were, in turn, driven primarily by the need to adapt to ever-changing material challenges. Of these, pressure on the food supply posed by rising human populations was thought to be especially significant. All patterned human behaviors, including the use of power, are explained when, first, they are set within the original adaptive systems in which they functioned, and second, their contributions to promoting those adaptations are identified.

Southern Mesopotamia became an important arena for understanding state formation processes because populations residing in this area during the 5th through 4th millennia BC were seen as especially precocious in creating this political form. Of the many Processual theories offered to describe and explain state formation here, we will limit ourselves to the influential approach proposed by **Robert McC. Adams** (see sidebar).

Robert McCormick Adams

Robert McCormick Adams was one of the major figures responsible for translating the principles of Processualism into research strategies pursued in southern Mesopotamia. Beginning in the early 1960s, Adams played an especially crucial role in introducing the methods of systematic settlement survey to the region. Since that time, these procedures have been increasingly enshrined as common practice by archaeologists working there and in other parts of the world. Through his settlement research, Adams encouraged all archaeologists to pay attention to the structures of ancient landscapes made up of sites of all sizes, inhabited by people of diverse classes, pursuing varied tasks, and adjusting to diverse ecological variables. As a result, we now have a broader appreciation for the complexity of ancient societies than when we concentrated primarily on the study of large cities. Adams's comparative research into processes of increasing sociopolitical complexity has also inspired numerous archaeologists conducting investigations within and beyond the Processualist school.

Cities, Storage, and Power

In several widely read books dating to the 1960s through early 1980s, Adams argued that power concentration, hierarchy, and social differentiation were coping mechanisms. They emerged to deal with spatial and temporal fluctuations in food and water supplies under conditions of rising populations. These ecological conditions challenged the capacities of southern Mesopotamia's inhabitants in a number of ways: evening out the effects of unpredictable floods and droughts over time; distributing food to people engaged in a variety of work; and balancing such complementary economic pursuits as herding in dry grasslands, farming along floodplains, and fishing in the delta. Population growth magnified pressure on people to increase food yields, which led to their specializing in producing goods appropriate to different ecological zones. This, in turn, promoted social differentiation. The advent of differentiation in turn required societies to create mechanisms for assuring general access to food and materials among those involved in different economic activities.

Cities emerged as a solution to these adaptive problems. It was here that institutions charged with collecting, storing, and distributing food emerged, initially under the leadership of priests acting as agents of powerful deities. These religious leaders came to dominate systems of tribute by which large quantities of basic foodstuffs were acquired, in the names of the gods, from diverse primary producers. Foods were then used in several ways: doled out to people in times of drought or flood; redistributed among those engaged in complementary economic pursuits; traded for essential goods not available in the immediate area; and used to support artisans producing a variety of items for both long-distance exchange and local consumption. Through their control of essential food supplies, priests came to occupy the upper reaches of society-wide hierarchies. From their social pinnacles, they exercised power over those who increasingly depended on them for the very means of survival. The exercise of such power ensured cooperation among growing populations in the common enterprise of adaptation.

The system's success was enhanced by the temple-controlled construction of ever larger irrigation systems that brought more land under cultivation. Newly watered land contributed the larger yields needed to sustain expanding populations. Management of extensive irrigation systems may not have inspired state formation, but mobilizing work parties to enlarge and maintain these canals invested ever more responsibility and power in state bureaucracies.

Processualism and the Expansion of Research Designs

Just as Culture Historical research required new methods to address novel issues, so too did studying the state through a Processualist lens lead to the development of new research designs. If the state is defined as a coherent body of functionally interdependent parts whose interactions are controlled by an administrative hierarchy, then research must be carried out in all portions of that integrated system to describe its operation and identify changes in it. It was essential that relations among members of different classes, occupations, and residential groups be understood so that the administrative functions of the state could be described and their emergence explained. If there was a causal relation among demography, food supplies, specialized production, and administrative structures, then information on such variables as the timing and rate of growth in population, storage facilities, irrigation canals, the crops and animals raised in different areas, and signs of administrative control must be documented. Gathering the requisite data meant that study needed to be done in rural areas surrounding urban centers, and not just in the large cities that had attracted virtually all archaeological attention up to that point. Rural settlements were discovered through systematic settlement surveys (Figure 5.3). Based on the distributions of sites of all sizes, archaeologists inferred changes in population numbers and distributions with respect to key environmental variables, such as watercourses. Variations in the extents of contemporary settlements and the dimensions of the buildings they contained were also used to infer the existence of, and shifts in, administrative hierarchies. These inferences were based on the notion that architectural scale correlated with the power of the elites who commissioned those buildings. Similarly, settlement size reflected the variable ability of leaders to attract and hold followers. Defining site hierarchies using these measures became a way of inferring the existence of power differences and administrative structures.

To figure out the range of ancient activities, excavations were also initiated in sites of diverse dimensions, time periods, and locations. If states administered complex economic and social relations for the benefit of all, then it was important to know about producers: Who were the workers? What did they make? How much did they manufacture? Where were the workspaces or workshops? Were tasks done year-round or seasonally? Finally, archaeologists wanted some sense of how these tasks were coordinated through the actions of various bureaucrats. Investigations were

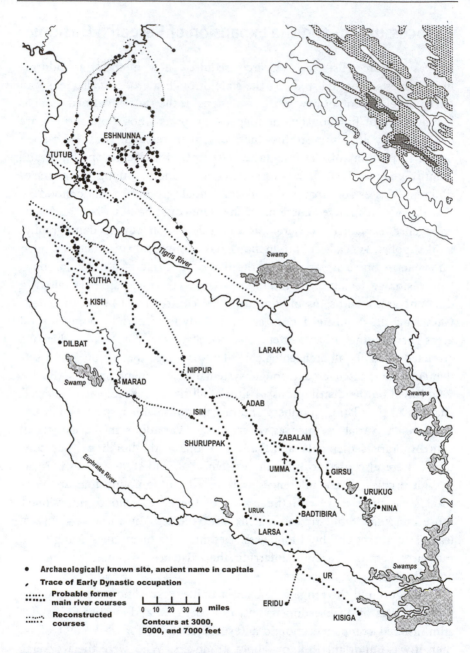

FIGURE 5.3 Example of a map depicting settlement distributions. In this case, the map graphically represents the disposition of sites with respect to watercourses during the Early Dynastic (2900–2373 BC) phase in southern Mesopotamia. Drawn after Figure 2 in Adams 1966.

greatly aided by the decipherment of cuneiform: texts in this writing system provided information on economic transactions among state institutions and their various constituents. Written accounts, however, did not yield all the information needed to map out adaptive relations among all segments of society. Archaeological survey and excavation were needed to test and amplify textual sources.

The search for evidence of behavioral variability across time and space also resulted in a dramatic expansion of the array of data collected by archaeologists. Chronology, based in part on changes in material styles, certainly did not wane as an important concern. Understanding the operation of adaptive processes required tracing changes among demographic, ecological, technological, social, and political variables over phases defined using Culture Historical techniques. Researchers increased their concern with studying the contexts of artifacts and features, not just to define temporal spans, but to see what those materials were used for at any one moment. Relations among finds, therefore, had a behavioral, not just chronological, story to tell.

The definition of what constituted archaeologically relevant materials was also enlarged. Faunal and floral remains, previously deemphasized, if not ignored, in excavations now were avidly sought. They provided information on past environments and the means employed to exploit them. Ecological data were especially relevant to assessing Adams's theory that coordinating the movement of matter and energy among social groups was a cause of state formation.

Processualism and the State

Adams's theory of state origins highlights certain basic assertions of Processualism:

- Society, not the individual, is the basic unit of adaptation;

- Societies are systems composed of closely interrelated parts that function together to promote the unity and physical survival of their members.

Based on these assumptions, archaeologists proposed that the core features of the state (power concentration, hierarchy, and social differentiation) arose not to enhance the lives of a few, but to preserve the integrity and coherence of entire societies. In this way, the physical survival of their members was assured. New methods were developed to reconstruct these social groups and the adaptive processes that shaped them.

Adams also argued through the early 1980s that processes of state formation are universal: the political changes seen in southern Mesopotamia are not unique to that locale. Instead, the structure of the Mesopotamian state is composed of the same basic elements of power concentration, hierarchy, and social differentiation that appear in other world areas. Similarities among early states are due to the operation of similar adaptive processes. To be sure, each state is an adjustment to specific ecological conditions. There is, therefore, no one factor, such as irrigation or environmental diversity, that drives state formation in all times and places. Rather, the state emerges as a way to meet the threat to social continuity and coherence posed by the universal problem of rising populations. Each instance, however, happens under certain specifiable ecological circumstances. One goal Adams and Processualists in general wanted to achieve was to identify which environmental, technological, and demographic variables combined to generate the administrative apparatus of the state in various times and places. If this could be done, archaeology could then develop a powerful set of laws governing relations between power and adaptation in all human societies.

Culture and history were dramatically redefined in Adams's research. Culture was now an adaptive system, not a body of stylistically distinctive traits to be traced over space and time. Within each cultural system, artifacts, features, plants, and animals functioned to promote the survival of societies and the individuals who belonged to them. In addition, the perception of history shifted. Initially, history was seen as a unique sequence of events shaped primarily by the cultural forces of diffusion and migration. In the new perspective, history became viewed as a process governed by adaptations that link aspects of culture and environment in predictable ways.

Marxism and the State of Power

Processualists tend to talk of power in the passive voice: relationships of inequality happened as a consequence of adaptive processes. Marxists of various stripes, in contrast, speak of power as an objective people seek, with the state as the means of gaining it. Just as there are a number of Processual theories of state formation in southern Mesopotamia, there

USE THIS Chapter
AND NEXT FOR PAPER (5+6)

2 schools of Thought
Marxist + ? Processualism
            Subsistence
            Materialism

are several Marxist-inspired approaches to explaining the emergence of this political form. We consider two of these here. The first, promoted by **Igor Diakonoff** (see sidebar), derives from the strong tradition of scholarship developed by researchers from the former Soviet Union. The second perspective, that of **Guillermo Algaze** (see sidebar), examines how the appearance of the state was tied up with developments in neighboring areas, especially northern Mesopotamia. Considering these two theories allows us to appreciate how the same basic principles can be applied by different researchers operating in the same school.

Seizing Power and Wealth with Class

Diakonoff contended that the state's emergence was intimately bound up with changes in the relations of production, the social means by which technology was put to use securing, processing, using, and exchanging resources. He argued that in the earlier, pre-state societies of southern Mesopotamia, small quantities of food were grown by, and more or less evenly distributed within, groups of relatives. These relations of production produced limited amounts of food, yielding what Diakonoff called a "hungry egalitarianism." Efforts to increase productivity required new relations

---

Igor Diakonoff

Igor Diakonoff was one of the most prominent students of ancient Near Eastern languages working in the 20th century. Throughout his career, he translated texts from different epochs of Near Eastern history written in Sumerian, Akkadian, Hebrew, Elamite, Hittite, Urartian, and Hurrian. Diakonoff's close analyses of these materials formed the bases of his studies of early Near Eastern political economies and general trends in human sociocultural evolution. He worked throughout most of his career firmly within a Soviet tradition that stressed the importance of Marxist principles, especially processes of class formation and exploitation, in explaining human behavior. Nevertheless, Diakonoff maintained close contacts with scholars from around the world who espoused different perspectives. In part because of the high regard in which he and his work were held by a wide range of students of the Near East, his publications were very influential beyond the field of linguistics and among non-Marxists. Archaeologists of different nationalities working in Mesopotamia especially drew on, and debated, his insights.

Guillermo Algaze

Guillermo Algaze has spent much of his professional career, beginning in the middle 1980s, conducting archaeological investigations in southeast Turkey. He has long focused on the impact southern Mesopotamian states had on the presumably smaller, more simply organized political units of northern Mesopotamia during the 4th millennium BC. In the course of grappling with this issue, Algaze became one of the first archaeologists working in the Near East to apply a modified version of World Systems theory to understanding processes of inter-societal interaction. Controversial from the start, Algaze's casting of northern Mesopotamia as a periphery of southern Mesopotamian cores continues to stir significant debate. As work by Algaze and other scholars has proceeded, especially in Turkey, there is increasing recognition that the northern Mesopotamian realms were not as small and politically simple as many had thought. Consequently, Algaze has modified his position to take account of these new findings. His book *Ancient Mesopotamia at the Dawn of Civilization: The Evolution of an Urban Landscape* (2008) provides a recent summary of his views on relations among local and inter-societal interactions in the creation of early southern Mesopotamian states.

of production. At the center of these were social classes distinguished by their different relations to property and surplus. The upper class, which had appeared by 3200 BC, was initially dominated by priest-rulers. In the names of the gods, they enjoyed privileged rights to large tracts of productive land watered by irrigation canals. These fields were worked, in turn, by members of a much lower class who were wholly dependent on their rulers for support. Those clients and slaves provided the labor needed to increase food production by cultivating extensive fields, herding numerous animals, and digging and maintaining the irrigation channels that made large-scale farming possible. Productivity was further enhanced by demands for tribute levied by rulers on members of an intermediary class made up of free farmers and herders. Though these "freemen" owned their own land, often as members of kinship groups, they were forced to develop means to increase yields to meet the demands of the state for food and other goods. Failure to do so could well result in loss of their land and removal to the class of temple clients and slaves. Thus, a "hungry egalitarianism" was replaced by a very productive economy, the outputs of which—in the form of land, food, and other goods—were unevenly distributed among people belonging to at least three distinct social classes. These exploitive relations generated tensions within southern Mesopotamia's early states.

As noted in Chapter 4, Marxists often invoke ideology, the body of beliefs generally shared by members of a society, to understand how such tensions can be calmed. Hence, priestly leadership was rationalized and placed beyond question by belief in divine rule: those who wielded power and accumulated wealth did so at the bidding of the gods and with their blessings. Belief, however, was bolstered in southern Mesopotamia by military threat. Priest-rulers invested some of their economic gains in subsidizing a permanent fighting force composed of temple clients. Since no other social group had access to comparable surpluses, no other group could support a force of arms even near the size, training, and organization as that maintained by the temple. Ideological and military power, based on unequal economic relations, were therefore concentrated in a few hands and marshaled in defense of privilege.

Diakonoff and his colleagues recognized that centralized power in Mesopotamian states was not absolute, nor did it necessarily follow clear class lines. From the very beginning, priestly authority was checked, to some extent, by councils of prosperous citizens whose economic well-being was threatened by the growth of temple landholdings and wealth. Further, by 2800 BC, secular leaders were challenging priests for political supremacy and the economic resources underlying it. Tensions among these factions sometimes broke out in open conflicts that could change who controlled the state and how they organized its relations of production. As noted in Chapter 4, Marxists tend to look to these sorts of competitions over the relations of production to explain political change.

Expanding the Scope of Analysis: The State, Colonies, and Interregional Exploitation

Many Marxist analyses of ancient states, like those conducted by their Processualist cousins, focus on developments that took place within particular societies. The crucial processes yielding hierarchical social relations and power centralization involved interactions among groups of people who lived together and drew resources from the same immediate environment. Inspired by **Immanuel Wallerstein's** World Systems theory (WST; see sidebar), some researchers began to challenge this perspective.

Wallerstein, a Marxist sociologist, wrote several influential volumes beginning in the 1970s that questioned traditional models of global relations.

Immanuel Wallerstein

Immanuel Wallerstein is a sociologist who early in his career was concerned with the unequal economic relations that pertain on a global scale and the historical roots of those inequities. Based in part on his early studies of post-colonial developments in Africa, Wallerstein rejected traditional Western approaches to economic development that imagined Third World nations as engaged in a steady process of transformation toward First World models of wealth and democracy. Instead, Wallerstein elaborated on earlier versions of dependency theory, which stressed that global capitalism has been and will continue to be predicated on the systematic exploitation of most of the world's populations by the leaders of a few core states. The utility of Wallerstein's World Systems theory has been much debated throughout the social sciences, one salient criticism being that he tends to emphasize economic processes at the expense of cultural variables in understanding interactions among nations. Nonetheless, some proponents of the anti-globalization movement have celebrated Wallerstein's early critiques of global capitalism. In addition, as illustrated here, some archaeologists have modified his insights to understand inter-societal dealings in non-capitalist contexts. Whatever this theory's fate, it continues to inspire interpretations of the past and present by calling attention to the spatially extensive economic, social, and political structures in which local developments occur and to which they contribute.

He argued that economic dealings among the world's populations have, since at least the 15th century, been increasingly structured to favor the leaders of a few core states at the expense of the rest. The process works as follows. Agents of the largest, most complexly structured core states use their superior military power and organizational structures to extract from smaller, more simply organized peripheries low-cost raw materials obtained through the cheap labor of those living there. These items are converted by core industries into expensive finished goods, which are exported back to peripheries at a high markup. Wealth thus consistently flows from peripheries to cores, where it finances core militaries and industries, and contributes to the growing power of core elites at home and abroad. Impoverished peripheries, in turn, lack the economic wherewithal to sustain complex hierarchical political structures; consequently, their political systems are far simpler than those of cores. This distinction only contributes to their continued exploitation, as they cannot muster the economic, military, and political means to resist core demands.

World Systems theory encouraged researchers to appreciate that:

1. all societies are linked in significant ways within expansive structures that include groups organized at varying levels of complexity;

2. understanding occurrences within any part of an interaction web requires specifying a society's place within the flow of goods that characterizes this network;

3. those transactions are inevitably unequal in character and effect, thus helping to create political and economic hierarchies at local and regional levels.

Guillermo Algaze applied these lessons to understanding the emergence of states in southern Mesopotamia. He argued that sustaining such large, complexly organized realms depended on acquiring commodities not available in the Tigris and Euphrates delta. Though rich in fertile soils, this area lacked such basic goods as timber, oils, stone, and metals used to make buildings, tools, weapons, and objects needed to distinguish people's positions within increasingly stratified societies. Consequently, the emergence of southern Mesopotamian states depended on the ability of their leaders to obtain reliable supplies of essential imported items, primarily from northern Mesopotamia, where sources for many of the needed raw materials were located. This goal was achieved in large part by the establishment of southern Mesopotamian colonies at strategic points along riverine and overland trade networks. Such enclaves were staffed by representatives from the different southern Mesopotamian realms who were competing for control of valued imports. In some cases, the outsiders were "guests" of established indigenous populations, settling in neighborhoods within preexisting settlements. In others, the colonies were more sizable, representing state imposition of southern Mesopotamian organizational forms and practices on native peoples. No matter what a colony's form or mode of establishment, it could be recognized by the appearance of distinctive styles of artifacts, features, iconography, and administration (especially modes of record keeping) that had clear ties with southern Mesopotamia but seemed out of place in northern Mesopotamian contexts. According to Algaze, the purpose of these enclaves was to promote the efficient transfer of goods back to the homeland.

Based on WST principles, Algaze predicted that, once established, trading relations contributed to the underdevelopment of peripheral societies. This is because the latter lacked the military forces and bureaucratic structures needed to resist the demands of their larger, more powerful, and complexly organized southern neighbors. Hence, the agents of core states could set the terms of exchange to their advantage. As a result, peripheral societies would become increasingly overspecialized in the extraction of resources for export, failing to develop local industries that might convert those assets into a diverse array of finished goods for local use and trade. Further, they would have been systematically stripped of raw materials by representatives of core states. Resources that might have been used to enrich local leaders and support the creation of independent, economically diversified northern Mesopotamian states were instead channeled southward, where they fueled the expansion of craft industries using foreign raw materials and contributed to the economic power of paramount lords who controlled those industries. Diakonoff had argued that the world's earliest states were founded on exploitive economic relations among classes distinguished by their variable control over property, labor, and surpluses. Algaze extended these exploitive relations to include the asymmetrical terms of trade that prevailed between core rulers and peripheral producers. That northern Mesopotamian societies were not as disadvantaged as might be expected given the expectations of WST was due to the relatively short duration of the southern Mesopotamian world system.

These and other Marxist approaches to state formation require that much the same sorts of data be gathered using many of the same methods employed by Processualists. In order to track relations among politics, production, and exchange, it is essential to obtain information on ecological, economic, social, and political variables from all sites that comprise a state, from urban capital to rural farmsteads to distant colonies. Research must therefore combine survey and excavation conducted at a wide array of settlements situated in diverse locales. Only in this way can data be acquired that are relevant to evaluating hypotheses based on theories such as the ones proposed by Diakonoff and Algaze. In part, the above methodological similarities are due to the materialist stances of both schools. Insofar as the physical conditions of life, especially the ways in which people extract and use resources from the environment, are critical to explaining social forms and changes, then ecological variables must be measured through survey and excavation. In addition, Processualist and Marxist approaches presuppose a view of cultures as systems of interrelated parts. These parts are differently defined by the practitioners of each school. In both cases, however, the behaviors through which cultural systems take shape and are transformed are variably enacted in different locales spread across and beyond an ancient realm. For example, whether irrigation is designed to feed many mouths or expand the productivity of estates worked by slaves, understanding its operation requires specific kinds of research. Essential are mapping canals and studying the different sites involved in their functioning, from the homes of primary producers to the administrative offices of state functionaries. No one site, no matter how large, is "typical" of an ancient state. Consequently, field research must be conducted in a wide array of locales.

Diakonoff's and Algaze's theories focus on ancient **political economies** (the ways in which processes of production, consumption, and exchange are manipulated by those seeking power). Political economies in both theories are structured according to exploitive relations based primarily on class differences. Changes in political structures result, in large part, from the ability of a few to mobilize and manipulate economic resources in efforts to centralize power in their own hands and create hierarchies that they dominate. Ideology and coercion may be mobilized to defend social privileges, but such efforts are never completely successful. Instead, the state is, and was, an arena in which social classes, and factions within them, contend for the reward of power by attempting to control economic resources (such as irrigation agriculture, alienated labor, and trade goods) in ways that benefit them and disadvantage everyone else. The scale at which these processes operate differs between the two perspectives. Diakonoff emphasizes unequal interactions within particular realms, whereas Algaze expands the analysis to include economic and power relations acted out across larger territorial expanses and involving multiple societies organized in different ways. As distinct as these theories are, they are unmistakable products of the Marxist theoretical school.

Material culture in both Processual and Marxist approaches is understood as serving to promote the operation of a society. It functions in large part to extract matter and energy from fields, herds, and crafts, and through trade, and to signal status distinctions. To Marxists, however, artifacts and features also figure in power contests, and these functions are as important as their roles in energy extraction. Adams, Diakonoff, and Algaze concur as well that the histories of each culture are not unique but conform to regularities that emerge from the action of universal causal principles. The difference, as noted in Chapter 4, lies in what drives that universal history, what goals societies and factions seek, and how behaviors and material culture function to meet these aims.

Interpretivism: Fragmenting the State

As discussed in Chapter 4, Interpretivists reject attempts to define universal phenomena (such as the state) that can be explained according to broadly applicable principles (such as adaptation and competition for power). In their view, it is more productive to describe the varied forms societies can take and to understand the unique histories out of which those arrangements arose. Consequently, one set of related topics that Interpretivists address in southern Mesopotamia include:

1. how people of different genders, ages, ethnic backgrounds, and classes experienced relations of power and hierarchy in their daily lives;

2. how these experiences gave rise to diverse social identities that fragmented the unity of ancient realms;

3. what distinctive historical sequences yielded these varied social and political forms.

In pursuing these interests, Interpretivists allow for more human agency in sequences of culture change than do their Processualist and Marxist colleagues. For them, human behavior occurs within a matrix of structural constraints, of which power relations are especially prominent. The constraints exclude and preclude some actions, enable others, but determine none of them. It is by making choices within this matrix of possibilities that cultures take shape and are reproduced. In addition, they are transformed by actors behaving strategically in pursuit of their own interests, though rarely are they aware of their actions' full set of implications.

Because Interpretivism encompasses such a wide array of approaches to understanding the past, it is hard to select one case that illustrates how its principles have been applied to the study of southern Mesopotamia. The extensive writings of **Susan Pollock** (see sidebar) on the region, however, provide a number of examples of this approach, from which we will draw one for consideration here.

Power and Gender

In one of her analyses, Pollock focuses on shifts in gender relations that occurred during the period of increased political centralization and hierarchy-building dating to about 3200 BC. Gender refers to cultural con-

Susan Pollock

Susan Pollock has been investigating developments in Mesopotamia and its environs for roughly three decades. Her approach might be characterized as a moderate version of Interpretivism. Pollock argues that Processual interpretations of sociopolitical and economic developments within southern Mesopotamia of the 5th through 3rd millennia BC stress the operation of broad forces, such as adaptation, that allow no room for human agency. They also tend to treat ancient societies as homogeneous wholes largely untroubled by internal divisions, except those of class. In contrast to these perspectives, Pollock has consistently argued for a vision of southern Mesopotamian realms as populated by different factions whose members enjoyed varying degrees of control over such essential economic factors as land, irrigation water, imports, and the labor to convert those resources into food and craft goods. Differential participation in these economic operations resulted in distinctions in the power wielded by members of various social groups. Pollock's attention to the linkage between political and economic processes in understanding culture change is an interest she shares with scholars working in the Marxist school. She looks, however, beyond the development of classes that Marxists often emphasize. Instead, she examines how social identities, especially those based on gender, were affected by and affected transformations in ancient southern Mesopotamian political economies. The sociopolitical structures that emerged from these struggles were diverse, products of their own unique histories. Those histories, in turn, were shaped by the variably successful strategies of agents working to secure the resources they needed to define and achieve their goals. This is a grassroots approach to understanding the genesis of the inequalities and oppressions thought to be characteristic of the state in general and its ancient Mesopotamian forms in particular.

structions of sexual differences. Gender is not sex but a culturally conditioned understanding of sex's social significance. Pollock argues that shifts in power and economic relations around 3200 BC provided an opportunity for some actors, primarily upper-class men, to define gender's meanings to their benefit. She pursues this point by exploring artistic representations of women and men at work. These appear primarily on carved seals used to mark claims of ownership to certain forms of movable property, such as grains and liquids.

Men appear on the seals engaged in a variety of tasks, sometimes acting alone, sometimes as part of groups doing such chores as herding and farming. Crucially, a few men wearing distinctive net skirts are occasionally shown in positions of authority—for example, leading troops and processions, and making offerings to the gods. Women are never shown as leaders. Invariably, they are part of groups carrying out repetitive, menial tasks (Figure 5.4). The participants in these chores are not distinguishable as individuals. Pollock sees in this pattern the emergence of a gender hierarchy that generally, if not invariably, subordinated most women to some men. Certainly, many males worked in menial jobs like their female counterparts. Members of both genders served as clients and/or slaves of large institutions such as temples. These powerful corporations, however, were always depicted as being led by men, never women, pointing to a rather firm limit on the aspirations of all women.

Art is not life. Art often represents life less as it is than as artists and consumers of art wish it would be. Ideologies that blatantly misrepresent social relations, however, are unlikely to be shown in pictorial representations that span centuries. Thus, the seals' depictions considered here have to be taken as legitimate statements about *some* aspects of ancient lived experiences.

Pollock's interest in this instance has less to do with general processes of state formation than with the ways changing political relations in one area at a specific point in time worked to divide societies into different interest groups. Each segment of ancient Mesopotamian society was characterized by diverse lived experiences. The change she highlights is the concentration of land and its products into the hands of powerful *oikoi*, or large households that employed clients and slaves to work their properties. Some temples were organized as oikoi, though the number of secular entities structured in this way apparently increased with time. Lacking access to the

FIGURE 5.4 Design from a southern Mesopotamian cylinder seal showing subordinate women and men in the process of offering goods to higher powers. Drawn after Figure 13.2 in Pollock and Bernbeck 2000.

means of production, laborers in oikoi depended on their employers for support in the form of standardized rations and/or access to land they could farm but never own. The gender hierarchy represented in carved seals emerged as part of these transformed productive relations. Women and men were conscripted into lives of clientage and slavery. Women almost never appear in any other context. This suggests that they suffered more from this kind of exploitation than did their male counterparts. Whether they were slaves captured in war or clients who had lost access to the productive resources obtained through membership in landowning kinship groups, women were especially vulnerable to incorporation within oikoi. By extension, their labor formed the backbone of productive arrangements that concentrated wealth and power in the hands of the few men who led these early corporations (the gentlemen depicted wearing net skirts). Political centralization and hierarchy-building were, therefore, not disembodied processes operating according to the dictates of abstract principles of adaptation or class formation. Instead, they came about through the decisions of actors who maneuvered successfully to exploit female bodies in strategies of economic domination initiated by, and benefiting, upper-class males. Rather than unifying society and benefiting all its members, as Adams argued, or uniting people within distinct classes, as Diakonoff contended, power concentration and hierarchy-building fragmented social groups along gender lines and disproportionately disadvantaged women.

The methods used to gather data needed to assess Pollock's hypothesis are much the same as those used by Processualists and Marxists. Exploring the ways in which societies are fragmented along lines of gender, class, ethnicity, and the like requires information collected from urban and rural sites as well as a wide array of settings in each one. If anything, the spatial and temporal scale of analysis must be particularly fine-grained for Interpretivists, since they cannot take for granted that information gathered from any one site, or portion of a settlement, is typical of behaviors and cultural patterns practiced throughout the place examined. There is every reason to suspect that the experience of being a woman, for example, varied by class, ethnic group, age, and occupation. The gender hierarchy depicted on seals may convey a general picture of interpersonal relations, but Interpretivists know that life is rarely that simple. Investigating this issue, therefore, would require extensive excavations covering a wide array of residential groups at specific sites. Such work should get past generalities to the specific strategies different groups of women in different structural positions employed to negotiate their relations with power.

Pollock's account of gender differences highlights the general Interpretivist notion that cultures are not homogeneous entities. They are fragmented by the diverse experiences of people who likely share broadly acknowledged premises but perceived those principles differently, based on their divergent life histories. Among the elements making up those histories are factors such as gender. But gender and other categories are not universal in their behavioral content or consequences. For this reason, the gender hierarchy outlined here was not inevitable. Instead, it arose from a specific set of circumstances that bore bitter fruit in one area at one moment in time.

Artifacts, features, and faunal and floral remains are of interest to Interpretivists for the meanings they conveyed to those who made and/or used them. Although these finds are still significant for how they functioned to promote adaptation or to gain power, in an Interpretivist perspective they are more important for looking at meaning. Understanding what it meant to be a woman or a man in 3200 BC in a specific community within southern Mesopotamia means inquiring into how different groups of people expressed who they were in their daily lives. To the extent that performances of identity involved the use of artifacts (such as carved seals), features, and elements of the physical environment, these views are accessible to archaeologists. Needless to say, it is not so much the objects themselves that convey this information as it is their relations revealed in contexts of discovery. On a larger scale, how these self-conceptions arose requires careful analysis of the complex histories of individual cultures and their variably well-integrated components. Histories, then, are unique, unlikely to have been replicated in other times and places.

Communication across Theoretical Schools

As outlined above, views on southern Mesopotamia's past have changed dramatically since the early 19th century. In the course of research conducted since that time, methods, along with concepts of culture, history, and the relation of material remains to both, have been debated. So has the role of southern Mesopotamia in understanding the human past. In the process, data have been collected by people operating under different sets of guiding principles. We conclude this section by considering how these findings are related to one another and to the theories under which they were gathered.

It is common to treat different theories as mutually exclusive, with their practitioners engaged in intellectual debates that cannot be reconciled. There is no doubt that each of the perspectives considered here is based on very different premises that specify why people act the way they do. An important point to bear in mind, however, is that the data generated by researchers working within different conceptual frameworks are used by those conducting investigations following other guiding principles.

The chronological framework developed through Culture Historical studies is employed as a time line by virtually all archaeologists working in southern Mesopotamia. Similarly, information Processualists gather about human–environment relations in the area are fundamental to all investigations, just as insights from Marxist and Interpretivist analyses inform research conducted by supporters of other theories. For example, insights into the operation of large oikoi provided by researchers like Diakonoff are incorporated into Pollock's account of gender. Notions of clientage, slavery, and exploitation are crucial to her analysis, even if she does not see in them the operation of those universal forces that Diakonoff perceives. It is also the case, as noted throughout the chapter, that methods developed by members of one school are readily appropriated by researchers from another. For example, the principles of stratigraphy elaborated by Culture Historians are essential to Processual research, just as settlement pattern studies developed to address Processual concerns are widely used by their Interpretivist and Marxist colleagues.

These crossovers of method and insight imply, for one thing, that the strong version of Interpretivism discussed in Chapter 4 is overstated. If theory determines findings absolutely, then communication among supporters of different conceptual structures would be nearly impossible. Yet people subscribing to distinct theories are capable of understanding and using results generated under other guiding principles. They can also adapt to their own uses methods developed within alternative perspectives. What does this say about the relationship between theory and data?

There is little doubt that the conceptual framework within which someone works directs attention to some aspects of ancient reality while discouraging the appreciation of others. Pollock sees evidence of women's subjugation to men within Mesopotamian realms in data that had long been available. Similar conclusions had not been drawn, or at least not emphasized, by others who were more concerned with issues of class, adaptation, or chronology. Now published, Pollock's interpretation can be incorporated in the work of all researchers.

It can also be said that the sorts of information a researcher generates about the past are very much conditioned by the theoretical perspective he or she brings to the investigation. Those data, however, are not so thoroughly shaped by their framing theories that they are unintelligible, and not useful, to others following very different conceptual paths. People may well argue about the significance of ecological variation, references to slaves in cuneiform texts, and how women are represented on seals, but they can accept that such variation, references, and representations exist. It is through communication among practitioners of different theories that the methods used to gather data, and the reconstructions of southern Mesopotamia's past resulting from their application, have expanded and become more sophisticated. It is easy to lose track of such cross-fertilization in the midst of cross-theoretical debates about how to explain what has come to light. Archaeological knowledge about developments in southern Mesopotamia, as in most world areas, may not advance in clear waves of harmonious agreement, but neither is the field so fragmented among different schools that each yields dissimilar and conflicting results.

Further Reading

Mesopotamia, General Discussion

Lloyd, S.
  1980   *Foundations in the Dust: The Story of Mesopotamian Exploration*. London: Thames and Hudson.

  This summary of 19th-century research in southern Mesopotamia is strong on the personalities and political intrigues involved in this work. You might want to pay attention to how Seton characterizes settlement studies at the end of the book for a sense of how a representative of the Culture History school viewed a methodological innovation promoted by Processualists.

Rothman, M.
  2004   Studying the Development of Complex Society: Mesopotamia in the Late Fifth and Fourth Millennia BC. *Journal of Archaeological Research* 12:75–119.

  Rothman provides an overview of shifting theoretical perspectives on southern Mesopotamian prehistory.

Theory, Interpretivist

Pollock, S.
  1999   *Ancient Mesopotamia: The Eden That Never Was*. Cambridge: Cambridge University Press.

  This is a lucid and concise synthesis of southern Mesopotamian prehistory from a moderate Interpretivist stance.

Pollock, S., and R. Bernbeck
2000 And They Said, Let Us Make Gods in Our Image: Gendered Ideologies in Ancient Mesopotamia. In *Reading the Body: Representations and Remains in the Archaeological Record*, ed. Alison E. Rautman, pp. 150–164. Philadelphia: University of Pennsylvania Press.

This is the source of the example of gender hierarchies discussed in this chapter.

Pollock, S., and R. Bernbeck, eds.
2005 *Archaeologies of the Middle East: Critical Perspectives*. Oxford: Blackwell.

This volume offers a selection of different perspectives on southern Mesopotamia's past, weighted toward Interpretivist accounts.

Theory, Marxism

Childe, V. G.
1936 *Man Makes Himself*. New York: Mentor Books.

Childe pioneered both Culture Historical and Marxist approaches to the study of the past in general, and to understanding developments in southern Mesopotamia in particular. Through time his viewpoints shifted, but Childe remains very influential in defining the parameters of study in the land between the Tigris and Euphrates. This specific book is interesting in part because of how Childe synthesizes elements of Marxism and Culture History in his interpretations of ancient southern Mesopotamia.

Diakonoff, I. M.
1969 The Rise of the Despotic State in Ancient Mesopotamia. In *Ancient Mesopotamia: Socio-Economic History, a Collection of Studies by Soviet Scholars*, ed. I. M. Diakonoff, pp. 173–203. Moscow: "NAUKA" Publishing House, Central Department of Oriental Literature.
1989 General Outline of the First Period of the History of the Ancient World and the Problem of the Ways of Development. In *Early Antiquity*, ed. I. M. Diakonoff and P. L. Kohl, pp. 27–66. Chicago: University of Chicago Press.

The above two sources provide an introduction to Diakonoff's work. Reviewing other articles in these collections will give you a general sense of how Soviet scholars interpreted developments in ancient southern Mesopotamia.

Zagarell, A.
1986 Trade, Women, Class, and Society in Ancient Western Asia. *Current Anthropology* 27:415–430.

Zagarell considers the effect of political and economic changes on gender relations in southern Mesopotamia during the late 4th millennium BC. You might want to compare this more strictly Marxist perspective with Pollock and Bernbeck's take on the subject (see above, under Theory, Interpretivist).

Theory, Processual

Adams, R. McC.

1965 *The Land behind Baghdad: A History of Settlement on the Diyala Plain*. Chicago: University of Chicago Press.

1966 *The Evolution of Urban Society: Early Mesopotamia and Prehispanic Mexico*. Chicago: University of Chicago Press.

1981 *Heartland of Cities: Surveys of Ancient Settlement and Land Use of the Central Floodplain of the Euphrates*. Chicago: University of Chicago Press.

Adams, R. McC., and H. Nissen

1972 *Uruk Countryside: Natural Setting of Urban Societies*. Chicago: University of Chicago Press.

These four sources will give you a good sense of Adams's approach to the study of the state in southern Mesopotamia and in comparative perspective. They also highlight the centrality of settlement survey to Adams's theoretical work.

Flannery, K.

1972 The Cultural Evolution of Civilizations. *Annual Review of Ecology and Systematics* 3:399–426.

This is a classic statement of how Systems theory principles might be applied to studying ancient states. Though Flannery was critical of many aspects of Processualism, his essay was and remains widely cited by those analyzing state formation processes from the Processualist perspective in southern Mesopotamia and elsewhere.

Wright, H., and G. Johnson

1975 Population, Exchange, and Early State Formation in Southwestern Iran. *American Anthropologist* 77:267–289.

This is a Processualist account of state formation in southern Mesopotamia, building on, but differing from, Adams's earlier work.

Theory, World System

Algaze, G.

1989 The Uruk Expansion: Cross-Cultural Exchange in Early Mesopotamian Civilization. *Current Anthropology* 30:571–608.

1993 *The Uruk World System: The Dynamics of Expansion of Early Mesopotamian Civilization*. Chicago: University of Chicago Press.

In this article and book, Algaze outlines his application of World Systems theory principles to the study of southern Mesopotamian states.

2008   *Ancient Mesopotamia at the Dawn of Civilization: The Evolution of an Urban Landscape.* Chicago: University of Chicago Press.

In this book, Algaze specifies how the trade mediated by southern Mesopotamian colonies had transformative effects on the states of southern Mesopotamia. His foci in this publication are the processes leading to the emergence of cities in southern Mesopotamia, and the economic and social bases for the dominant role that southern Mesopotamian states played in their interactions with those in northern Mesopotamia. Algaze no longer relies as heavily here on World Systems theory to explain these transformations as he has in earlier works.

Kohl, P.

1987   The Use and Abuse of World System Theory: The Case of the Pristine West Asian State. *Advances in Archaeological Method and Theory* 11:1–35.

Kohl offers an overview and critique of how World Systems theory has been applied to archaeology; the article provides a good list of published sources dealing with the topic up through the middle of the 1980s.

Stein, G.

1999   *Rethinking World Systems: Diasporas, Colonies, and Interaction in Uruk Mesopotamia.* Tucson: University of Arizona Press.

Stein offers here a rebuttal of Algaze's World Systems–based approach to the study of relations between southern Mesopotamian states and their northern Mesopotamian neighbors.

Wallerstein, I.

1974   *The Modern World System*, Vol. 1. New York: Academic Press.
1980   *The Modern World System*, Vol. 2. New York: Academic Press.

These volumes articulate the basic principles of World Systems theory as they apply to modeling the expansion of capitalist economies from the 15th century onward.

CHAPTER 6

MULTIPLE VIEWS OF STONEHENGE

I N GEOFFREY OF MONMOUTH 's *History of the Kings of Britain*, written in about 1136, he claimed that Stonehenge was built by Merlin. Around AD 485, the sorcerer magically brought its massive stones from Ireland to help King Ambrosius, a probably mythical early king of the Britons, construct a victory monument.

As outrageous—or as silly—as this "history" may seem today, like all history it is based on theoretical positions: about how to calculate the age of a monument; the ways to determine who was king of the Britons; who, indeed, the "Britons" were; who interacted with the Britons; and the nature and responsibilities of kingship. The previous chapter looked at theory in terms of how different schools of thought approached social and political change in southern Mesopotamia. Here we switch focus to see how one particular site, Stonehenge on Salisbury Plain in southern Britain (Figure 6.1), has been interpreted by different parties—although we'll leave Geoffrey's ideas for you to evaluate.

As in Chapter 5, we review how practitioners of various archaeological schools have understood much the same set of archaeological remains from different perspectives, emphasizing in particular the work of Culture Historians, Processualists, and Interpretivists. Marxist takes on Stonehenge have not been common and are excluded here to make room for a discussion of Stonehenge's place in debates that involve non-archaeologists. People outside our profession often have a stake in understanding the past. Stonehenge offers a particularly clear example of how archaeological interests in antiquity crosscut the views and concerns of others and often exist uncomfortably

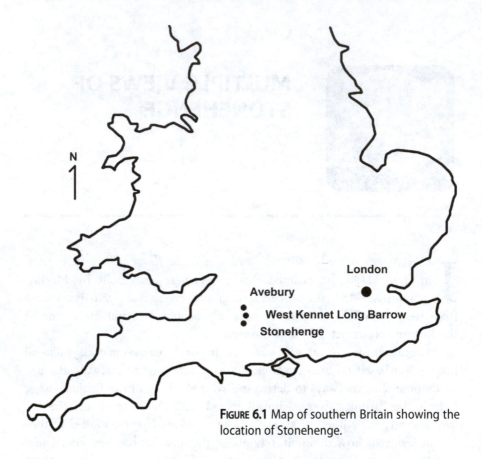

FIGURE 6.1 Map of southern Britain showing the location of Stonehenge.

with them. At the end of the chapter, we reserve a few pages for a brief consideration of this topic and its relation to broader issues of theory.

Stonehenge Today

Stonehenge's massive blocks can be seen for several miles across the rolling terrain of Salisbury Plain, about 129 km (80 miles) west of London. The site is best known for its large, shaped, upright sarsen stones, some of which still support lintels of the same material. In fact, Stonehenge is composed of a complex array of nested circular constructions, fashioned in a variety of ways, which were put in place over a long span of time (2950–1700 BC; Figure 6.2). Let's begin with the stone part of the monument.

The outermost stone circle is composed of 30 surviving squared uprights made of a very hard kind of sandstone known as *sarsen*. These are laid

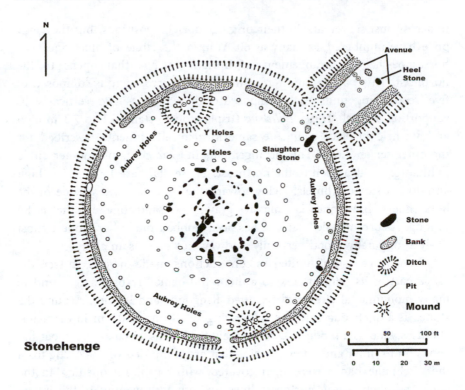

Figure 6.2 Map of Stonehenge showing the major features discussed in the text. The Aubrey holes are arranged around the inner perimeter of the ditch and bank. Drawn after Figure 4 in Burl 2007.

out to form a circle measuring about 30.5 m in diameter, each sarsen stone separated by approximately 1.1 m. Stone lintels once spanned these gaps, originally creating a continuous circle sitting about 4.9 m above today's ground surface; at present the entire south and southwest portions of the circle are missing, and only three lintels remain in place. The lintels are joined to each other and to their supporting upright using techniques that are more in keeping with carpentry than masonry. One member of each pair of lintels has a vertical groove at one end, into which the projecting tongue of its neighbor fits. The top of the supporting sarsen is outfitted with two low knobs of stone, each of which corresponds to a cup-shaped depression in the base of the corresponding lintel. The lintels are fitted over these projections and joined to each other, increasing the stability of the entire construction.

Set within this outer ring is a circular arrangement of bluestones that are about 2 m high and now lack lintels. They form a ring measuring 23 m across; just six remain in their original upright positions, but they may once have numbered as many as 60. Within the circle of bluestones is a horseshoe-shaped arrangement of upright sarsens that opens to the northeast. This configuration measures 13.7 m across and is composed of five freestanding units, each composed of three stones—two vertical slabs supporting a lintel. These *trilithons* (triple stones) stand 6.1 to 7.3 m high and are held in place using the same form of attachments described for the outer sarsen circle. This arrangement, in turn, contains another circle of bluestones, also open to the northeast. These slabs are 1.8 to 2.4 m high and do not support lintels. Lying toward the base (southwest) side of the horseshoe of bluestones is a massive gray-green sandstone slab that is 4.9 m long. It currently lies flat and has been dubbed the "Altar Stone"; most likely it originally stood vertically and was not used as an altar.

Stonehenge is not limited to constructions made of rock. In fact, the *henge* part of its name refers to a ditch-and-bank arrangement found in many monumental sites of the United Kingdom and Ireland. Around the stones is a ditch dug into the underlying chalk; it is 101 m in diameter, about as wide as a modern U.S. football field. This circular dry moat has banks on its inner and outer margins that are composed of chalk dug from the ditch; the banks were then covered with earth. An opening in the bank-and-ditch at the northeast lines up with the opening in the inner-most sarsen and bluestone horseshoes. This gap also matches up with a formal walkway called an "avenue." Like the circular ditch, the avenue is bordered on the northwest and southeast by ditches with low earthen banks. This avenue is 21.3 m wide and continues to the northeast past the modern highway; eventually it reaches the Avon River. Located near the center of this walkway, just outside the ditch, is the large rock known as the "Heel Stone." This sarsen is 4.9 m high and was shaped by nature, not human activity. A second, narrower, entrance through the encircling bank-and-ditch lies on the south but does not seem to have been marked by stones or to have connected to a formal avenue.

Two isolated sarsen stones are found within the bank; one is on the northwest and the other on the southeast sides of this circular chalk-and-earth construction. Each of these so-called Station Stones may have been paired with other comparable blocks, although any possible companions have disappeared. The "Slaughter Stone," another block of sarsen, cur-rently lies flat on the east edge of the gap in the ditch-and-bank.

At varying distances from Stonehenge, within and around Salisbury Plain, are large earthen mounds, or *barrows*, that largely predate and postdate Stonehenge's creation. These constructions take many shapes but seem to have functioned primarily as tombs.

This describes what visitors to Stonehenge see today and have for quite a while. Vandalism and some stone robbing have taken their toll over the past three millennia or so, but Stonehenge has generally been undisturbed by developers. Until recently, the site was not much fought over as property, but its intellectual significance and place in national history have been much contested.

Antiquaries and Stonehenge

Stonehenge was visited numerous times since it abandonment sometime around 1600 BC, but records of what these visitors thought of the place do not appear until the Middle Ages. From that time through the 19th century, there were numerous attempts to grasp the significance of Stonehenge within British history, some more systematic than others. These efforts occasionally involved investigations conducted at the site. As was the case for early studies of Mesopotamian prehistory, however, the emphasis was not on establishing what happened at a certain location and when it occurred: early investigators did not use careful studies of materials recovered in well-recorded contexts. Rather, attempts were made to tie the massive stone-and-earth constructions of Stonehenge to individuals and cultural groups mentioned in known documents. The Bible was of less concern here than it was in the land between the Tigris and Euphrates. With several notable exceptions, research at Stonehenge was guided not by a search for the roots of Europe's Judeo-Christian heritage, but for indications of how British history fit within Europe's past. Classical authors, such as Julius Caesar, were used as sources to place the monument in history as it was understood at the time. Stonehenge's unusual size and form made it a tempting target for such analyses. Early researchers thought that if it could be related to constructions recorded elsewhere on the continent, then important insights into Britain's early history would be revealed.

Much of this debate centered on the role that the Romans played from AD 43 to 410 in shaping Britain when that land was part of their empire. Rome was generally seen in these early times as a civilizing force. Romans changed the conquered barbarians, such as the Britons, into people who respected and perpetuated forms of social organization that could be called "government." In contrast to supposedly unorganized barbarians, Roman-style rule would guarantee order and restrain base human impulses. The mythical King Ambrosius, for example, was seen as the inheritor of Roman civilization, ruling after the Romans left, as was the probably equally mythical King Arthur.

Inigo Jones (see sidebar), in the 17th century, conducted one of the first detailed surveys of Stonehenge. His model of architecture was derived from the Romans, and his map of Stonehenge matches his ideas. For Jones, Stonehenge was, to be sure, a simple and imperfect version of far more elaborate imperial Roman constructions, but he thought the arrangement of its parts was inspired by principles of Roman architecture. On the one hand, Jones's work demonstrates a feature of archaeological research we have discussed before: he used field data (his map of Stonehenge) to evaluate an idea about past human relationships. On the other, it also demonstrates one of the weaknesses of conducting investigations based on deeply cherished world views. His map was intentionally or unintentionally drawn to yield the results he expected to see. Even some of his contemporaries recognized that Jones's diagram was inaccurate and did not prove what he claimed. Despite problems with these interpretations, for many years to come Romans, and occasionally Greeks, continued to be championed as Stonehenge's builders. The enduring appeal of such claims was often rooted in the great skill and engineering knowledge needed to fashion the constructions at Stonehenge. Many thought that the crude and rude "savages" the Romans encountered could not possibly have known how to move, shape, and set in place the materials used in the monument. In a world view that saw clear differences between civilized people and barbarian savages, the native Britons were definitely not civilized. So, Stonehenge could not be a product of local hands.

Inigo Jones

Inigo Jones was an architect of some note in England during the early 17th century. His studies in Italy provided him with the skills and inspiration to bring elements of Italianate Renaissance architecture to England. Some of Jones's grandest constructions for the English aristocracy and the royal court still stand, including the Banqueting House at the Palace of Whitehall, the Queen's House in Greenwich, and Covent Garden Square in London. He also worked in stage design and served under King Charles I as Surveyor of Works. It was in this last capacity that Jones turned his architectural skills to making the first formal map of Stonehenge.

From the beginning of investigations at Stonehenge, however, there was an alternative view that promoted native Druids as Stonehenge's creators. Early **antiquaries** (people who collected old artifacts and natural objects—for example, fossils), such as **John Aubrey** (see sidebar) and **William Stukeley** (see sidebar), advocated this view and gathered field evidence to support their claims. They initiated systematic surveys of Stonehenge in the 17th and 18th centuries, creating maps that were remarkably accurate, especially given the available technology. Part of what drove this work was a desire to identify the source of inspiration for Stonehenge by providing a map of its overall shape and a detailed account of the site's architectural details. Just as Inigo Jones looked for Roman inspiration in the forms and relations among the stones, so men like Aubrey and Stukeley looked to other groups. They used their data to refute claims about Romans, or Phoenicians or Egyptians, trying to link the site to what they saw as its true source: Druids and/or Celts. The maps that emerged from this work exposed Jones's errors. Further, these diagrams provided a firmer basis than existed before for comparing Stonehenge with stone circles known from elsewhere in the British Isles. Though some of these monuments covered larger areas than Stonehenge, none were as complex in their arrangement as the example found on Salisbury Plain. Despite their differences, all these sites shared basic similarities of form. It was very likely, therefore, that Stonehenge was part of a broad tradition of stone

John Aubrey

John Aubrey was a member of the landed gentry in England during the 17th century. Though suffering from debts throughout his life, Aubrey managed to live a relatively leisured, if peripatetic, life as he traveled among the houses of his more financially solvent friends. He used these connections to write copiously, if not always with great accuracy, about the people he came to know. The resulting anecdotes were collected in a manuscript entitled "Brief Lives." Though not published, these short accounts served as the bases of biographies written about Aubrey's subjects by others, especially Anthony Woods. Aubrey's wide-ranging fascination with the world around him extended to the study of Britain's past. This interest led him to conduct surveys in search of ancient monuments. In the course of one such study, he came upon the large Neolithic stone circle at Avebury in southern England. It was also in the course of this work that Aubrey recorded Stonehenge.

William Stukeley

William Stukeley studied medicine in early 18th-century England, went on to become a vicar at All Saints' Church in Stamford, and wrote a memoir of his friend Sir Isaac Newton. He is perhaps best remembered, however, for the investigations he conducted at the Neolithic stone circles of Avebury and Stonehenge in southern England and which he reported in publications that appeared in 1740 and 1743. These studies comprise the earliest systematic research carried out at both monuments, and they set the stage for later archaeological investigations at those sites. Stukeley's fascination with the religion of the Druids led him to mistakenly associate Stonehenge and Avebury with that religious sect. This interpretation dominated understandings of British Neolithic stone circles generally and Stonehenge in particular into the 19th century. Ultimately, the claims made on Stonehenge by neo-Druids today owe a great deal to Stukeley.

circle construction, native to Britain and unrelated to architecture originating with groups living along the Mediterranean's shores. That most of these numerous circles were found in areas never subdued by Romans supported the indigenous origin of Stonehenge.

But why were Druids identified as the creators of these monuments? In answering that question, we have to bear in mind two points about the conceptual structure in which the antiquaries worked. First, they took for granted the biblically based chronology of the world which specified that the earth was no more than 6,000 years old. Thus, all sites had to fit within a very short span of time. Second, successful interpretation of stone circles and other remains meant associating them with, preferably, some group of named people who dominated this brief history. Since in their view the human presence on earth was short and fairly well known from written accounts, it only made sense that all sites must have been created by those groups whose names scholars already knew. If the Romans were not Stonehenge's creators, then some of the people they mentioned upon their arrival in Britain might be. Roman writers such as Tacitus described the Druids as religious leaders among the Britons who often incited resistance to Roman arms. Since the antiquaries saw stone circles as places of ancient worship, there was a strong tendency to link Druids to these supposedly sacred locales. There were problems with this interpretation, not the least of which is that there is no mention of stone circles in Roman reports of Druidic worship. In fact, most such religious observations were supposed to have been conducted in natural settings, often around venerable oak trees. Though some of these difficulties were recognized at the time, for those who saw Stonehenge as a native construction, the Druids were in the right place at the right time to play the role of its creators.

Once again, we see here an uneasy mix of theory and world view. Aubrey and Stukeley, in particular, set out to gather data with which to answer the question of who built Stonehenge. In the process, they produced results still used by archaeologists today. Once having refuted a Roman origin for the site, however, they did not question received wisdom concerning the antiquity of people in Britain before the Romans' arrival, or investigate alternatives besides groups named in Roman accounts of Britain's inhabitants. They exercised the doubt on which scientific investigations are based, but only within narrow limits. It was acceptable to debate who among recorded groups might have built Stonehenge but not to wonder if the builders belonged to groups who predated these better-known societies.

Excavations conducted at Stonehenge and in the surrounding barrows through the early 19th century tended to be casual affairs about which little was recorded and less published. Caches of animal remains that were retrieved from the monument, for example, were quickly seen by many as evidence for rituals involving blood sacrifice. Still, as was the case for southern Mesopotamia, these discoveries were not interpreted with reference to their contexts of recovery (which would have been, minimally, their vertical and horizontal relations with other finds). As noted in Chapter 5, archaeology is based on ignorance about the past, ignorance that can only be reduced through careful recording of recovered materials in context. Aubrey, Stukeley, their predecessors, and contemporaries worked from a position of presumed knowledge: they knew Stonehenge's date was recent, its builders named, its purpose as a religious center clear. The crucial point was to decide who among the available candidates were responsible for the site as it appeared on Salisbury Plain when it was mapped. Doing any more would have required developing new techniques with which to collect and record the vertical and horizontal contexts of recovered materials. Doing so would have required admitting doubts about the site's date, use, and origins.

It would be as misguided to criticize British antiquaries for their treatment of Stonehenge as to dress down early researchers in southern Mesopotamia. We all work within conceptual frameworks that highlight certain areas for study while obscuring other lines of inquiry. Early research on Stonehenge, therefore, was characterized by arguments that were rigorous and empirically based but limited by assumptions of which few, if any, of the participants were consciously aware. Once those assumptions were exposed, the nature of the debate broadened considerably.

Addressing History in Context

Recognition that the question of who built Stonehenge might be more complex than it initially seemed required (1) insights derived from research in Salisbury Plain, and (2) shifts in general archaeological theory. In the first case, excavations conducted during the early to middle 19th century into large burial chambers, or long barrows, overlooking Stonehenge revealed communal interments that lacked grave goods made of iron. They did, however, yield chips of sarsen stone likely derived from the nearby monument. It seemed reasonable to assume, therefore, that the people interred in these mortuary chambers were alive when the great stone circles were being raised and prior to the period immediately preceding the Roman invasion, when iron implements were widely available in southern Britain. Such discoveries did little to support the notion that Stonehenge dated to the last centuries BC.

At about the same time, researchers in Scandinavia were developing a scheme for categorizing the many artifacts that were coming to light there and in the rest of Europe. They organized these materials according to whether they were made of stone, bronze, or iron. Though not initially proposed as an evolutionary scheme, this taxonomy was soon treated as one. Increasingly, scholars recognized that, through time, iron replaced bronze in the making of tools in Europe, and bronze, in its turn, had displaced stone. If iron was the dominant metal used during the centuries preceding the Roman incursion into Britain, and if the long barrow burials were contemporary with Stonehenge's construction, then the absence of iron from the barrows suggested that Stonehenge's builders were not the Druids described by Tacitus and others. No one could tell at this point how old Stonehenge was. There was a strong possibility, however, that it was the product of a very ancient and unknown culture.

Investigators of Stonehenge had arrived at much the same position as had those studying early societies in southern Mesopotamia. In both cases, unexpected evidence pointed to older predecessors of the more recent cultures that had long been the primary focus of study. Shadowy Sumerians gave rise to better-known Babylonians and Assyrians, just as an unnamed people were now discerned as ancestral to the much-discussed Druids. Figuring out who was responsible for Mesopotamian civilization and Stonehenge required shaking off dependence on texts and developing techniques that would allow scholars to write history from material remains. It was in this context that the techniques and theory of Culture History were born.

To be sure, changing research strategies in Britain and Mesopotamia were related, often being instigated and practiced by people who worked in both areas. In fact, these Culture Historical investigations belonged to a broader revolution in archaeological practice that increasingly emphasized:

1. defining ancient cultures by identifying patterned associations among objects with distinct styles;

2. organizing these cultures chronologically by charting changes in their diagnostic styles across stratigraphic sequences revealed in deep excavations;

3. explaining shifts in those styles by movements of people and/or ideas.

Augustus Lane Fox Pitt-Rivers (see sidebar), perhaps the premier British archaeologist of the late 19th century, was among the first to recognize that achieving these aims carried certain responsibilities:

1. the excavator must be present at all times when fieldwork was being conducted and must keep precise records of all that was found, including notes, drawings, and photographs;

2. no site should be completely excavated, since later archaeologists would likely have better techniques to apply to its study in the future;

3. any work should be published, and made available to the public;

4. the materials recovered should be placed on public display since they were owned by the citizens of the places where these items were discovered.

Though these practices seem quite standard today, they constituted a break from previous approaches. The recognized importance of context motivated this greater attention to controlled excavation and publication of results. Once it was acknowledged that questions about the past do not depend on matching remains to cultures and individuals mentioned in written accounts, it became imperative that relations among all uncovered

Augustus Lane Fox Pitt-Rivers

Augustus Lane Fox Pitt-Rivers was born in Yorkshire in 1827 and served in the British military from 1841 to 1882, retiring with the rank of Lieutenant General. Just before leaving the service, in 1880, he inherited the considerable Rivers estate from his great-uncle, adding the name "Rivers" to his own as part of the bequest. Pitt-Rivers had long shown an interest in past material culture and went on to conduct excavations at his estate in Dorset as well as elsewhere in England. Pitt-Rivers's work was distinguished, especially for the time, by the care with which recorded finds and their locations as well as his insistence that archaeological materials be put on display for the education of the public. Pitt-Rivers's extensive collections eventually found a permanent home at Oxford University where they were installed in an annex to the University Museum. The organization of the items was designed to illustrate general principles of cultural evolution, pieces being arranged so as to reflect presumed progressive changes of material culture toward ever greater degrees of complexity, efficiency, and rationality. The Pitt-Rivers collection is still on display at Oxford.

materials be described in detail. It is from such carefully uncovered, analyzed, and reported finds that previously unknown cultures can be identified, their distributions mapped, and their temporal relations reconstructed.

Early Culture History work in Britain was not conducted at Stonehenge. As it turns out, the site has a long history, but the sequence of events through which it was created is not neatly laid out in clear stratigraphic levels. Initial Culture Historical research focused on excavating the burial mounds, or barrows, that are widely dispersed across southern Britain. Painstaking comparison of materials recovered from these interments, as well as from other sites, led to the creation of a chronological sequence marked by changes in a variety of materials. Styles of pottery tended to dominate the trait lists, but scholars also paid attention to the forms of stone and metal tools.

Ironically, excavations at Stonehenge did not initially benefit from this attention to context. The investigations immediately following World War I, for example, stripped soil from large portions of the monument and turned up many artifacts. Records of this work are poor, failing to provide sufficient information on context to reconstruct ancient behaviors and infer the site's chronology. Nonetheless, as the 20th century progressed, increasingly sophisticated approaches implemented by better-funded projects succeeded in piecing together the site's complex history.

It turns out that Stonehenge's current appearance is the product of a long sequence of events stretching from 2950 to 1700 BC (Figure 6.3). Very briefly, the first major set of activities involved making the henge by digging the encircling ditch and piling up chalk to form its bordering embankments. Roughly contemporary with this major building effort was the digging of 56 holes, each about 1 m in diameter and 1 m deep. Called the Aubrey holes, they are spaced more or less evenly in a circle within the site's inner bank and may have originally held wooden posts or stone pillars. Additional wooden constructions of uncertain shape seem to have been put up closer to the center of the monument during 2950–2550 BC. Beginning around 2550 BC, as many as 80 bluestones were brought to the site and arranged in two concentric rings composed of closely spaced, paired columns. This set of stone circles is best preserved on the northeast; it had an interior diameter of 20 m and was located near the middle of the space defined by the ditch and embankment. The bluestones themselves likely came from the Preseli Mountains, 250 km to the west in what is now Wales.

By 2400 BC, the bluestones had been removed from their original locations and the great sarsen rings erected. The sarsens derive from quarries roughly 40 km north of Stonehenge. Thirty of them formed an outer circle, each upright linked to its neighbors by a continuous curve of lintels. Contained within this space is the sarsen horseshoe. It is open on the northeast and composed of the 15 sarsens that comprise the five trilithons described earlier. By 2150 BC, two constructions employing bluestones were erected: one, a continuous circle of upright slabs set within the sarsen circle, and the other an oval arrangement of vertically set bluestones nested within the sarsen horseshoe. Around 1900 BC, the northeast portion of the inner bluestone oval was removed, converting it into a horseshoe arrangement along the lines of the sarsens that enclose it. The Station Stones, Heel Stone, and the avenue running from Stonehenge to the Avon River were also introduced during the period from 2550 to 1900 BC, though the Heel Stone may belong to an earlier point in the sequence.

The above account simplifies a complex history in the interests of space; please refer to some of the sources listed at the chapter's end if you want to know more of the details. Stripped down as it is, this outline raises an important point about many archaeological sites: what we see on the surface is often the result of rebuildings and accretions and not the expression of a timeless vision held in the minds of the original builders. Archaeologists deal with static remains that were once part of dynamic cultures. It is very tempting to treat the arrangement of buildings and

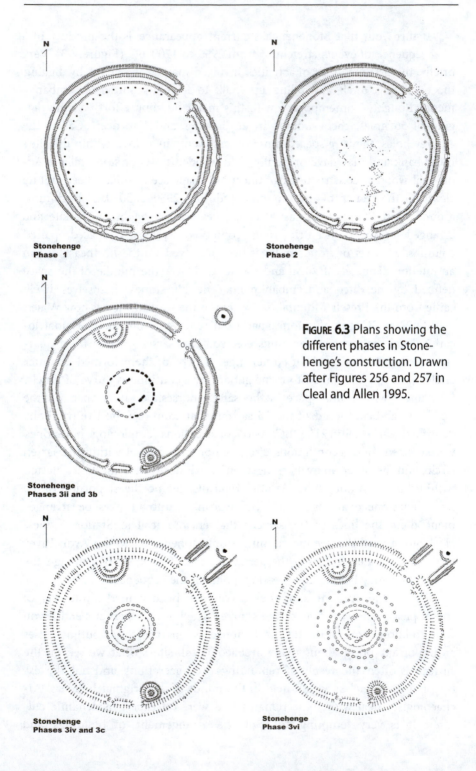

FIGURE 6.3 Plans showing the different phases in Stonehenge's construction. Drawn after Figures 256 and 257 in Cleal and Allen 1995.

N

Stonehenge
Phase 1

N

Stonehenge
Phase 2

N

Stonehenge
Phases 3ii and 3b

N

Stonehenge
Phases 3iv and 3c

N

Stonehenge
Phase 3vi

features at sites as unchanging configurations that survived from first construction to abandonment. As work at Stonehenge revealed, this is far from the case. Understanding Stonehenge's place within the prehistory of Salisbury Plain depends on charting its shifting form, and this is only possible through the techniques of Culture History.

From the late 19th century to the present, research based on the principles of Culture History has been pursued at Stonehenge and in its environs. Throughout this period, techniques of dating, much helped by the advent of carbon-14 analyses, have greatly refined our understanding of Stonehenge's changing form, just as studies of soils, flora, fauna, and artifacts have enhanced our ability to describe shifts in ancient behaviors and in the surrounding physical environment. All of this work was driven, in part, by that initial question of who raised the monument. As discussed in Chapter 4, those following the precepts of Culture History in the early to middle 20th century tended to answer that question by referring to processes of diffusion and migration. Once Stonehenge's pre-Roman date was acknowledged among researchers, the search was on for a culture whose members could have inspired the creation of such a complex, labor-intensive monument. One supposition that persisted from earlier debates about Stonehenge's origins was that native Britons were too "primitive" to have fashioned such an engineering marvel on their own. They surely needed outside help, and the most likely place to find that inspiration was in what Europeans long considered a major hearth of civilization, the Mediterranean basin.

About the time that Stonehenge's origins were being reconsidered, new information on the hierarchically structured, architecturally impressive civilizations of Minoan Crete (2300–1450 BC) and Mycenaean Greece (1600–1100 BC) was coming to light. The Minoans and Mycenaeans seemed to be likely sources of the engineering knowledge and organizational skills needed to move large stones long distances and arrange them into awe-inspiring monuments that could last for ages. The discovery in the early 1950s of shallow etchings of daggers and axes in a style reminiscent of Mycenaean examples on several of the sarsens at Stonehenge seemed to confirm this view. The scarcity of Mycenaean trade goods in Britain generally, and their complete absence at Stonehenge, was not a major obstacle to accepting the idea of diffusion of architectural knowledge and masonry skills from the Mediterranean to southern Britain. As noted in Chapters 1 and 2, theories exercise great power over our imaginations. Given the stress on external contacts in explaining the

cultural transformations identified by increasingly detailed Culture Historical reconstructions, researchers were strongly encouraged to look outside Britain for the roots of something as locally unusual as Stonehenge.
Deep-seated and pervasive assumptions about the cultural capacities of
native Britons made the civilizations bordering the Mediterranean appear
to be plausible candidates as those who could have inspired the locals to
make the monument. A few carvings of Mycenaean design thus assumed
great interpretive significance. Therefore, Stonehenge must have been
built by Britons under the tutelage of foreigners.

This diffusionist view was undermined by newly developed methods
of carbon-14 dating that were applied to remains from Stonehenge and
other comparable sites in Western Europe. Radiocarbon dating placed
the origins of Stonehenge within the British Neolithic (4000–2000 BC)
and helped relate its history to that known from other monumental and
domestic sites in southern Britain. What had been seen as Stonehenge's
unique features could now be related to local innovations made within a
cultural sequence of great time depth. The most economical explanation
of Stonehenge's form was to see it as arising from the efforts of local people operating within their own gradually changing cultures. Contacts
with populations in France who raised similar monuments were likely.
No longer was it necessary, however, to explain Stonehenge's creation as
a simple and direct consequence of such interactions. These shifts highlight once again how extant theories can give rise to research that dis-
proves them.

Why Was Stonehenge Built?

Over the years, Culture Historians have cast much light on who built
Stonehenge and how they did it. Through their investigations, techniques
such as careful stratigraphic analysis, and concepts like the importance of
context, have become central to the conduct of all archaeological studies
in Britain and beyond. Similarly, the basic phases defined by Culture Historical research, each marked by distinctive artifact styles, continue to be
used by scholars of all theoretical persuasions to divide the continuum of
time into distinct periods. Diffusion may now be less heavily relied on to
explain culture change than it was in the early 20th century, but much attention still centers on reconstructing when sites were occupied, with
whom (which other settlements) they were associated, and how the resulting settlement system changed over time.

That said, developments in archaeological theory throughout the late 20th century had impacts on how Stonehenge was viewed. The advent of Processualism, in particular, led to an emphasis on a new set of questions concerning why this massive monument was built. The traditional view, regardless of who was thought to have raised the stones, was that Stonehenge was a center of religious devotion. The size of the place and the way in which it dwarfs human visitors seemed in keeping with a religious center where puny mortals confronted powerful supernatural forces. That general position has not been seriously questioned in recent years. By the mid-20th century, however, it became increasingly important to know how those devotions fit within the overarching cultural system centered on Stonehenge. Explaining the center's size, form, location, and history depended on identifying the functions it served within the cultures that created it.

Several different approaches to addressing Stonehenge's function were pursued by scholars. The perspective with the greatest appeal outside archaeology stressed Stonehenge's function as an observatory used to track celestial events important in the daily lives of early farmers and herders. The two most significant are the rising of the sun at the summer solstice and its setting on the winter solstice (around June 21 and December 21, respectively, in the Northern Hemisphere). These dates mark crucial points in the yearly cycle: first when the sun is at its zenith in the north; and second, when hours of daylight there have reached their minimum. Dependent as early farmers and herders were on the sun for their survival, it makes perfect sense that they would organize their year around the above events and be very concerned to predict their occurrence. It had long been known that someone standing near the center of Stonehenge's trilithon and inner bluestone horseshoes and looking along the alley would be facing a point on the northeast horizon where the sun rises at the summer solstice. Just as importantly, processions marching into the horseshoes would have been walking toward the sunset on the winter solstice, perhaps marking that event and conducting ceremonies to ensure the sun's return.

These observations were refined and further tested by archaeologists and **archaeoastronomers** (those who study ancient knowledge of the sun, moon, and stars), leading to the identification of other possible alignments between pairs of stones and various celestial observations. Lunar eclipses could be calculated using the 56 Aubrey holes, while sunrises at the fall and spring equinoxes (when daylight and darkness are about equal) were supposedly determined using combinations of sight lines from the Station Stones and a hole by the Heel Stone. There were problems with many of these interpretations, not the least of which were the almost endless possibilities of alignments one could envision among the constructed features at Stonehenge, many of which could be linked to a variety of solar and lunar events. Nonetheless, the idea that Stonehenge functioned as a celestial calculator gained considerable popularity and was offered as an explanation for its construction. The notion that its features were arranged to predict where the sun would rise at the summer solstice and set at the winter solstice is still generally accepted and is included in most accounts of Stonehenge's use throughout much of its history.

To be sure, many of those who proposed that Stonehenge functioned to predict the movement of the sun and moon were not Processualists; one of the most widely read of these proponents, **Gerald Hawkins** (see sidebar), was an astronomer. Still, explaining Stonehenge's form by reference to its presumed function (as an observatory) fits well with Processual approaches, which tend to equate the reasons for a phenomenon's existence with its purpose.

The question still remained, however, as to why so much effort was devoted to creating a setting for observing the sky. A few well-placed sticks coupled with years of careful observations could have accomplished the same purpose. What goal was achieved by making Stonehenge so large? One answer offered from a Processualist stance turned on issues of power. Many Processualists viewed changes in power relations as ranging along an evolutionary sequence, from small-scale egalitarian societies to

Gerald Hawkins

Gerald Hawkins was an astronomer with a long-standing interest in the ways in which ancient people arranged monumental constructions, such as Stonehenge, to track and predict the movements of celestial bodies. He also examined the form and arrangement of such large features as the Nasca lines in southern Peru and the Amun temple in Egypt for evidence that they, too, were built to conform with astronomical observations. One of Hawkins's innovations was to use a computer to compare alignments among features at Stonehenge with the reconstructed positions of the sun, moon, and certain stars in the sky above Salisbury Plain at the time of the monument's construction and use. Though much criticized by archaeologists at the time, Hawkins's view on the astronomical alignments seen at Stonehenge quickly gained wide acceptance in the popular literature dealing with that site. From its first publication in the 1960s to this day, his argument that the monument was an observatory has figured to varying degrees in many interpretations of Stonehenge proposed by professionals and amateurs alike.

hierarchically structured, populous states. Occupying an intermediate position in this supposed universal progression were **chiefdoms**. Chiefdoms, societies of moderate size whose populations are usually measured in the thousands, are organized according to a rudimentary ranking system with a few elites leading many followers. The latter retain considerable control over their own lives, thus limiting the power of their leaders. Two of the principal ways chiefdoms are recognized archaeologically are by the size of the constructions they were able to raise, and marked differences in the lavishness of their burials. The first criterion speaks to the ability of leaders to harness large labor forces in the accomplishment of significant projects. The second reflects variations in wealth thought to correlate with distinctions between rulers and ruled.

The nature of chiefdoms was much debated by Processualists. **Colin Renfrew** (see sidebar), for example, noted that there was a tendency to treat all such societies as organized under the leadership of charismatic individuals who stood out from all others by the relative opulence of their material possessions and the respect they were accorded. This model did not match with the evidence from places like Stonehenge. The burials found within Stonehenge's encircling bank are largely simple cremations with few clear grave goods. There are rich interments in some of the round barrows surrounding the monument, but these postdate Stonehenge's main period of use. In short, Renfrew noted a contradiction that applied to Stonehenge and some other European cases where people also raised large stone monuments during the 3rd millennium BC: the amount of work involved in building such centers was considerable, but there was no sign of the chiefs who supposedly directed these efforts. This led Renfrew to argue that power in chiefdoms could also be exercised through corporate bodies, or groups of people who cooperate in accomplishing a set of activities. Leadership in corporate settings is provided by elites who work together in directing the actions of their subordinates. These notables may not stand out by their dress or other possessions in daily life, and are not overtly celebrated at death. Still, they can motivate people to work together in the name of the group. Stonehenge therefore functioned as an expression of this collective power.

Stonehenge's great size could thus be seen as a tangible statement of social unity and the political structure that made that unity possible. This and other easily visible monuments may also have been used by their builders to stake clear claims to land. For populations whose members were dispersed across the landscape in small settlements—as was then

Colin Renfrew

Colin Renfrew is, and has been since at least the late 1970s, a major figure in the archaeology of Europe. He has written broadly on such topics as Aegean prehistory, the spread of Indo-European languages, and, as seen in Chapter 6, the sociopolitical significance of megalithic monuments. Renfrew was one of the first researchers to synthesize results from the carbon-14 dating of European and Near Eastern materials. He used these findings to question the traditional diffusionist view that such basic cultural features as agriculture, herding, and monument construction first developed in the Near East and spread westward into Europe. This shift in viewpoints was influential in turning the attention of archaeologists to local factors in explaining processes of culture change throughout Europe, rather than relying on external influences to account for these transformations. Renfrew adopted key facets of the Processualist approach in presenting his own accounts of the past. He insisted, however, that the adaptationist and local foci of this perspective had to be balanced with an appreciation for inter-societal interactions in shaping culture change. The latter aspect of his work is most systematically expressed in his theory of Peer Polity Interactions. Peer Polity Interaction stresses that shifts toward increasing sociopolitical complexity are rarely accomplished by the members of individual societies acting alone. Instead, these developments often involve intense cultural, social, political, and economic interactions among neighboring political units which together form a system of closely interrelated, mutually inter-influencing parts. Unlike World Systems theory, Peer Polity Interaction deals with inter-societal transactions that took place over relatively short distances among societies that were roughly equivalent in their size and level of complexity. Renfrew remains influential throughout archaeology, his intellectual reach extending well beyond Europe and Processualism.

thought to have been the case for the late Neolithic people who constructed Stonehenge—this may have been critically important. Widely spread out populations would have found it difficult to maintain contacts with one another. Having a massive center to which members of the wider group returned on a regular basis during the year helped solidify bonds that weakened during periods of absence, just as ceremonies conducted there revivified feelings of commitment to group members, the land, their leaders, and whatever supernatural powers governed society and nature. Stonehenge, and other large stone monuments, might thus have functioned as religious centers in which rituals were tied to movements of the sun and moon. Their size and form, however, went beyond these obvious functions and reflected their role as focal point for organizing large, dispersed populations under the leadership of councils. Stonehenge was less a means for conducting celestial observations than a medium for ensuring social continuity.

The above views parallel Processualist approaches to explaining the emergence of the state in southern Mesopotamia in several ways:

1. the society is the basic unit of action and analysis;

2. emphasis is placed on how ancient people maintained the integrity of that unit;

3. power differences play a crucial role in ensuring such solidarity by providing direction to large groups of people;

4. material culture is central to the activities by which unity is achieved and preserved.

Consequently, once Stonehenge's function in sustaining the cultural system of those who built it was identified, its existence had been explained.

Creating Culture through Experiences of the Material

In keeping with the general tone of Interpretivist approaches to the past, perspectives on Stonehenge founded on the premises of this school are quite diverse. They are united by a general desire to move away from a search for supposed universal processes that animated past behaviors. Interpretivists seek instead to identify the meanings that all elements of material culture, including monuments, had for those who made and used them. In this view, Processualist explanations of Stonehenge as an expression of social solidarity and the power that ensured such unity are problematic: they rely too heavily on the notion that all cultures are systems that naturally seek balanced relations among their constituent parts. As discussed in Chapter 4, Interpretivists insist that people act for reasons that make sense to them and not because they are driven by forces of which they are not aware (such as seeking social equilibrium). Asking why Stonehenge was built and why it assumed the different forms it took over its long life depends on grasping those culturally specific motivations.

There are many ways this can be done, and we focus here on how two particularly influential researchers, **Julian Thomas** and **Michael Parker Pearson** (see sidebar), went about this task. In essence, Thomas argues that past people must be understood in their own terms and not by projecting our understandings of life and culture onto them. This emic view is possible in the absence of living informants because the material remains we recover archaeologically were infused with meaning by these ancient people. Studying patterned relations among these surviving objects can reveal some sense of what those meanings were.

Thomas is careful to point out that artifacts are not secondary to thought. Rather, people in general use objects of all sorts to think about themselves and the world; without them, we could not live meaningful and coherent lives. But material items do not have inherent meanings. Rather, their significance is culturally determined and historically contingent. That is, what we make of a plate with a certain decoration or a house of a certain form is an outcome of the beliefs, values, and dispositions that are unique to the culture in which we participate, as that culture exists at a certain moment in time. To be sure, cultures are not homogeneous entities, and people participate in them to different degrees and in different ways, depending on such factors as gender, age, social class, and ethnicity. Still, these different perspectives exist within a cultural and temporal framework that is unique and lends to them some loose unity; at the very least, what we see are different takes on shared cultural themes and emphases.

Julian Thomas and Michael Parker Pearson

Julian Thomas and Michael Parker Pearson were two of the directors of the Stonehenge Riverside Project briefly discussed in Chapter 6. Though their theoretical positions are not identical, Thomas and Parker Pearson are both important contributors to the vital Interpretivist school in Britain. Their work on the island's Neolithic and Bronze Age has challenged Culture Historical and Processual accounts of the period by stressing the importance of grasping the ways in which ancient people imbued the landscapes in which they lived with meaning. Rather than seeing constructions, such as Stonehenge, as direct expressions of ancient political and social forms, Thomas, Parker Pearson, and their colleagues view them as having played active roles in shaping cultural principles and, through those principles, human behavior. Hence, Stonehenge was less a symbol of chiefly power than an arena in which distinctions between the powerful and powerless, the living and the dead, were made real, as different people directly but to varying degrees engaged with this symbolically rich setting.

How does Stonehenge fit into this scheme? One way of looking at the monument is that the builders manipulated a variety of materials to think in certain culturally distinct and historically specific ways about the world and people's relations to one another and to the cosmos (Figure 6.4). Just as importantly, once built, Stonehenge became an important part of that world. Experiences with the monument inspired feelings and dispositions that were essential to the culture of those who created and used the site. Stonehenge, in this view, was a product of a certain culture, as well as a means for re-creating its core principles generation after generation. Explaining Stonehenge's existence and appearance depends on figuring out how it fit within the matrix of beliefs and values that characterized the culture of those who used it for more than a thousand years.

What can we discern of this meaningful structure? Stonehenge during its final phase, when the stones we see today were in place, is characterized by a complex arrangement of features. Entering the innermost part of the stone circles required passing through a series of barriers. Further, the way the stones and bank are set up means that different parts of the center hosted groups of varying sizes. Only a few people could be accommodated within the central horseshoe of bluestones, more could have

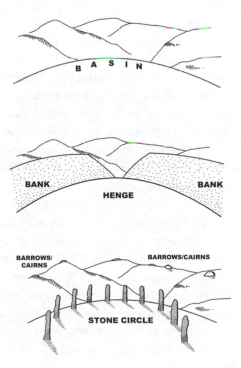

FIGURE 6.4 An example of how access to an open space, such as that defined by Stonehenge in Salisbury Plain, can be redefined and compartmentalized with the erection of a ditch-and-bank or stone circle. Drawn after Bradley 1998: Figure 40.

clustered in the area between the encircling bank and outer sarsen circle, while still more could have found space to stand outside the ditch. These gathering areas correlate with variations in the ability of ancient people to experience through all of their senses what was happening within Stonehenge. Those stranded beyond the ditch may have had only a vague sense of what was being said and done within the inner sanctum, even as the noise, actions, and smells of this crowd created their own distractions. Individuals in the intermediate position, between the sarsen circle and bank, would have been better able to see, hear, and smell (e.g., if incense was used) what was happening around the Altar Stone but were still excluded from participation in those ceremonies. The way Stonehenge was built, therefore, constantly re-created differences within the society: people experienced the monument in a variety of ways that made those differences concrete. Every time people attended ceremonies here, they were reminded of their varying relations to one another and, presumably, to whatever supernatural powers were propitiated at the monument's center. These distinctions may well have correlated with power differentials, from those of higher rank who conducted the rites, to those of lower status standing outside the bank-and-ditch. The point, however, is that Stonehenge was not constructed to reflect these political distinctions; it did not exist apart from them, as Processualists argued. Power and social difference were not abstract principles represented by physical symbols. They were directly experienced by all who variably participated in ceremonies conducted at the monument. Stonehenge was an important symbolic arena in which cultural principles came alive in performance; without it, the culture of its builders would not have existed in the form it took. Thomas's perspective combines performance theory with aspects of what is called *embodiment*—that is, how people physically experience the world. There is more to both perspectives than we indicate here, of course, and we have noted resources at the chapter's end for you to pursue if you are interested in learning more about them.

Embodiment looks at experience at a micro-level: a single person. Performance can be thought of as acting at multiple scales, from individuals to large groups. But delving further into Stonehenge's meaning requires examining it at larger scales. For Stonehenge, this requires looking at the entirety of Salisbury Plain. This perspective is called **landscape archaeology**. The study of landscapes began in the Cultural Historical school and continued in the work of Processualists, with most attention directed to how humans interacted with the environment. In these views, the physical aspects of a place's setting were the most significant; for example, the questions asked centered on where a site was located with respect to crucial resources, and how these materials were exploited. An Interpretivist approach, however, looks at meaning more than at resources and adaptation. To get ourselves into this perspective, we would like to take you on a walk.

Aubrey Burl, a contemporary expert on Stonehenge and similar monuments, suggests that a trek following a 2-mile path from the site of Durrington Walls to Stonehenge gives the walker a sense of how prehistoric residents might have experienced the sites. One of the first things to notice is the barrows mentioned above. Then, moving from Durrington Walls, we walk to the southwest. The path contributes to an optical illusion: that we are walking over a large, low, artificial mound. This was first suggested by Stukeley, but recent excavations have shown that the rise is natural. Passing by and through a number of barrows, the Old and New Kings groups (named this, but not containing the burials of kings), we go by or over another monument known as the Cursus. From this point, the land rises again, and we see the sarsen stones of the henge, and its Heel Stone. If we align ourselves with the Heel Stone and the center of the circle, we just need to walk straight ahead toward the worn banks of the avenue, which was once flanked by rows of standing stones, and then a bit farther to the monument itself. Burl and others think that the avenue existed to channel processions to Stonehenge proper. Today, what Burl calls the "enchantment" of the walk is spoiled by fencing, a parking lot, and a highway, but in prehistoric times the experience of Stonehenge would have been unmarred.

Of course, what is seen today on this walk may not have been what ancient people saw; and what we feel is likely not what they felt. Still, by experiencing a site directly, as in our walk, we can get a sense of the grandeur of some places, the peace of others, and the cleverness of the designers and builders as they reworked the henge and its surroundings.

The burial mounds around Stonehenge have long been known; many predate Stonehenge and were already ancient by 3000 BC. Researchers have also realized for some time that the monument itself contains cremated human remains. Building Stonehenge in the midst of these mortuary constructions was likely part of a purposeful attempt to evoke a connection to the ancient dead by means of the ceremonies conducted at the center. Those interred at the site may have been other honored deceased individuals. Bodies, stones, earth, and sight lines to long barrows might thus have been manipulated in order to think about ancestors, the supernatural, and to root both in great antiquity.

Recent research in Stonehenge' s immediate environs elaborates on this view. In particular, Durrington Walls turns out to have been a sizable settlement contemporary with at least the monument's final phase of major construction. Associated with Durrington Walls are two circular arrangements of large wooden posts. Durrington Walls and its "woodhenges" are linked to the Avon River by a formal avenue, as is Stonehenge. Based on these findings and ethnographic analogies, Parker Pearson argues that the occupants of Salisbury Plain in the last half of the 3rd millennium BC used different materials (stone and wood among them) to create a landscape in which they could directly experience abstract distinctions between life and death as these were understood by members of that culture. Durrington Walls, in this view, is the land of the living, its posts made from living trees that showed the signs of decay associated with life cycles. Stonehenge, at least by 2400 BC, was a place of the ancestors, its seemingly unchanging stones imperturbable and permanent. Movement along the avenues and the Avon River from Durrington Walls to Stonehenge—our walk outlined above—was a journey from the world of the living to the world of the dead (Figure 6.5). This interpretation argues that movement across the Salisbury landscape would have been a powerful way of experiencing relations between the ancestors and their descendants, culminating, presumably, in ceremonies conducted at Stonehenge timed to the summer and winter solstices and the equinoxes. Answering the question of why Stonehenge was remodeled as it was in 2400 BC thus requires two mental activities: inferring the cultural context in which it was created; and grasping how people living within that context used different materials to invoke and encounter physically, in the process of various bodily experiences, meanings that were central to their existence. The material patterns relevant to this attempt exist at varying scales, from the specific arrangements of stones and ditches at Stonehenge to the relation of that site to the natural and created environment of Salisbury Plain. Thomas and Parker Pearson are concerned to point out that this was not a static symbolic structure. Stonehenge itself was modified considerably throughout its long history, its radically different forms likely conveying and instilling very different structures of meaning. The landscape in which the monument was situated also changed. For example, where Stonehenge' s avenue intersects the Avon River there was once a circle of bluestones, nicknamed Stonehenge' s "Little Sister." These uprights were removed and may have been reset at the larger site. Such shifts imply that not only do site forms change, but these transformations can be instrumental in instigating novel views of the world and people's places in

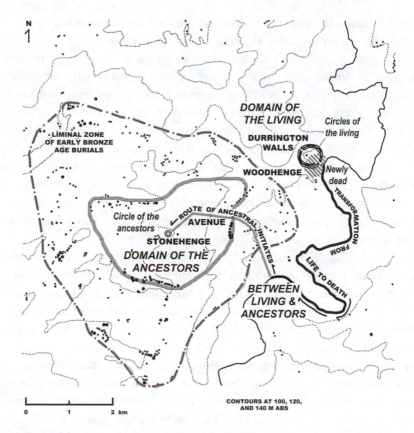

FIGURE 6.5 Map showing relations among different constructed and perceived features of Salisbury Plain's landscape as reconstructed by members of the Stonehenge Riverside Project. Drawn after Pitts 2001: Figure 51 (originally appeared in Parker Pearson and Ramilisonina 1998).

it. Thus, Salisbury Plain was likely a contested landscape in which objects were redeployed as different factions gained the ability to express themselves materially.

Continuing Contests for Stonehenge

Disputes over Stonehenge and its meaning are not limited to those that occurred in the 3rd millennium BC. Unlike most of the sites we discuss in the book, this center continues to exercise a considerable effect on the human imagination. In fact, we would guess that many people in the Western world, if asked to name an archaeological site, would respond with "Stonehenge."

Such widespread recognition does not translate into unanimous opinions on what the site means today and how it should be protected. In a sense, arguments over Stonehenge's significance and future are notably prominent examples of debates that involve a host of sites in many parts of the world. They tend to pit people with very different views of past remains against one another. These include, but are not limited to, private landowners who want a free hand in developing their property; national governments who claim elements of the past that they see as icons of the country and its history; tourists who want to maximize their chance to experience ancient remains as directly as possible; people with perceived stakes in a site due to religious or other cultural concerns; and archaeologists who are interested in pursuing research questions at particular sites. The central point this debate raises for our purposes is, to put it crudely, Who owns the past?

Answering that question takes us into a complex situation wherein conceptual schemes of different sorts intersect, often uncomfortably, at a specific moment in time. On the one hand, legal principles that have been articulated in many countries over the past century contend that a nation has the right to hold particularly valuable sites in common for the good of the country. Thus, Stonehenge, which was in private hands for much of its recent history, passed to government control in 1918. State interest in the land was underwritten by a novel legal premise that prioritized national concerns over the rights of property owners. The Ancient Monuments Act, first passed in weak form in 1882 and given greater powers to take control of sites in 1913, was one manifestation of this change in British legal principles. Similar arrangements are now found in many parts of the world, as seen, for example, in U.S. government control over such icons of U.S. history as the Yorktown battlefield and the Statue of Liberty.

At the same time, clauses in many constitutions that guarantee freedom of religion have been used to question absolute national sovereignty over archaeological sites. Thus, groups like the Ancient Order of Druids, recognized in Britain as practicing a legitimate religion, see Stonehenge as a sacred site linked for millennia with their faith (Figure 6.6). Consequently, they argue that full expression of their religion requires that they have access to Stonehenge at crucial points in their ceremonial calendar (the winter and summer solstices, in particular). Interestingly, these claims are founded in part on a mix of archaeological interpretations concerning who built Stonehenge and what it was used for. That some of these views, such as the association of Stonehenge with the Druids, are no longer accepted in the profession has done little to damage ties between it and latter-day Druids.

Further afield, various people in the last several decades have built replicas of Stonehenge from such diverse materials as cars (near Alliance, Nebraska) and refrigerators (outside Santa Fe, New Mexico, and Gordonton, New Zealand). Construction of these monumental replicas of the Salisbury Plain prototype was apparently inspired by diverse motivations, including a desire to honor a deceased loved one (Carhenge); an aesthetic impulse; and the pure fun of creating something incongruous. These variably exact replicas of Stonehenge are generally not seen as foci of religious devotion, though some people do time their visits to Carhenge and, while it existed, Fridgehenge to coincide with the solstices. What they signify, in part, is the widespread appeal of Stonehenge as a powerful symbol of human antiquity and accomplishment.

Archaeologists' claims to Stonehenge are, in turn, founded in part on their ability to clarify the original builders' purposes through the application of specialized knowledge, including an array of investigative techniques. Some archaeologists go so far as to cast themselves as arbiters among different interest groups, based on our empirically founded understandings of Stonehenge's past. This last contention derives, to a significant degree, from the assumption that data-based appreciations of the monument and approaches to its treatment are more valid than views arrived at through religious faith and bureaucratic procedures. Needless to say, this position is not shared by those whose world views and powers we challenge.

FIGURE 6.6 Neo-Druids at Stonehenge (from *http://religion-compass.com*).

Stonehenge is, therefore, not merely a nexus of different interpretations offered by proponents of varied archaeological schools. It is also competed over by people from varied backgrounds and with distinct interests who measure their arguments based on very different criteria of law, faith, academic credentials, aesthetics, and data. Attempts to negotiate among parties operating from such disparate backgrounds tend to generate some uncertainty concerning the best ways to deal with Stonehenge. Hence, national policies concerning the site and its setting have oscillated over recent years between providing open access to the monument to closing down direct contact with it almost completely. Similarly, some archaeologists have argued for the absolute prominence of their views, while others in the profession have countered that we should be open to, and take seriously, such "alternative histories" as those offered by the neo-Druids.

We raise these points for two purposes. First, it is easy to think that archaeological debates occur, and have their consequences, primarily within our field. On the contrary: what we have to say about the past is conditioned by events occurring within the societies in which we were raised and continue to work. Further, our interpretations are variably picked up by nonspecialists who may adopt some of them while categorically rejecting others. For example, neo-Druids draw some inspiration from archaeological accounts of solar observations at Stonehenge while denying the validity of our conclusion that the site was not built by Druids. We exist in a complex world, where our research is influenced, though not determined, by the context in which we conduct it, our studies contributing in unanticipated ways to that context.

Second, we want you to think about these connections. There is no formula for navigating among the demands of governments, religious congregations, and other interest groups. You have to decide how and to what extent your work will be influenced by the concerns and sensibilities of those with whom you deal outside the profession. It is almost always best to tell any audience what you believe the materials you study have to say about important issues, just as it is crucial to lay out your reasons for advancing those interpretations. In this way, you stay true to a basic precept that unites just about all archaeologists across theoretical divides—that is, we owe the people we study as complete and unbiased an account of their lives as we can provide. That said, it is wise to be as aware as possible of how your statements fit into wider discourses on the past, and against what criteria your remarks will be evaluated. This does not mean trying to avoid upsetting some by agreeing with everyone. It does mean acknowledging that people are interested in the past for different reasons, and not all of them are founded on the doubts and questions that motivate archaeological research. We can respect neo-Druidism as a religion even if we do not choose to treat their interpretation of Stonehenge as good archaeology. The precepts of both are different, as are the means by which their members decide what constitutes the truth.

Stonehenge and Identity

A theme that runs through much of this discussion concerns issues of **identity,** or the sense one forms of oneself in the context of interacting with others within a specific cultural setting. The identities we enact are based on constructs available to us within our culture and operate at variable levels, from those unique to specific individuals, to affiliations we share with members of groups, ranging from families to nations, from religious congregations to professional associations (such as those to which archaeologists belong). These linkages are often also expressed through the use of material symbols, such as when we wear flag pins to express national allegiance or display religious symbols in our houses. There is, therefore, a complex and shifting relationship among our sense of self, the culture providing the categories of identity on which we can draw, the contexts in which we express those affiliations, and the items used to express them. The authors, for example, are simultaneously parents in a nuclear family, participants in book groups, professional archaeologists, employees of a college, members of occupation-based associations, and citizens of a town, state, and nation. We do not proclaim these identities all at once, and some are more important in certain situations than others. Hence, when attending graduations at our college, we wear garb that distinguishes our profession (scholar-teachers) and indicate where we obtained our PhDs. The acts we engage in on such occasions mark our association with that institution (including processions, songs, and speeches that highlight the importance of the college in our collective lives). When attending a professional meeting, however, our collegiate identity is overshadowed by our archaeological affiliation, which is usually marked by wearing distinctive badges and engaging in acts that set us apart as members of the field (such as attending sessions where research reports are presented, and trading stories of our investigations).

While we cannot and should not project the specific range of identities defined in modern Western societies back into the past, it is likely that prehistoric people also had a variety of intersecting affiliations. The different schools of thought considered here have, to differing degrees, broached the issue of identity and its relation to material culture with respect to Stonehenge. How their practitioners have grappled with this set of issues reveals a great deal about the nature of these theoretical perspectives.

The antiquaries were very concerned to assign a named cultural affiliation to the people who constructed Stonehenge. They collected data pertaining to the site's final form in efforts to decide whether Romans, Druids, or some other historically known group was responsible for this architectural marvel. Their work was underlain by the assumption that each of the candidates for Stonehenge's creators possessed a distinctive, relatively unchanging culture that informed all that they did, including arranging massive stone blocks. Because of this direct and fairly unambiguous link between culture and behavior, ancient culture groups could be unequivocally recognized in their material remains.

The Culture Historical version of identity is the "archaeological culture," defined on the basis of a regularly occurring assemblage of stylistically distinct artifacts and features. The appearance of similar materials in limited spatial distributions was assumed to signal the former existence and distribution of a particular social group. These entities were often named after a characteristic artifact. For example, in the Stonehenge area, one of the most important artifacts used to define an archaeological culture was a kind of pottery vessel called the *beaker*: a tall, flat-bottomed vase with a gently outflaring neck, usually decorated with geometric designs etched into the surface. These distinctive ceramics date to 2400–1800 BC and are distributed through the Iberian Peninsula, Holland, Belgium, parts of France, Germany, Britain, and Ireland. A widespread shared "culture" is inferred from these observed material patterns. References can still be found in the literature to the "Beaker People," though today often with qualifications to show that there was no monolithic "Beaker Culture."

There are some similarities in the ways in which Culture Historians and antiquaries approached the relation between material remains and identity. Both drew a direct connection between the values and practices of a specific culture, on the one hand, and the nature of the objects they produced, on the other. Ancient cultures could thus be recognized in distinctive arrangements and styles of artifacts and constructions. Culture Historians, however, drew on a wider array of materials in identifying past cultures than did antiquaries, paying close attention to styles in ceramics, stone and metal tools, as well as architectural forms. More attention was also devoted within the Culture Historical framework to changes in these reconstructed cultures over time. Still, there was an enduring assumption that each culture was characterized by certain diagnostic items; study the latter and you could reconstruct the former. There was also a tendency in Culture Historical research to submerge the individual within the group. Identity was a culture-wide phenomenon; the precepts and practices that defined a culture were widely shared among all its members.

Processualists retained this focus on group identity. Cultures were now defined by their integrated subsystems, with a particular focus on the means by which those entities adapted to their physical environments and maintained solidarity. Individuals and their decisions were relatively un-important; people did what was essential to ensure group survival, whether or not they realized the consequences of their actions in promoting adaptation and social equilibrium. Social differences within groups were not ignored: differential distributions of goods, housing, and/or foods could signal social distinctions expressed in power and wealth. So factions were recognized but were usually interpreted in terms of hierarchical distinctions. As noted above, these divisions were not seen as fragmenting society, but as providing the leadership needed to maintain its integrity and coherence.

Interestingly, as much as Processualists defined themselves in opposition to the precepts of Culture History, they adopted as basic units of analysis the territorially bounded cultures defined by members of the latter school. Whereas Culture Historians saw the cultures they defined as packages of traits that manifest values and practices shared by a group, Processualists viewed these cultures as reflections of functioning systems composed of in-terrelated parts. Material culture, to Processualists, was both a marker of cul-tural identity and the means of instigating and preserving cultural unity and survival. In both cases, however, identity was lodged at the group level.

Interpretivist approaches stress that there are no bounded entities, and that within groups, however they are defined, there are factions with agendas that sometimes intersect but also diverge. Such divergence can cause conflict. Individuals do not share equally in all aspects of culture: some have more knowledge, better skills, a greater interest in one realm of action—say, pottery making—than another—say, fashioning stone tools. Everyone has to survive, but not everyone needs to have the same ideas, nor do they have to act in the same ways. Hence, people in any cul-ture may operate within a shared frame of meaning and expectation but negotiate their relations to that frame differently. In the case of Stone-henge, the monument's form was instrumental in forging experiences in which people directly confronted differences based, for example, on how close they were to the center of ceremonies performed there. Because this is a purely prehistoric case, we do not know how these distinctions related to such differences as those between men and women, old and young. What an Interpretivist approach to Stonehenge highlights, however, is how material culture may have figured in the creation of a symbolic environment, existing within and among sites, through which the unity of past cultures was simultaneously affirmed and fragmented as people participated in the same ceremonies. The search for identity has now shifted to the subcultural level; material remains are assessed for how they might have figured in the creation of interpersonal differences.

Stonehenge continues to serve as a touchstone for complicated identities in groups as large as the European Union (EU) and as small as the local archaeology society, as well as in individuals. Stonehenge is a symbol of national identity with meaning at least in a bureaucratic sense for cultural heritage managers in Britain. There have also been efforts to associate Stonehenge with the Celts, thus pushing that ethnic identity into the deep past—which is a highly debatable enterprise—and uniting the people of Britain with those in the EU who also claim Celtic ancestors. Since Celtic speakers were once found from Turkey to Ireland, a case has been made that Celts are a foundational population in Europe. Integrating "Celtishness" into modern identity thus pulls together the past and present, and unites people of different nationalities. Going back to the individual, for a neo-Druid, the EU–Celt linkage might not be important, but Stonehenge's religious symbolism may well be crucial in defining a person's sense of self as an individual and member of a group of like-minded believers.

Stonehenge is thus **polysemous**: that is, it means many things to many people, on a wide variety of scales. Archaeologists are implicated in these processes, offering interpretations that are variably adopted by those constantly using material culture to redefine themselves in relation to others and the past. This is one arena in which archaeological research has modern relevance. It is here that our theories intersect data and current concerns, often yielding results we could not have imagined and can rarely control. Think about this the next time you look at an image of Stonehenge and contemplate what it means to you. Most likely, those thoughts are influenced by what you have read about the site, what you want to believe about the past and its relation to the present, and what you might have experienced through a visit. Stukeley's Stonehenge is not your Stonehenge, nor our Stonehenge, nor Britain's Stonehenge. It is all of these and more—and less as well, perhaps.

Further Reading

Archaeologies, Alternative

Lovata, T.

2007   *Inauthentic Archaeologies: Public Uses and Abuses of the Past.* Walnut Creek, CA: Left Coast Press, Inc.

     This volume reviews the ways in which people use reconstructions of archaeological sites to establish meaningful relations with the past. The interview Lovata conducted with Adam Horowitz, Fridgehenge's creator, is especially relevant to the material covered in this chapter.

Stonehenge, General Discussions

Bradley, R.

1998   *The Significance of Monuments: On the Shaping of Human Experience in Neolithic and Bronze Age Europe.* New York: Routledge.

     Bradley offers an Interpretivist approach to understanding the significance of ancient European monuments to those who made and used them. Though not focused on Stonehenge, his remarks are certainly applicable to that site.

Burl, A.

2007   *Stonehenge: A Complete History and Archaeology of the World's Most Enigmatic Stone Circle.* New York: Carroll and Graf Publishers.

     Burl offers a good summary of early research at Stonehenge, followed by a detailed account of the history of the site and its setting in Salisbury Plain.

Chippindale, C.

2004   *Stonehenge Complete.* 3rd edition. New York: Thames and Hudson.

     As the name implies, this is a comprehensive account of research at Stonehenge. It is particularly strong on early studies of the site through the mid-20th century.

Cleal, R., K. Walker, and R. Montague

1995   *Stonehenge in Its Landscape: Twentieth Century Excavations.* London: English Heritage.

     This tome provides a detailed summary of research conducted at Stonehenge up through the late 20th century. Here you will find perhaps the most carefully constructed and thoroughly documented arguments for the sequence of changes that shaped this monument.

Hawkins, G.

1963   Stonehenge Decoded. *Nature* 200:306–308.

1965   Stonehenge: A Neolithic Computer. *Nature* 202:1258–1261.

These two articles summarize Hawkins's influential, if much criticized, interpretations of Stonehenge as a center for observing and predicting celestial events.

Theory, Interpretivist

Aronson, M., ed.

2010 *If Stones Could Speak: Unlocking the Secrets of Stonehenge*. Washington, DC: National Geographic.

Contributions to this volume by Michael Parker Pearson provide information on the results of the Riverside Project, which is exploring Stonehenge and its landscape. See also *http://www.shef.ac.uk/archaeology /research/stonehenge* for recent findings from these investigations.

Thomas, J.

1999 *Understanding the Neolithic*. New York: Routledge.

Thomas discusses Stonehenge within the context of his overarching view of the active roles played by material culture in shaping people's beliefs and actions. The example of an Interpretivist approach to Stonehenge summarized in this chapter is drawn from this book.

Theory, Processual

Renfrew, C.

1974 Beyond a Subsistence Economy: The Evolution of Social Organization in Prehistoric Europe. In *Reconstructing Complex Societies: An Archaeological Colloquium*, ed. C. B. Moore, pp. 69–95. Bulletin of the American Schools of Oriental Research, Supplement 20. Cambridge, MA: American Schools of Oriental Research.

In this article, the author lays out the Processualist explanation for Europe's Neolithic stone monuments from which the account outlined in this chapter is drawn.

CHAPTER 7

CULTURE, HISTORY, AND ADAPTATION IN THE NACO VALLEY

Introduction

A s LONG AS WE HAVE BEEN TEACHING —over three decades now— students have asked us personal questions such as: Why are you an archaeologist? Why not a cultural anthropologist? Why do you study Mesoamerica, and not, say, Greece? Why Honduras in particular? How do (now did) you manage with two children? Where do you get your ideas? And, Do you enjoy what you do?

None of these are trivial questions, and all have a bearing on how we approached our initial research in the Naco Valley. Theory and data come together through the actions and beliefs of individuals who employ the first to understand the second. This insight, developed most fully by those who subscribe to Interpretivism, applies to all research conducted in archaeology. You certainly do not need to know our biographies in any detail to understand how theory and data are interrelated in the investigations we conducted. But it does help to be familiar with some aspects of our pasts if only because these variables played a significant role in our choices of theories and where to conduct research. So this is the first goal of the present chapter.

Second, we use a few pages to outline the history of investigations in the Naco Valley in particular, and **Southeast Mesoamerica** in general (Southeast Mesoamerica encompasses the adjoining portions of Guatemala, Honduras, and El Salvador; Figure 7.1). This review highlights how

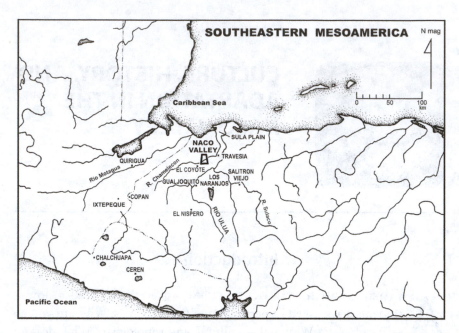

FIGURE 7.1 Map of Southeast Mesoamerica showing sites mentioned in the text.

developments in archaeological theory shaped research agendas within Southeast Mesoamerica. We were not immune to these currents, which strongly affected how we conducted investigations in the Naco Valley beginning in the 1970s. Many of our initial ideas continued to haunt our research for the next two decades. Understanding why we made the choices we did when we started work, therefore, requires understanding something of the historical context in which we began our studies.

Our third goal takes up most of the chapter. We talk about the basic theory that guided our initial investigations and the goals we sought to achieve, and then examine the fieldwork conducted in pursuit of those objectives. Finally, we mention the problems encountered in the course of our studies and the steps we took to deal with these difficulties.

Our Beginnings

As we mention a number of times in the first four chapters, no one ever embarks on a research project without cultural, theoretical, and personal predispositions. We do not begin investigations in places chosen at random, nor are our questions drawn out of thin air. Crucial decisions about what to ask, and where to ask it, are shaped by a wide array of factors not often discussed in research reports. In part, trying to separate the scholar as person from the scholar as investigator derives from the Modernist notion that pursuing an objective study of any phenomenon depends on taking ourselves out of the picture. From that point of view, what we observe and how we interpret it ideally should be unaffected by who we are.

It is true that we want to suspend as many of our more blatant biases as possible. Nevertheless, even the most self-aware investigators begin work with preconceived notions that, whether intentional or not, lead them along certain research paths and away from others. This was definitely the case in our Naco Valley investigations. There is probably no end of personal details we could relate that would have some bearing on our research. These might include the initiative Pat showed in the fall of third grade to organize a group of friends into a hunting-and-gathering band roaming her neighborhood in search of edible plants (from frost-bitten gardens) and dangerous megafauna (local dogs who objected to our being in "their" backyards). This was inspired by the section on Neanderthals in a Time-Life book about ancient humans her parents bought for her at a local grocery store. Let's just say that our interests in archaeology lie deep within our respective childhoods.

Neither of us entered college expecting to become archaeologists: Ed started out in history, and Pat was persuaded by her high school English teachers that she had a great career as a literary critic (they were so very wrong). Archaeology was something that drew us in the more courses we took. At least as important as the classes was our participation in actual archaeological fieldwork during our undergraduate years. Pat attended a formal field school in Colorado, while Ed volunteered on several excavation projects in England, Delaware, and the Guatemalan highlands. You can learn a lot from good teachers and texts (in fact, we are counting on it). It is one thing, however, to be in love with the idea of archaeology: if we had a dollar (or 10) from all the people who told us how much they just *loved* archaeology, we would have retired years ago. It is another thing to be crazy about *practicing* it. Archaeological fieldwork is like any job: it has its boring sides, and the places most of us work are often remote from such taken-for-granted services as drinking water (or running water at all), electricity, telephones, and the Internet. Do you still feel that passion for studying the past you first sensed in a classroom when the temperature has just passed 100 degrees F, the square you are digging has not yielded an artifact for three days, and something unspecified just took your lunch down its burrow and is not inclined to share? If the answer is yes, then your interest in archaeology runs deep.

Choosing an area in which to work is often a very personal matter. Ed enjoyed the projects he worked on in England and Delaware but fell in love with the field in Guatemala. Pat first experienced Latin America in Panama when visiting her parents, who were living and working there. Deciding where to work is certainly based, at least in part, on the sorts of issues that can be studied in particular places. This was true in our cases, or became true with time and education. But a big part of Latin America's appeal for us was the vividness of the life we experienced there. Houses in Panama and Guatemala were painted in bright colors not seen in, say, western Pennsylvania steel and coal towns; buses rumbled by loaded with people and animals—chickens hanging from side-view mirrors at times— and everywhere we looked life seemed to be infused with vitality. Being in Latin America felt *right*. Just as one theory is not necessarily the best in any absolute sense, so too there is no "best" place to do research. That locale is no more or less than where you feel most comfortable and excited to be, and whether or not the area has the potential to be intellectually challenging (in addition, many times, to being physically challenging).

Both of us came out of our undergraduate field and classroom experiences with little doubt of the career we would choose and where we would pursue it. Consequently, we headed off to graduate school to gain the advanced training and degrees needed to make that plan a reality. Here we came to one of the major forks in the road to becoming professional archaeologists. The graduate program in which you enroll plays a major part in introducing you to various ways of approaching the field. Schools usually provide distinct theoretical takes on anthropology in general, and archaeology in particular. This is not to say that everyone in a graduate program marches in intellectual lockstep. Still, faculty members tend to hire people with whom they feel some sense of commonality, and shared theoretical orientations can contribute to that feeling. Who you study with, then, will influence the theoretical school in which you choose to begin your career.

We ended up in 1974 at the University of Pennsylvania (Penn) in Philadelphia. Penn had, and still has, an excellent reputation for research on **Mesoamerican** prehistory, especially the **Maya lowlands**. Mesoamerica consists of central Mexico and runs south through Guatemala and Belize into western Honduras and El Salvador. The Maya lowlands cover portions of Belize, Mexico, and Guatemala where some of the principal manifestations of prehistoric Maya culture are found. When we started graduate school, Penn had a strong tradition stressing intensive field training and an open approach to theory. To the extent that Penn professors expounded a single conceptual framework in 1974, it was that of Culture History, though scholars such as Robert Sharer were also exploring ways of synthesizing Culture History and Processual approaches to study the lowland Maya past.

To be honest, our interest in theory was muted at this stage in our careers. We did not enter archaeology because we loved theory, but because solving the puzzle of ancient behaviors by studying patterns in material remains was deeply fascinating. We were, however, aware of the conceptual currents flowing through the field at this time. Virtually every issue of such major archaeological journals as *American Antiquity* appeared with an article about Processual archaeology. Many of these essays included programmatic statements—that is, sections telling us how it should be done, even if archaeologists were not yet carrying out these ideal plans. There was a palpable sense that a new paradigm was being worked out in ever greater detail; publications and presentations by the architects of that framework, such as Lewis Binford, led to many heated discussions in which we participated.

Selecting a Research Area

But why did Pat choose to pursue her dissertation research in the Naco Valley? As one of Pat's committee members once asked her, "[Expletive deleted], why work in that backwater? Do they even have architecture there?" This well-known archaeologist was putting into admirably explicit terms what many others only implied: important investigations were to be done in the Maya lowlands, the core of the culture area, not in its margins.

Pat came to work in the Naco Valley as the result of a happy accident. She had studied with John Henderson, a prominent Mesoamerican archaeologist, while still an undergraduate at Cornell University. John was, in 1974, at the point of initiating systematic archaeological research in the Naco Valley and generously invited Pat to direct the settlement survey. The timing could not have been better. Pat was in a position to begin what would become her dissertation research, and, while the Naco Valley was on the perceived fringes of the Maya culture area, it was close to that core. In addition, field-based dissertation topics were not that easy to find (for women, especially— it was easier for men in those days). Ed was doing his PhD research in the nearby lower Motagua Valley, west of the Naco

Valley and over the mountains defining the border between Honduras and Guatemala. He therefore helped Pat conduct her settlement studies from 1977 to 1979, while she returned the favor, assisting him with the lower Motagua research in those same years. Neither had lusted after the Naco Valley as a research site: it had simply been presented as an opportunity that Pat happily snatched up. It was one of the best professional decisions we ever made. The value of that choice, however, was not immediately obvious, in part because very little was known about the valley's prehistory. Why that was the case is a matter of theory.

Southeast Mesoamerican Prehistory: A Marginal Matter

John Henderson was drawn to the basin by the site of Naco's renown as a Late Postclassic (AD 1300–1532) trading center. Largely buried by the modern town of the same name, Late Postclassic Naco was a sufficiently important Precolumbian economic node that it attracted the attention of such leading lights of the Spanish Conquest as Hernán Cortés. Cortés sent ambassadors (of sorts—more like advance scouts) to Naco soon after completing his defeat of the Mexica (or Aztecs). He wanted to establish his authority over what would become Honduras, an area also claimed by rival *conquistadores* from points south and by restless subordinates from what is now Guatemala. Partly as a result of this strife, Naco appeared fairly often in early Spanish documents, some of which have been published in recent times. Because of colonial documents, Naco figured in discussions of Southeast Mesoamerican prehistory going back to the early 20th century, and even attracted some early archaeological research: a three-week program of excavation and mapping was conducted at Naco and several nearby sites in 1936. No follow-up investigations were pursued here for another 38 years.

Why did nearly four decades pass between research projects in the Naco Valley? The situation is not unique to this basin. Most surrounding portions of Southeast Mesoamerica suffered from similar neglect. It was not that Southeast Mesoamerica was harder to get to than other areas that enjoyed far more attention; nor was Honduras a particularly dangerous place. No, the reason is because the archaeology of Southeast Mesoamerica was not considered important. Why it was not thought to be significant has a lot to do with how the area was perceived through the lens of prevailing Culture Historical perspectives.

As noted in Chapter 4, Culture Historians during the early to middle 20th century were very interested in identifying cultural boundaries by tracing the distribution of material traits across space. The ancient world was thus seen as a patchwork of cultures that were internally homogeneous but distinct from one another.

How did application of this Culture Historical perspective marginalize the study of Southeast Mesoamerican prehistory? Beginning in the 19th century, the attention of archaeologists and the public alike was riveted on the dramatic discoveries made at lowland Maya centers such as Tikal, Chichén Itzá, and Copan. Early archaeological work, therefore, set out to define the limits of Maya culture. Researchers spread far and wide, enduring malaria and uncooperative mules, in search of sites bearing the distinctive hallmarks of this civilization. Traits thought to be characteristic of Maya culture included hieroglyphic inscriptions, massive temples and palaces arranged around extensive plazas, stone monuments, and elaborately decorated ceramics bearing distinctive motifs. Most of the pioneering research in Southeast Mesoamerica was directed toward tracing the distribution of such features. Once the limits of Maya culture were determined, research intensified inside this zone and abruptly declined outside it.

Diffusion and migration, the great causal mechanisms in Culture Historical explanations, helped to direct attention away from Southeast Mesoamerica. Since no large centers with dramatic public artwork were known in the Southeast outside the lowland Maya capitals of Copan (in Honduras) and Quiriguá (in Guatemala), it was highly unlikely that ideas or populations from this area played significant roles in the genesis of lowland Maya culture. Innovations might have diffused from the Maya lowlands to the Southeast, sparking developments there, but influences did not flow the other way.

With cultural boundaries drawn by the 1930s, even the sporadic research that Southeast Mesoamerica had enjoyed up to that time declined in frequency as work in the Maya lowlands intensified. Southeast Mesoamerica was not inherently uninteresting. It failed to attract scholarly attention because research there did not seem rewarding within the predominant theory of the time. Useful knowledge and successful careers would come from investigations in the Maya heartland.

Intensified Interest: Southeast Mesoamerican Research in the 1960s–1970s

Culture Historians increasingly shared the archaeological stage with Processualists by the late 1950s. Causation was now sought in relations among material and cultural factors—in particular, how people adapted to their physical environments determined the course of human history. Initially, these shifts did little to stir interest in Southeast Mesoamerican prehistory in general, and the Naco Valley in particular. Those boundaries drawn by Culture Historians still defined the basic units of analysis. Understanding Maya history required work within an identifiable culture, though now attention focused on interactions between people and their immediate physical environments. Processualist archaeology could have been successfully applied to studying Naco Valley prehistory, but why would anyone bother? Earlier investigations had relegated Southeastern Mesoamerica to the margins of lowland Maya developments. If you wanted to investigate such major questions of the time as how and why social hierarchies developed and cities grew, you were better off working where these processes had achieved obvious heights, where the sites were large and the political structures extensive. The Naco Valley was a sideshow to the main event.

By the late 1960s, however, there was increasing recognition among Processualists that every culture was connected to others from which its members received essential goods needed for their survival and societal functioning but which could not be found at home. Trade studies had begun. Defined as the peaceful movement of items among people living in different cultures, trade was increasingly seen as a possible trigger for culture change. William Rathje, for example, argued that the exchange of goods was crucial to the development of lowland Maya realms. Lacking many basic resources, especially stone needed to make tools, the lowland Maya were forced to secure these goods from distant sources (compare this argument with the one proposed by Algaze, outlined in Chapter 5, for the development of southern Mesopotamian states). Such trade required organizing:

1. people who produced and collected the items to be exported;

2. folks to transport them to wherever they were to be exchanged for needed resources;

3. individuals to bring the imports home;

4. distribution of the imports in the recipient society.

Such needs gave rise to political hierarchies whose leaders saw to the conduct of trade that was essential to their society's survival. Trade studies like the one conducted by Rathje were initially conducted in a Processualist mode. Importing goods could be another way of adapting that complemented such local processes as farming and hunting. Similarly, hierarchies were seen as means of organizing large groups of people to do what was necessary to adjust to their environments, including securing goods from great distances. But now, cultures, still the basic units of study, had porous borders.

Even areas that seemed remote might have contributed through trade to the appearance and persistence of major states. It was only a matter of time before someone would think to take another look at Southeast Mesoamerica. By 1968, archaeological investigations in the area had begun in earnest, and John Henderson rode this wave into the Naco Valley six years later. We washed up in the valley 12 months after that. It is important to realize here that it was not changes in the Naco Valley itself that led to its study. It was still pretty much the same place in 1974 that it had been in 1944 and 1904, with the exception that the main road had been paved in the early 1960s. It was changes in theory that at first marginalized, and later emphasized, the area for study. Even so, Southeast Mesoamerica was not necessarily being investigated during the 1970s because it was seen as important in its own right. The area was examined for what it might contribute to studies of lowland Maya developments. Perhaps the Southeast was a source of trade goods that Maya notables could use to enhance adaptation and gain power. The Naco Valley went from being beyond the margins of lowland Maya culture to being part of its periphery. As such, the Southeast Maya Periphery, as it was now called, might have been a source of goods, but its people were not seen as active participants in innovations occurring in the core. Still, it was a start and this is the perspective we happily brought with us when we joined John Henderson in Honduras in 1975–1979.

Setting

The Naco Valley encompasses 96 km^2 of gently rolling terrain ringed by steep hills that rise 2,000 m or more from the valley floor (Figure 7.2). Cutting southwest to northeast through the basin, the Chamelecon River is the main source of water. This stream follows the line of a geological fault, dividing the basin into two unequal segments: roughly two-thirds of the valley lies west of the stream, while the remainder is compressed between the Chamelecon and the eastern mountains. Despite its location in the tropics, the Naco Valley does not conform to the common image of a rainforest. First, the vegetation is tropical but deciduous: almost all trees lose their

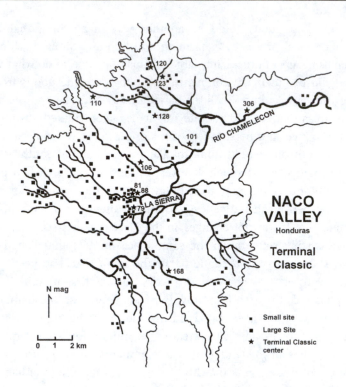

FIGURE 7.2 Map of the Naco Valley showing the distribution of sites, including political centers, dating to the Terminal Classic. As excavated Terminal Classic sites were generally also occupied in the Late Classic, Figure 7.2 also illustrates the pattern of Late Classic settlement.

leaves during the dry season, though many also flower then, making it look somewhat like spring. Second, the temperature is warm to hot year-round (averaging 27 degrees C; 81 degrees F); but, third, rain is not evenly distributed over all months. Most precipitation falls during May–November; the rest of the year is relatively dry. Still, timing and amounts of rain vary annually, causing serious anxiety for people dependent on adequate moisture for their crops. This is the case today, and rain is a constant topic of conversation from planting to harvest. Concern over rainfall was certainly at least as important to the valley's ancient inhabitants.

Just as significant to farmers in any period is soil quality. The general impression of tropical soils is that they are difficult to farm because they are alternately leached of nutrients by rain and then baked by the sun. About 5 percent of the Naco Valley is taken up by fields that match this expectation of low productivity. Most of the basin's soils are of good quality, however;

they are easily capable of supporting at least one crop per year of basic staples such as corn, beans, and squash. Roughly 5 percent of the valley's soils are so fertile that two crops can be cultivated sequentially in one year if there is sufficient rain just at the end of the dry season to carry the plants through to harvest.

Many Naco Valley farmers today can only look wistfully at the land, imagining how much it might yield. By 1975, a few landowners controlled the most fertile tracts. They have recently been replaced by agrobusinesses, sometimes subsidiaries of multinational companies, raising cattle, plantains (cooking bananas), and sugarcane for export. Since the mid-1990s, much land has been occupied by factories owned by foreign corporations. Growing along with the factories are increasing numbers of housing developments for the employees. The few remaining small producers have to work on the poorest fields. Subsistence farming is fast disappearing, with wage labor, supplemented by cultivating cash crops (such as watermelons and pineapples), barely providing for most people's basic needs.

Widespread and dramatic modifications of the landscape due to centuries of farming and modern changes have also threatened most native species of plants and animals. Tapirs, deer, and jaguars once moved in the deciduous forest on the valley floor and into the hills, which used to have many oak trees in addition to soft woods. Now there are large expanses of grassland deliberately created for the cattle, along with cultivated fields, factories, and housing developments. The hills have fewer trees every year, since many people who still have to cook with wood cut from these slopes; and instead of a mixture of trees, the hills mostly have pines, rather than the oaks of yesteryears. The older people say even the rivers yield fewer fish, shellfish, snails, and crustaceans than they did several decades ago, statements we can support with our own observations. Now iguanas, lizards valued as a source of food, are rarely seen, where before they were numerous and impressively large. These changes are the latest in a series of modifications brought about largely by human action in the Naco Valley over its three millennia of occupation.

The basin's population was never isolated from people in neighboring areas. The Chamelecon cuts a valley providing easy access to close-by areas: about 15 km to the northeast lies Honduras's massive and fertile Caribbean coastal plain; to the southwest, the major lowland Maya center of Copan is approximately 120 km distant. Paths run to the northwest and southwest over the mountains, leading eventually to Guatemala's lower Motagua Valley—another extensive Caribbean coastal plain—and

Quiriguá, a large lowland Maya site about 90 km to the west-southwest. Evidence recovered from archaeological excavations suggests that the basin's residents maintained contacts with members of societies living in these and other surrounding areas at various points in the valley's occupation.

Outline of Naco Valley and Mesoamerican Prehistory as Understood in 2011

Occupation of Mesoamerica dates back to before 10,000 BC, when hunter-gatherers first moved into the area. Plant domestication began in a few portions of highland Mesoamerica about 2,000 to 4,000 years later, agriculture becoming the economic foundation of societies stretching from central Mexico through Guatemala, Honduras, Belize, and El Salvador by at least 2000 BC. The earliest evidence of habitation in the Naco Valley, however, dates to the Middle Preclassic, stretching from 1200 to 400 BC (the general trends in Naco Valley prehistory are summarized in Table 7.1). During this time, population was widely scattered around the valley, hunting, fishing, and farming on a small scale. There were a few particularly influential social groups who occasionally commandeered the labor of their less well-positioned brethren to build large earthen platforms atop which these elites lived. Some of their constructions reached 3 m high. Such power centers shifted periodically over the eight centuries of the Middle Preclassic, no one group sustaining its pre-eminence for more than a limited period. Despite their exalted living arrangements, these notables did not enjoy privileged access to foreign valuables, such as jade or marine shell jewelry. Everyone, regardless of the size of their residence, pretty much lived similar lives, using comparable artifacts. Differences between leaders and followers were muted, and distinctions between rich and poor were not marked and were perhaps non-existent.

These social developments are fairly modest when compared with the emergence at this time of populous societies dominated by powerful rulers in such places as the Gulf Coast of Mexico and the lowland forests of Guatemala. In fact, population was growing throughout Mesoamerica during this period, and expressions of political hierarchies, including the construction of large buildings, were becoming increasingly widespread.

The succeeding Late Preclassic (400 BC–AD 200) in the Naco Valley may have witnessed a population decline. Fewer sites dating to this interval are known than for just about any other period in the valley's prehis-

Table 7.1. Summary of the salient trends in the Naco Valley's culture history, from the first known occupation to the Spanish Conquest in AD 1532

PERIOD	DATES	SOCIOPOLITICAL ORGANIZATION	POPULATION LEVELS	INTENSITY OF EXTERNAL CONTACTS
Middle Preclassic	1200–400 BC	Political fragmentation, minimal development of hierarchy.	Widely dispersed, fairly low.	Evidence for the spread of ideas, but not goods, from neighboring areas.
Late Preclassic	400 BC–AD 200	Political centralization at one major valley capital; evidence for hierarchy is unclear.	May mark a period of significant population decline.	Signs of inter-societal exchange remain weak.
Early Classic	AD 200–600	Political fragmentation among at least three competing polities; hierarchy is not strongly developed.	Population increases considerably across the valley.	There remains relatively little evidence of inter-societal exchange.
Late Classic	AD 600–800	Power is highly centralized at La Sierra; evidence for a valley-wide hierarchy is strong.	Population continues to rise, filling all parts of the basin.	The intensity of inter-societal transactions increases significantly.
Terminal Classic	AD 800–1000	Power is divided among as many as 13 political centers; heterarchy replaces the valley-wide hierarchy.	Population increases throughout the valley.	Inter-societal exchanges continue at relatively high levels.
Early Postclassic	AD 1000–1300	The power commanded by surviving elites was minimal and fragmented; hierarchy is barely recognizable.	Population drops precipitously and is concentrated in the central and northern valley.	Evidence for inter-societal exchanges is minimal.
Late Postclassic	AD 1300–1532	Power was increasingly concentrated in the rulers of two valley centers; signs of hierarchy increase.	Population rises markedly but is still largely found in the central and northern valley.	Ethnohistoric accounts indicate an increase in inter-societal exchanges; material remains confirm this view to some extent.

tory. Interestingly, a major political center, Santo Domingo (Site 123), was built in the Late Preclassic (Figure 7.3). Its 23 massive, stone-faced platforms are nestled against the foothills on the basin's far northwest margin. Some people, therefore, were able to command the labor to erect the densest concentration of large buildings the valley had seen up to this point. How they managed this feat, and why a seemingly dwindling local population acceded to their demands, remain unknown.

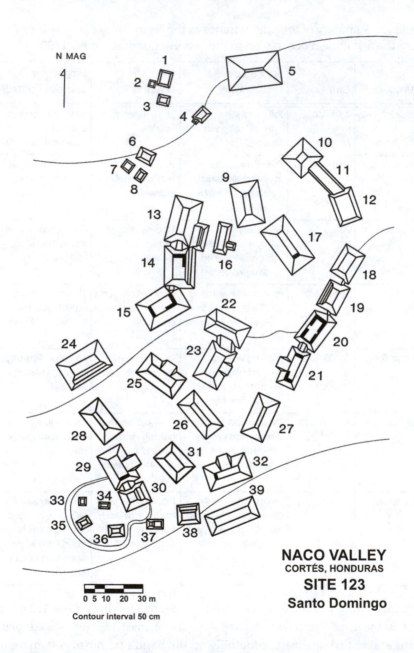

FIGURE 7.3 Map of Site 123, Santo Domingo,
Late Preclassic capital of the Naco Valley.

This period was marked by considerable social and political change throughout Mesoamerica. While some areas suffered demographic losses similar to those apparently faced in the Naco Valley, others witnessed dramatic shifts in the opposite direction. The region's first clearly defined states (politically centralized, hierarchically structured realms; see Chapter 5 for a definition of this political form) emerged now in the highland valleys of Oaxaca and Mexico. Each was commanded from large capitals—Monte Alban in Oaxaca and Teotihuacan in the valley of Mexico—whose influence extended well beyond their immediate hinterlands. Closer to the Naco Valley, such lowland Maya sites as Tikal and Calakmul to the northwest were also taking on the trappings of major political, population, and economic centers.

The apparent centralization of control over the Naco Valley represented by Santo Domingo was shattered during the Early Classic (AD 200–600). Leaders of at least three political units divided the basin among themselves at this time, each ruling from a small capital with no more than 28 structures apiece. Within each of the three centers were several monumental platforms (defined for the Naco Valley as structures 1.5 m or more in height). Population, based on the number of sites with evidence of Early Classic settlement, was rising. This political decentralization contrasts with the continued growth of the major Mesoamerican realms focused on Monte Alban, Teotihuacan, Tikal, Calakmul, and other comparable capitals. Perhaps most significant for the basin's inhabitants was the establishment of a powerful royal dynasty in the 5th century AD at nearby Copan by notables who hailed from Tikal. That Tikal's rulers were, by this point, descended from interlopers from Teotihuacan highlights the political dynamism of the Early Classic and the close ties that linked at least members of the period's principal royal houses. Very little of these connections is evident in the materials recovered from the Naco Valley for this time.

A major shift occurred during the Late Classic (AD 600–800). The leaders of one of the Early Classic centers, La Sierra, won out against their competitors and established control over the entire valley (Figure 7.4). The new capital, with 468 surface-visible constructions, is fully 10 times the size of its next largest contemporary. La Sierra's site core, comprised of 21 massive platforms organized around two concentrically arranged plazas, also provides the most significant evidence of labor control seen anywhere in the Late Classic basin (Figure 7.5). In addition, La Sierra's elite enjoyed a locally unprecedented ability to attract subordinates to their center; roughly one-third of all known Late Classic structures are found in La Sierra and within a 1-km radius of the capital. No matter how this aggregation was achieved—by force, positive incentive, or both—it is a testament to the power of these newly established lords. Throughout the Late Classic, population in the Naco Valley was rising; almost every environment was occupied and the number of sites proliferated rapidly.

The ascendancy of La Sierra's elites occurred at a time of great political turmoil in Mesoamerica. Teotihuacan and Monte Alban were in de-

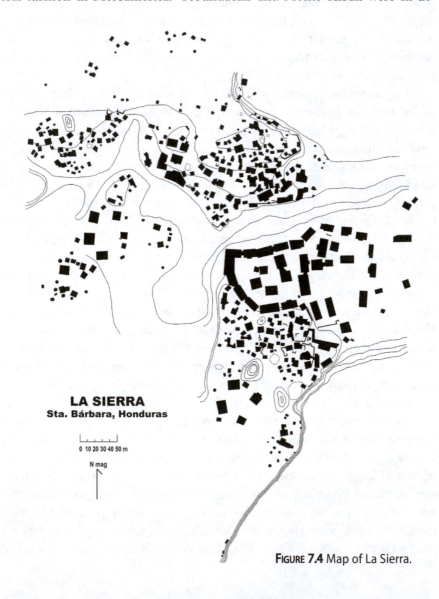

LA SIERRA
Sta. Bárbara, Honduras

0 10 20 30 40 50 m

N mag

FIGURE 7.4 Map of La Sierra.

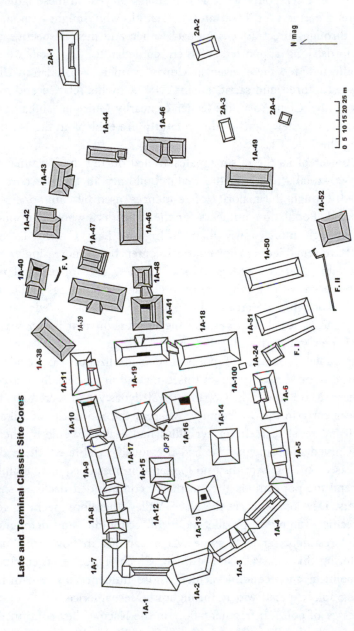

NACO VALLEY
LA SIERRA

Late and Terminal Classic Site Cores

FIGURE 75 Map of the La Sierra site core. The structures shaded in gray were built in the Terminal Classic, while those shown in white date to the Late Classic.

cline, while the nearby lowland Maya centers were embroiled in an esca-
lating series of inter-polity wars. The primary players in these latter conflicts were the rulers of Tikal and Calakmul, who sought regional supremacy through direct attacks on each other and their respective allies.
Copan's lords, long supporters of their confederates at Tikal, were ad-
versely affected by these events. Copan's ruler, Waxaklahun-Ub'ah-
K'awil, was captured and sacrificed in AD 738 by his relative and former
ally, K'ak' Tiliw' Chan Yo'at, the leader of nearby Quiriguá and a new ally
of Calakmul. Very few signs of this volatility are evident in the Naco Valley during the Late Classic.

The power of La Sierra's magnates waned during the Terminal Classic (AD 800–1000). Some of the major buildings in the site core were
abandoned, though the majority of residences used by commoners were
still occupied. Population numbers for the valley as a whole continued to
increase, though more slowly than during the Late Classic. La Sierra
seems to have remained a major political center, but it increasingly shared
the stage with other contenders. At least 12 new seats of political power
appear now, each with its own core of monumental buildings and cadre of
supporters. Though La Sierra's rulers still may have had an edge in these
political contests, it is hard to escape the impression that power was slip-
ping from their grasp, diffusing out to upstarts.

Comparable processes of political decentralization are evident in
many portions of Mesoamerica at this time and are especially marked in
the southern Maya lowlands. Copan's royal dynasty had seemingly fallen
from power early in the 9th century, whereas the monarchs of Tikal and
Calakmul and most of their former allies had ceased to rule by the 10th
century. Carved monuments that had previously celebrated these divine
leaders ceased to be raised, they no longer commissioned major building
projects, and the populations they formerly commanded declined sharply
in numbers. Developments in the Naco Valley, therefore, seem to represent a specific example of broader political, economic, and demographic
trends. Interestingly, at least some Maya capitals in northern Yucatan
thrived during this interval. One of them, Chichén Itzá, even emerged as
a major political and economic center whose influence, as seen in its art
and iconography, spread widely throughout Mesoamerica.

Processes of political fragmentation in the Naco Valley continued un-
abated through the Early Postclassic (AD 1000–1300), when La Sierra
was largely abandoned. Population numbers, which had been on a more
or less continuous ascent for roughly six centuries, now went into a steep

decline. Most people were concentrated in the central and northern parts of the valley during the Early Postclassic, abandoning some of the most fertile soils across the southern third of the basin. Signs of political power are also few: there were only two minuscule centers, each with 16–19 structures, none of which were taller than 2.75 m. The ability to command the labor needed for large-scale projects had definitely ebbed. Similar developments are also noted throughout the Maya lowlands during the Early Postclassic. Even the realms in northern Yucatan declined in population and political importance at this time.

The Late Postclassic (AD 1300–1532, and the Spanish Conquest in our area) sees the rapid rise of the site of Naco to both local and regional prominence. Covering roughly 1 km^2, Naco was one of the largest valley centers ever built and a center of long-distance trade. A second center, Viejo Brisas del Valle (Site PVN 306), lies a scant 2 km northeast of the Naco Valley on the north bank of the Chamelecon River. This large site, with an estimated 120 structures and 223 artifact scatters covering 0.5 km^2, may have been one of Naco's major competitors. Alternatively, Naco and Brisas might have been part of the same large site that the Spanish called Naco.

Late Postclassic rural settlements are difficult to identify on survey, in part because most buildings raised during this period were made of perishable materials that leave little trace; any mounds used were made of earth, but most buildings were constructed on ground surface. Nevertheless, the large sizes of Naco and Brisas, coupled with early Spanish accounts of 10,000 people living in Naco by the early 16th century, suggest that population was definitely on the rebound. It was, of course, at this point that the indigenous history of the valley came to an end. Fought over by rival Spanish factions, mercilessly raided for slaves, and overwhelmed by diseases brought from the Old World, native populations and cultures in the basin quickly declined and eventually disappeared. This tragic situation was repeated frequently throughout Central America.

The Late Postclassic sees a resurgence of powerful, often expansionistic states throughout Mesoamerica. The Aztecs and their perpetual rivals, the Tarascans, established their empires during the final Precolumbian centuries in central and western Mexico. Closer to the Naco Valley, Mayapan was, until the mid-15th century, the capital of a realm that encompassed most of northern Yucatan. Even though the Late Postclassic was marked by another round of increasingly intense armed conflicts, it also seems to have been characterized by growth in long-distance commerce, population numbers, and the development of novel political forms. This resurgence was tragically curtailed everywhere by the Spanish Conquest and its legacy of disease.

We concentrate here on developments dating to the Late and Terminal Classic periods (dated to AD 600–1000). The large quantities of material relevant to this interval that we have analyzed provide ample scope for examining how theories guide research, are then evaluated, and subsequently change. Other phases in the basin's long prehistory are given short shrift in this review because we feel that a relatively tight temporal focus is needed to highlight our central theme of relations among theory, field investigations, and data.

Developing Our Initial Theory

The theoretical stance Pat crafted by the time she began her dissertation research in the Naco Valley combined elements of the Culture History perspective so strong at Penn and strains of Processualism prevalent in archaeological writings at the time. On the one hand, she was convinced that constructing basic time-space frameworks was a first priority. Linking the cultures and phases defined in this process to those known from surrounding areas was also important. Specifically, Pat would try to correlate developments in the Naco Valley with those reported from the better-studied neighboring Maya lowlands. This made practical sense: very little was known about the prehistory of the Naco and surrounding valleys in 1975. Establishing the local chronology and placing this sequence in its broader context would require comparing Naco Valley finds with Culture Historical sequences recorded in the intensively studied Maya lowlands.

She was also working within an intellectual framework that gave pride of place to the basin's lowland Maya neighbors during the period AD 600–900 (the Late Classic period as it was then defined). As noted above, it was commonplace to assume that royal agents from centers such as Copan and Quiriguá exercised considerable influence on the smaller societies of Southeast Mesoamerica. Significant transformations in political organization and population numbers, along with any shifts in other cultural patterns, were thought to have resulted from contacts initiated by representatives of the closest lowland Maya capitals. Reconstructing those interactions was of the utmost importance because such relations presumably played a crucial role in motivating local culture change. This argument is based on a diffusionist idea that innovations arising in culture cores are adopted by those living on their margins. In this case, lowland Maya centers were seen as particularly creative locales from which influential concepts spread to their neighbors. These neighbors, for whatever reason, were not nearly as creative as the Maya but certainly knew a good idea when they heard or saw one.

We must admit that the causal connections between contact and change were not at all clear in our own minds at this time. To some extent, Pat presumed that upwardly mobile segments of Naco Valley populations would envy the power and achievements of lowland Maya rulers. Consequently, these peripheral elites would do everything they could to capture some of that charisma by importing valued goods and adopting distinctive practices associated with Maya lords. Such diagnostics of elite Maya power as elaborately painted ceramic vessels, carved jade, temples, and ballcourts would thus be concentrated at Late Classic Naco Valley political centers. The portable items likely arrived through inter-elite gift exchanges. Lowland Maya architectural forms, in turn, were replicated to serve as venues for the performance of sacred rites. In these ceremonies, Naco Valley rulers were thought to have interceded with powerful supernaturals on behalf of their communities, much as Maya notables did in their own capitals. In both cases, the potency of Maya lords was appropriated by their Naco Valley counterparts, who engaged in ceremonies that they alone within the basin could do, using valuable foreign goods that only they could acquire. Still, Pat presumed that Naco Valley rulers did not command the power and prestige of their role models. What her theory led her to expect was the creation of a pale reflection of Maya greatness in the basin from AD 600 to 900.

From the Processual side, Pat was committed to describing and explaining variations in the behaviors that shaped the basin's material record. As noted in Chapter 4 and illustrated in Chapter 5, Processualists argued that no one site typifies the full range of actions and interactions conducted in past cultures. Pat thought it essential, therefore, to survey the Naco Valley and describe its ancient settlement patterns. Excavations would then be conducted at sites that spanned the full range of settlement forms, locations, and sizes. In this way, Pat hoped to secure a representative sample of materials that would cast light on the complete spectrum of behaviors practiced in the valley in all periods. Such descriptions would form the basis for mapping out changing relations among such variables as natural resources, population numbers, activities, and modes of interaction.

The survey program was particularly designed to determine how ancient populations adapted to the Naco Valley's natural environments. Pat looked at the spread of people across the landscape, how these patterns changed over time, and the ways the patterns were related to the distribution of such basic physical resources as water and arable land. This approach is based on the notion that people's decisions on where to live and what to do were strongly conditioned by their evaluations of the valley's physical features. Areas blessed with a happy combination of water, fertile soils, and easily acquired stone and wood for construction would, in this view, have attracted relatively large numbers of people. Places lacking these resources would have been avoided or supported only very small populations. This hypothesis derives from a more comprehensive Processual model in which human efforts to adapt to their environments significantly affect cultural choices and practices. Some of those adaptive processes should be visible in ancient settlement patterns.

This was not a terribly coherent conceptual framework. Looking back on that interpretive structure, we are impressed by how the disparate principles of Culture History and Processualism shared the same conceptual space. Ideas of diffusion linked with notions of unique culture histories coexisted with processes of adaptation thought to be widely applicable. Pat was borrowing ideas from distinct sources to address different questions, without devoting much thought to forging a coherent approach to Naco Valley prehistory.

There was also nothing inevitable about the perspective she took to the field. Though Interpretivist musings were still unheard in archaeology, Pat could certainly have begun her studies from, say, a Marxist stance. That she was not attracted to these views has much to do with the time and place where we began our careers and what we made of the research potentials offered by those circumstances. Marxist theories had made little inroads into lowland Maya studies. Pat could have sought them out in the literature but was not inclined to do so, as their relevance to her research was not obvious at the time. We eventually embraced this theoretical school, but it would take a while.

Summary of Our Overarching Theory

We can summarize our overarching theory in reference to the issues of causation, agency, and generalization raised in Chapter 3. The variables given pride of place in describing and explaining local developments were:

1. elements of the natural environment crucial to pursuing agriculture (fertile soils, water, building materials, and stone for tool production, in particular);

2. a marked distinction between Maya and non-Maya, the latter being recipients of innovations offered by the former;

3. an equally important division between elites and commoners.

Processes linking these variables in causal chains were, first, adaptation (supposedly explaining settlement choices made by all Naqueños [pronounced Nah-ken-yos, these are Naco Valley residents]), second, diffusion (from culture core to periphery), and third, emulation or outright copying (of elite lowland Maya political and religious innovations by their Naco Valley counterparts). Though there was some room for individual action in this formulation, it was a weak form of agency at best: people settled near basic resources; local elites imitated the practices and material culture of their foreign superiors; and the commoners pretty much did as they were told. As to generalization, Pat thought that the basin's history was shaped by the convergence of locally distinctive events and broad adaptive processes.

Setting to Work

Research activities pursued during 1974–1979 directly followed from the above theory and the need to construct a local chronology. John Henderson's excavations at La Sierra aimed to reveal the full temporal sequence of valley settlement. Stratigraphy would, we hoped, help identify changes in artifact styles crucial to determining the different phases of Naco Valley occupation and their relative order. The stratigraphic work was concentrated at La Sierra because, as the largest known site in the area, it was most likely occupied for the longest period of time. There was, therefore, a good chance that deep, undisturbed deposits spanning multiple phases, each marked by its own distinctive material styles, were preserved there. This supposition was based on the reasonable argument that sizable sites reached their final dimensions as a result of accretion: the longer people lived someplace, the more remains they would leave behind. This was the same reasoning that led early archaeologists to dig at major ancient cities in southern Mesopotamia (Chapter 5). Such correlations between a site's extent and age do not always hold true, but they provide a good premise from which to begin research.

La Sierra's considerable size, and the presence of large-scale architecture there, further suggested that it was the most likely place to find evidence of external contacts. This proposition is founded on the notion that valley rulers commanded more labor to build their houses and associated structures than could those of lesser rank. The concentration of massive stone-faced platforms at La Sierra, therefore, pointed to an equally marked centralization of power at the center. If, as seems to be the case generally, transactions among ancient, hierarchically organized societies were conducted primarily by the nobility, then it is in their capitals that evidence for these contacts is most likely to be found. Since the theory in use predicted that local elite power was based, in part, on interactions with Maya nobles, what better place to look for evidence of those transactions than at the Late Classic valley capital?

Pat and her survey teams, in turn, set out to track the distribution of people across the landscape. She hoped survey results would provide initial measures of population size and show the importance of certain combinations of natural resources in determining settlement choices. It rapidly became clear that finding sites was not going to be a problem, though dating them would be. By and large, prehispanic Naco Valley settlements yield few artifacts on the surface with which to date their periods of use. To make up for this lack, test pits were to be dug at a sample of sites to recover artifacts. Dating would be done by comparing these finds with those recovered in the deep stratigraphic tests being conducted at La Sierra. In this way, Pat could estimate how population sizes and distributions changed over time.

When Pat began the survey in 1975, most ancient settlements were identifiable by the presence of low mounds (0.5 m or less in height) generally arranged around two or more sides of a central space, or patio. The mounds are the remains of earth-filled, stone-faced platforms that supported houses fashioned of clay applied over woven stick frameworks and capped with thatch roofs. Though the summit buildings did not survive, their supporting platforms did. Settlements lacking platforms were recognized from surface scatters of artifacts. Such clusters of material came to light where the soil had been disturbed by plowing or other activities. As mentioned earlier, these conditions were rare in the Naco Valley throughout the 1970s, so the majority of all settlements recorded on survey contained platforms of various sizes.

In Southeast Mesoamerica, it is generally assumed, and frequently confirmed through excavation, that each cluster of buildings surrounding a patio belonged to an ancient **household**. Households are basic social units, usually consisting of people closely related by birth and marriage whose members cooperate in carrying out life's daily tasks. Differences in the power and wealth of households are reflected in the sizes of the buildings that surround their central patios, the degree to which these structures are decorated with, or fashioned from, materials that are difficult to work or obtain, and the array of valuable goods to which a household's residents had access. Households, therefore, were basic units of analysis in the settlement survey.

Problems and Compromises

The chronological tests excavated at La Sierra were generally unsuccessful in revealing clear stratigraphic sequences. One problem, from our perspective, was the ancient Naqueños' precocious concern with recycling. The valley's residents had the archaeologically frustrating tendency to reuse old trash when raising later buildings. No sooner had garbage begun to accumulate in one place than it was scooped up and redeposited in the core of a platform under construction. Such practices make sense: working without the benefit of metal tools, probably using such objects as deer shoulder blades for shovels, prehistoric Naco Valley occupants would have found it much easier to dig up fairly recent trash than to dislodge large chunks of undisturbed soil. The building boom experienced at La Sierra from AD 600 to 900 worsened this penchant for recycling. What such reuse means is that cultural debris was not allowed to collect in one place for any considerable span and so stratigraphy at La Sierra was virtually nonexistent.

Perhaps the situation would be different in other parts of the valley. At smaller sites, the pace of construction was more relaxed, and trash might have been allowed to accumulate in peace. Unfortunately, this was not the case. Rural sites dug in the 1970s were not occupied long enough to generate the deep trash deposits spanning many years that are needed to identify and order shifts in material styles so important for constructing temporal sequences through stratigraphy.

Since she found no stratigraphic sequences, Pat used another of archaeology's chronological tools, seriation, to create a temporal order. As discussed in Chapter 4, seriation orders components and phases based on changes in the frequencies of artifact styles. Pat's application of this method focused on fragments of ceramic vessels, or *sherds*. They are abundant at every excavated Naco Valley site and exhibit the greatest stylistic variation of all valley artifacts. Recovery of items imported from other areas where chronologies were better understood allowed Pat to test her sequence, to see if she had gotten it right, and relate it to well-established temporal orderings. Pat did not have the funds to pursue similar tests through carbon-14 analysis.

Accomplishing these basic Culture Historical tasks required digging at a fairly wide range of sites beyond La Sierra and excluding Naco. Ultimately, Pat excavated 19 of the 130 sites found on survey in 1975–1979, choosing those that spanned the full range of size and building arrangements then known for the valley. Criteria of size and form were emphasized because she suspected that these differences were related to when and how people lived at the settlements in question. The ways buildings were arranged at sites probably changed over time. Settlements that varied in their appearance therefore might yield materials dating to a number of the valley's prehistoric phases. Size, in turn, might reflect the attraction a particular locale held for people. Investigating a variety of sites of diverse sizes would probably help her figure out what was attracting so many individuals to certain spots, and how they were exploiting the resources found there.

In order to obtain the information needed for chronology building, larger-scale excavations had to be conducted at more sites than she anticipated. This expansion was necessary to recover enough artifacts for seriation (small collections yield unreliable results). Because time and money are not infinitely expandable, the new demands on the survey program required making hard choices. Resources invested in carrying out the necessary excavations meant that the area surveyed had to be cut back and fewer sites could be dug. It was no longer possible to walk the entire valley in search of ancient settlement. Segments of the basin, chosen to represent the full range of recognized environmental diversity, were investigated: roughly 50 percent of the valley's floor was covered between 1975 and 1979.

It was still crucial to identify those Maya innovations that were supposedly so central to culture change here. John Henderson's 1979 excavations at La Sierra were doing just that. Here he concentrated on the two adjoining plazas that make up the site core. Initial results yielded considerable information about architecture. A **ballcourt**, for example, was identified in the southern portion of the core. This construction consists of two parallel, stone-faced platforms 1.8 m high. They border a playing alley measuring 10 m across and 29 m long, oriented slightly west of north. Ballcourts are common components of Southeast Mesoamerican political capitals during the centuries in question. At lowland Maya centers such as Copan, ballcourts are usually situated between major public plazas on the north and more secluded areas of elite ritual and residence on the south. This layout physically reinforces the ball game's conceptual significance, mediating relations between supernatural forces associated with the heavens (linked to the north) and the underworld (associated with south). Rulers participating in this "sport" occupied a central place in cosmic dramas, interceding with supernatural powers that controlled the lives of all on earth.

Pat presumed that the game had similar sacred meanings and political implications for La Sierra's rulers. The organization of the La Sierra court, in fact, strongly suggested that what Henderson was excavating was modeled on a prototype acquired directly from Copan. The La Sierra and Copan main courts are both oriented roughly north–south and backed on the south by a steep rise. At Copan, the massive, human-made **acropolis**, the ritual and administrative center of the ruling elite, serves as the backdrop to the main ballcourt. La Sierra's architects built stone terraces into a natural ascent that overlooks their court. They thereby replicated the general organization of the Copan model without going through the trouble of building an acropolis from the ground up. These similarities between the Copan and La Sierra courts indicated that an important component of the basin's capital was inspired by a lowland Maya model.

Site core excavations overall, however, yielded very few artifacts useful for reconstructing external ties. Not only were imports few in number, but cultural materials of local origin were equally rare. Apparently, these imposing edifices were kept admirably clean of all debris. What was learned of external relations, therefore, came primarily from artifacts unearthed during excavations at sites found on survey. Here, minuscule numbers of sherds from imported pottery vessels were recovered, mostly elaborately painted cylinder vases that may have originally come from the nearby Comayagua Valley and the Caribbean coast. More common goods of foreign derivation were **obsidian** blades. Obsidian is a volcanic glass highly prized in Mesoamerica for fashioning cutting tools. At the time, the closest known source for these implements was about 200 km to the southwest, at the Ixtepeque flows in eastern Guatemala. Somehow, even the humblest Late Classic householder in the Naco Valley had access to these imported stone tools.

Unanticipated developments led to changes in the research strategy. All of these modifications were made within the context of the overarching theory described earlier and were geared to accomplishing objectives defined as important from the outset of investigations. Reconstructing the valley's chronology, determining the distribution of ancient settlements, and inferring the range and nature of external connections were still central to John and Pat's studies. They just had to change how these topics were to be addressed. By the conclusion of the 1979 field season, approximately 50 percent of the valley floor had been surveyed, 19 of the 130 recorded sites excavated, and roughly 45,000 artifacts analyzed. Six structures at La Sierra had been dug, five of which were large platforms in the monumental site core, and deep probes had been sunk to reconstruct the local temporal sequence. About two-thirds of what was thought to be La Sierra's full extent was mapped. All of what remained of the Late Postclassic site of Naco was recorded by Tony Wonderley, who dug there in 1977 and 1979.

Interpretations

The data were skewed and Pat knew it. Most of the information gathered between 1974 and 1979 came from survey and excavations conducted in areas outside La Sierra. Nevertheless, what was found so nicely matched expectations that she simply noted the biases and embraced the results. The chronology was long, stretching from the Middle Preclassic (800–400 BC was our best guess for its dates as of 1979) through to the Spanish Conquest. The Late Classic (AD 600–900, its temporal definition at the time) and Late Postclassic intervals were identified as periods of maximum political complexity. During both spans, nobles living at sizable capitals (La Sierra in the Late Classic and the site of Naco during the Late Postclassic) ruled the entire valley. The Late Classic also witnessed a marked growth in population. The numbers of people living in the basin exceeded those reached in earlier and later periods. This interpretation was based on those excavations conducted at sites found during survey. In other periods, the Naco Valley was apparently divided among small political units, the capitals of which paled in comparison with their Late Classic and Late Postclassic counterparts.

These fluctuating political fortunes matched Pat's expectations. She already knew that Naco was a major economic center when the Spanish arrived, so this site's local preeminence during the last Precolumbian centuries, as revealed in Wonderley's investigations, was no surprise. Simi-

larly, it was understandable that the Naco Valley underwent a political flo-
rescence during the Late Classic, given that neighboring lowland Maya
realms also enjoyed greatly accelerated growth at the same time. This correlation made perfect sense, based on the fundamental assumption that
Naco Valley developments would be inspired by influences emanating
from the Maya lowlands. Similarities in the layout of the La Sierra and
Copan ballcourts seemed to confirm the notion that lowland Maya rulers
provided models that catalyzed changes observed in the Naco Valley.

Further confirming the guiding assumptions was the impression that
La Sierra was only a modest political center, its rulers exercising relatively
little control over their subordinates. The mapped portions of La Sierra
suggested that even though the site was large by local standards, it was far
smaller than any known lowland Maya capital. Along the same lines, the
56 Naco sites dated to the Late Classic comprised a sizable proportion of
the total number of settlements found during survey (43%) but did not
suggest a population that was large in any absolute sense. No evidence of
craft production was identified in any of these early excavations. It was
hard to escape the impression, therefore, that pretty much everyone in the
Late Classic Naco Valley engaged in the same round of productive tasks,
feeding themselves and fashioning the few items they needed. Survey indicated that all sites, including those pertaining to the Late Classic, were
situated close to essential assets such as fertile soils, building stones, and
year-round sources of water. Such a distribution confirmed that each
household, no matter how small, met most of its own physical needs by its
own efforts.

La Sierra's rulers were able to extract modest food surpluses and labor
from these people; after all, someone had built the large platforms that
made up the capital's site core. The size and frequency of these demands
were almost certainly limited by the economic autonomy of followers. Pat
thought that the basis of Late Classic elite power, such as it was, derived
from the association of rulers with distant Maya realms, especially Copan,
and the goods they obtained from these contacts, such as imported pottery and obsidian. These valuable imports were, based on the excavations
pursued at rural settlements, handed around to supporters throughout the
valley as gifts (or bribes) to ensure their loyalty. The preponderance of ritual structures in the La Sierra site core—for example, the ballcourt—further suggested that the preeminence of rulers was also founded primarily
on ceremonies they performed for all valley residents, possibly as inter-
cessors with the supernatural. That the ballcourt was seemingly based on

a Copan model implied to her willing eyes that these elite rites were of Maya inspiration.

The above hypothesis of an economically self-sufficient peasantry ruled by those who controlled access to foreign valuables and the supernatural fit well with interpretations then current of Late Classic lowland Maya political organization. The primary difference was that the realm centered on La Sierra was far smaller than the prototypes on which it was presumably modeled.

In short, nothing *observed* during 1975–1979 led Pat to question that the largest, most complexly organized political unit in the Naco Valley's long prehistory was anything but a weak reflection of the lowland Maya models that supposedly inspired its creation. She was taken aback, however, by how little evidence there was for external connections in all periods but the Late Postclassic. During the Late Classic peak, interactions with neighboring regions were signaled by two things: the small amounts of obsidian found at all excavated settlements, including La Sierra; and a handful of sherds from elaborately painted polychrome vessels of diverse origins. None of these containers came directly from Copan. In addition, the distinctive caches (ritual deposits), burials, monuments, and hieroglyphic inscriptions that characterized lowland Maya capitals were not found at La Sierra; nor did the arrangement of large buildings here replicate the organization of temples and palaces seen at lowland Maya political centers. This should have signaled that something was wrong with her assumptions. If Copan loomed so large in La Sierra's history, why were so few items and material patterns traceable to that center? Happily ignoring that discordant note for the moment, however, she supposed that La Sierra and its realm were simply located on the margins of interaction networks.

The Late Classic Naco Valley, therefore, was coming across as a "backwater," despite its position on a seemingly important communication corridor following the Chamelecon River. In fact, a colleague politely described the basin as a "fascinating case of inner marginalism," a periphery's periphery, as it were. Pat had not expected this degree of isolation and was at a loss to explain it. Looking back, we both should have realized that these findings contradicted our shared presumption that Late Classic Naco Valley developments were inspired by lowland Maya influences. Evidence for these influences was surprisingly slight, implying that local cultural patterns owed little to external stimuli. Still, the theory she used led her to attribute exaggerated importance to the few signs of lowland Maya contacts recorded (that ballcourt again), and to downplay the considerable evidence that such interactions were neither regular nor intense. We saw a similar phenomenon in our discussion of the great importance attributed to the carvings of supposed Mycenaean style found at Stonehenge (Chapter 6). No evidence is more important than that which you expect to find.

Pat's inference to the best explanation, therefore, accounted for most of the recovered data in ways that made sense within the portion of the world where she worked during the period in which she conducted her study. The guiding theoretical positions accepted by most researchers in Southeast Mesoamerica at this time strongly encouraged her to view the Naco Valley as marginal to, but inspired by, major social, political, and economic developments occurring within the Maya lowlands to the west. Given the available data and the prevalent theories, she therefore opted for the interpretations outlined here as the best available ones.

The Naco Valley held few intellectual charms for us after 1979, and we moved off to study along the middle Ulua River drainage roughly 45 km to the south. This area seemed to be linked more directly to Copan by a series of valleys and passes. If Copan's monarchs were not receiving a warm welcome in the Naco Valley, perhaps the network linking them to other portions of Southeast Mesoamerica ran along the Ulua and not the Chamelecon River. We were still trying to understand how the actions of lowland Maya notables affected developments among less complexly organized, smaller neighboring societies. The Naco Valley did not offer much hope for pursuing this topic, so we went in search of a more promising locale. We did not return to the Naco Valley until 1988, and then our intention was to tie up a few loose ends. Instead, we managed to ensnare ourselves in a Gordian knot that we have yet to unravel.

The Naco Valley, AD 825— As We Saw It in the Early 1980s

Based on what we knew about the Late Classic Naco Valley in 1979, we saw the area as an essentially peaceful place far removed from the hustle and bustle associated with centers such as Copan and Quiriguá. Households of folks lived scattered across the basin, their members going out each day to tend their fields, get wood, do some hunting and collecting of wild foods, and secure water. Most essential tools were made from time to time by the residents of individual domestic units, people fabricating just enough to meet their needs and those of their co-residents. The daily routine was occasionally broken by attendance at ceremonies conducted at

La Sierra. Life in the capital differed little from that in the countryside, except that it was conducted on a slightly larger scale. Rulers and their families were fed from surpluses surrendered by valley farmers, in return for which notables interceded with the supernatural through rituals celebrated near their large residences in the site core. Subordinates also occasionally contributed their labor to construction projects at La Sierra. These efforts were probably widely spaced in time and never involved more than a few hundred or so laborers at any one period. Valley leaders were careful to avoid imposing demands for food and work that their followers would think excessive. Surpassing those limits could lead to a withdrawal of loyalty and support. If that happened, potentates might rail about it, but they could do little to change the situation.

Visitors from afar came through the valley, bringing such exotics as obsidian blades and polychrome pottery as gifts for the rulers. Imports acquired in this way were used by elites, passing some down to subordinates as gifts used to win and hold their loyalty. The flow of imports into the valley and down the hierarchy was no more than a trickle. Travelers may have been treated politely, but any requests they made to establish more intensive trading relations with the locals probably fell on deaf ears. Faced with a rebuff, petitioners could at least console themselves with the feeling that they were dealing with unenlightened yokels who did not even know how to organize their capital properly. La Sierra's rulers may have made occasional trips elsewhere, at least one of these excursions bringing them to Copan. Here they might have witnessed a ball game, no doubt intended to impress them with the sophistication of lowland Maya cosmological principles. Unknown to their hosts, however, the visitors from La Sierra saw something entirely different which they then replicated back home.

We believed that throughout the Late Classic, the Naco Valley was known as a place whose residents preferred to be left alone, a place where innovation was frowned upon and tradition valued, a place that was, from the perspective of lowland Maya nobles, a bit boring.

Further Reading

Archaeology, Households
Hendon, J.
    1996   Archaeological Approaches to the Organization of Domestic Labor: Household Practice and Domestic Relations. *Annual Review of Anthropology* 25:45–61.

Hendon's review of household studies offers a fresh perspective on these crucial units of analysis.

Wilk, R., and W. Ashmore, eds.
1988 *Household and Community in the Mesoamerican Past*. Albuquerque: University of New Mexico Press.

This influential collection of essays, focused primarily on studies of the Maya lowlands, deals with the structure and organization of ancient Mesoamerican domestic groups.

Archaeology, Methods

Renfrew, C., and P. Bahn
2008 *Archaeology: Theories, Methods, and Practices*. London: Thames and Hudson.

This textbook provides a thorough review of archaeological dating techniques (Chapter 4) as well as approaches to survey and excavation (Chapter 3).

Sharer, R., and W. Ashmore
2002 *Archaeology: Discovering Our Past*. Mountain View, CA: Mayfield.

Sharer and Ashmore offer another, clear account of the different dating techniques used by archaeologists (Chapter 9) and how surveys are conducted (Chapter 6).

Mesoamerica, General Discussions

Adams, R.
2005 *Prehistoric Mesoamerica*. Norman: University of Oklahoma Press.

This text provides an overview of prehistoric developments in Mesoamerica, from the arrival of the first people to the Spanish Conquest.

Ashmore, W.
1991 Site Planning Principles and Concepts of Directionality among the Ancient Maya. *Latin American Antiquity* 2:199–226.

Ashmore's article summarizes the ways in which cosmological principles were expressed through the arrangement of monumental buildings at major Classic period (AD 200–900) lowland Maya centers.

Ashmore, W., and J. Sabloff
2002 Spatial Orders in Maya Civic Plans. *Latin American Antiquity* 13: 201–215.

This essay is an updated version of Ashmore's earlier position that takes account of the effect a site's history has on how ideological and political principles are expressed in its arrangement.

Kirchoff, P.
 1952 Mesoamerica: Its Geographical Limits, Ethnic Composition, and
       Cultural Characteristics. In *Heritage of Conquest*, ed. S. Tax, pp. 17–
       30. New York: The Free Press.
       Though dated, this article conveys an idea of how culture areas
       were defined by those pursuing research in the Culture History
       school.

Rathje, W.
 1972 Praise the Gods and Pass the Metates: A Hypothesis of the Develop-
       ment of Lowland Maya Rainforest Civilization in Middle America.
       In *Contemporary Archaeology*, ed. M. Leone, pp. 365–392. Carbondale:
       Illinois University Press.
       This is the essay from which the example of the importance of
       trade to Classic period Maya societies was drawn.

Sharer, R., and L. Traxler
 2006 *The Ancient Maya*. Stanford, CA: Stanford University Press.
       The most recent successor to Morley's 1946 overview, Sharer and
       Traxler's account is an up-to-date summary of Maya prehistory.

Naco Valley

Henderson, J., I. Sterns, A. Wonderley, and P. Urban
 1979 Archaeological Investigations in the Valle de Naco. Northwestern
       Honduras: A Preliminary Report. *Journal of Field Archaeology* 6:169–
       192.
       This article summarizes where the Naco Valley research stood at
       the close of the 1977 field season.

Urban, P.
 1986 Precolumbian Settlement in the Naco Valley, Northwestern Hon-
       duras. In *The Southeast Maya Periphery*, ed. P. Urban and E. Schort-
       man, pp. 275–295. Austin: University of Texas Press.
       This summary expresses Pat's understanding of Naco Valley pre-
       history as of the end of the 1979 field season.

Southeast Mesoamerica, General Discussions

Boone, E., and G. Willey, eds.
 1988 *The Southeast Classic Maya Zone*. Washington, DC: Dumbarton
       Oaks.
       The essays compiled here present a diverse set of views on the pre-
       history of Southeast Mesoamerica. Though the focus is on Copan,
       articles by Demarest, Hirth, Joyce, and Urban and Schortman cover
       research in El Salvador and Honduras.

Fash, W.

2007 *Scribes, Warriors, and Kings: The City of Copan and the Ancient Maya.* London: Thames and Hudson.

Research at Copan has been going on for over a century and continues as of this writing. Thus, there is no definitive last word on developments at this lowland Maya center. Fash's book synthesizes the results available at the time and gives a clear outline of Copan's long prehistory. Keep an eye out, however, for volumes and articles that have appeared in the journals *Ancient Mesoamerica* and *Latin American Antiquity*.

Glass, J.

1966 Archaeological Survey of Western Honduras. In *Handbook of Middle American Indians*, Volume 4, volume eds. G. Ekholm and G. Willey, series ed. R. Wauchope, pp. 157–179. New Orleans: Tulane University Press.

This article captures fairly well the state of knowledge about Southeast Mesoamerican prehistory as it stood by the mid-1960s. You might find it interesting to compare this account with what P. Healy has to say (see below).

Healy, P.

1984 The Archaeology of Honduras. In *The Archaeology of Lower Central America*, ed. F. Lange and D. Stone, pp. 113–161. Albuquerque: University of New Mexico Press.

Healy recapitulates what was known about Honduran prehistory as of the late 20th century. See also the article by P. Sheets in this volume dealing with the prehistory of El Salvador,

Joyce, R.

1988 The Ulua Valley and the Coastal Maya Lowlands: The View from Cerro Palenque. In *The Southeast Classic Maya Zone*, ed. E. Boone and G. Willey, pp. 269–295. Washington, DC: Dumbarton Oaks.

1991 *Cerro Palenque: Power and Identity on the Maya Periphery.* Austin: University of Texas Press.

This book and article by a leading researcher in Southeast Mesoamerica summarize her research in the Sula Plain on Honduras's north coast. Joyce's investigations comprise some of the work to which we referred when discussing the diverse trajectories followed by Southeast Mesoamerican societies during the Late-to-Terminal Classic transition.

Sharer, R.

1990 *Quiriguá: A Classic Maya Center and Its Sculpture.* Durham, NC: Carolina Academic Press.

Sharer directed the most recent spate of investigations at Quiriguá (1974–1979) and summarizes those results here.

Webster, D., A. Freter, and N. Gonlin
2000 *Copan: The Rise and Fall of an Ancient Maya Kingdom.* New York: Harcourt College Publishers.

This volume tells the Copan story from an avowedly Processualist stance; you might compare it to the Fash book cited earlier.

CHAPTER 8

CRAFTING POWER IN THE LATE CLASSIC NACO VALLEY

Introduction

THIS CHAPTER REVIEWS HOW we came to rethink all we were sure we knew after 1979, and how we came to see our previous inference to the best explanation as not the best at all. In the process, our hybrid Culture Historical/Processualist perspective gave way to a Marxist-inspired focus on ancient political economies, especially processes of political centralization. The focus was now on the ways in which trade and craft production might have been interrelated through the actions of aspiring elites seeking power over their fellow valley residents. Adjusting our conceptual lenses required paying attention to new questions concerning craft manufacture, questions we had never thought relevant to understanding Naco Valley prehistory. A brief review of how we handled these heretofore unconsidered data sets is included to give you some idea of what is involved in changing theoretical stances. Before addressing these issues, however, we need to review why we returned to the Naco Valley at all.

Shifting Conceptual Ground

The theoretical landscape of archaeology had changed between 1979 and 1988. Processualism was still the dominant conceptual framework, at least in the United States, but many of its practitioners were not as confident about finding general laws of human behavior as they had been in the

1970s. Applications of Systems theory in Processualism were also raising serious questions of whether supposed causal chains stretching from the technology-demography-environment nexus to the rest of society might actually be far more complex than originally thought. Perhaps, such presumably **dependent variables** (those shaped by the operation of other factors) as ideology and social structure could damp down or encourage culture change in ways that were not predicted by more straightforward approaches that assumed the causal primacy of adaptation (also called **techno-environmental determinism**). The basic materialist principles were still intact, but their operation was far more complicated than first acknowledged.

Investigations of trade and its sociopolitical consequences intensified over this period. Many trade studies still focused on the adaptive significance of goods exchange—for example, how members of ancient societies used imported commodities to meet their basic needs. There was, however, a growing literature inspired by Immanuel Wallerstein's World Systems theory (WST) that cast trade as a resource used in power struggles occurring at a wide array of spatial scales. As noted in Chapter 5, true to their Marxist roots, World Systems theorists saw trade networks not as benign economic webs in which all participants benefited. Rather, these interaction systems were structured such that the flow of goods consistently enriched those leading the largest, most complexly organized societies (cores) and impoverished their smaller, more simply structured neighbors (peripheries). World Systems theory also inspired some archaeologists to see economic, social, and political processes as occurring not solely within the bounds of individual realms, but across structures that spanned great distances and incorporated societies organized in very different ways.

Applying New Theories to the Naco Valley

World Systems theory provided, to our eyes, a more systematic framework for understanding inter-societal interactions than did diffusion. In particular, we entertained the idea that the Late Classic peak of both population and political power revealed by the 1974–1979 research in the Naco Valley might have been spurred by intensifying contacts with members of surrounding societies, especially, but not limited to, Copan's rulers. If La Sierra's paramount lords exercised exclusive control over the foreign transactions by which such valued goods as obsidian and imported polychrome vessels were acquired, then they would have had a decided edge in local power competitions. The labor and surpluses of subordinates would have been surrendered in exchange for gifts of exotic blades and pots available only from rulers. Once begun, this process might have set in motion a whole host of changes in Late Classic Naco Valley society. For example, agricultural production may have intensified when rewarded by gifts of foreign goods to compliant farmers. Bureaucracies staffed by lesser nobility might have been amplified as rulers sought to exercise greater control over these surpluses. Trade monopolies therefore may have become the pillars on which an ever more complex hierarchy dominated by La Sierra's rulers was built.

Several features of our earlier hypotheses had shifted along with the theoretical ground in which they were rooted. Copan, though it still loomed large in our thinking, was no longer simply a source of ideas mimicked by the rulers of peripheral societies. Instead, valuables and concepts acquired from Copan and other realms were resources strategically manipulated by La Sierra's nobility to convert their former peers in the basin into subordinates. Power had, in short, moved to the center of our analysis, becoming the primary variable on which the 1988 investigations would focus. In addition, like many of our colleagues, we did not subscribe to a strict application of World Systems theory in which peripheries were structurally constrained to be impoverished *with respect to* cores. Instead, Copan, or any lowland Maya center, was a source of ideas and items that were creatively used by Naco Valley rulers to obtain their own ends. The result was not the **development of underdevelopment** predicted by World Systems theory, but the enhancement of local notables' status through their strategic use of high-value foreign goods and ideas. This situation was based on the inability of elites from any lowland Maya core state to dictate the terms of interaction through their overwhelming military, economic, or political advantages. Copan might have been a far larger, more populous, and complexly organized realm than any of its Southeast Periphery compatriots, but its rulers and their agents did not control their near neighbors.

Some degree of individual agency had crept into the theory: we believed that La Sierra's rulers played active roles in shaping valley society by manipulating their privileged ties with distant lords. Nevertheless, the vast majority of the population had little say in the matter. Trapped within dependency relations, they could do little but admire the accomplishments of their leaders and hope, by dint of good behavior, to benefit from their generosity or, more likely, gain from the elites' desire to acquire and manipulate clients. Power therefore was conceptualized as both the ability of people to achieve their goals and as the structure of unequal relations that resulted from the success a few individuals enjoyed in achieving their objectives at the expense of a great many others. This mix of structure and agency, combined with an increasing attention to structural power, indicates a decided shift toward Marxist interpretations in our work.

The changed perspective sketched above derives far more from shifts in our ways of thinking than it does from any new discoveries in the Naco Valley. The data were the same as they had been in 1979, but our understanding of them had changed. As noted in Chapter 2, estimations of what constitutes an inference to the best explanation are based, in part, on the array of hypotheses and the theories underlying them that researchers see as relevant. Our new appreciation for the utility of WST in our work opened an array of interpretive possibilities of which we were not previously aware.

Part of this change in our viewpoints followed from research we conducted in 1983–1986, 45 km southeast of the Naco Valley along the middle Ulua River with Dr. Wendy Ashmore (at the time of writing, with the University of California at Riverside). Our understanding of this Middle Ulua work led us to rethink how trade might have figured in elite efforts to gain and hold power. In particular, within the Late Classic middle Ulua, power was concentrated in the hands of those notables best positioned to control contacts with a wide range of neighboring societies. Their capital, Gualjoquito, lies where passes connecting the middle Ulua valley to areas on the west, east, north, and south converge. Imports coming from all these places, including Copan, were concentrated here. Large constructions at Gualjoquito were also organized according to models derived from Copan, suggesting that middle Ulua rulers welcomed both goods and site planning principles from the lowland Maya. This correlation among strategic position, evidence of foreign connections, and concentration of power implied that the above factors were causally related. It also suggested that we needed to take a closer look both at the trade and World Systems literature and at La Sierra, where evidence of similar external contacts might have been concentrated in the Naco Valley. The hypothesis outlined above helped us to make sense of the middle Ulua data, and we had high hopes that it would also clarify processes of political centralization in the Late Classic Naco Valley.

Adopting a novel theory also encouraged us to reappraise Urban and Henderson's earlier work, highlighting biases in the data we had acknowledged but not thought significant. Excavations at La Sierra had previously concentrated in the architecturally interesting, but artifact-poor site core.

Perhaps investigation of other residential portions of the center would yield better information on external contacts. Digging in rural settlements, we reasoned, would not turn up much evidence of inter-societal interactions if their occupants were at the end of the receiving line for imports. Rather, it would be residents of the capital, living close to the elites who engaged in long-distance exchanges, who would be the primary recipients of goods acquired from afar.

Pat recognized this bias in 1979 but ignored it because her results fit with her notion of the area's marginal position with respect to lowland Maya developments. There were also practical considerations: lack of money, time, and permission to excavate at La Sierra. Returning to the world of ideas, however, recent shifts in trade and World Systems theories questioned whether any society could be as remote from external contacts as we both imagined the Late Classic Naco Valley to have been. These changes in ideas led us to reconsider old data in a new light.

To be sure, some aspects of our theory had not changed. Lowland Maya rulers of Copan and, to some extent, Quiriguá were still thought to have played primary roles in catalyzing Southeast Mesoamerican developments. We assumed that the great size and complexity of these realms provided lowland Maya monarchs with the *means* and *incentives* to establish contacts over long distances. Organizing such large political units gave Copanec and Quiriguá aristocrats the experience needed to structure the inter-societal ties that kept goods flowing into their centers. Further, these imports were essential to providing large lowland Maya populations with basic commodities, such as obsidian used to make essential tools, and exotic jewelry and pottery that served as badges of ever more intricate hierarchies. Thus, Copan's and Quiriguá's foremost lords' search for imports initiated political and economic shifts among their smaller, more simply structured neighbors. Once begun, however, these processes took on lives of their own.

We also continued to presume that these power contests yielded only moderately complex, fairly small political units in the Naco Valley. To our thinking, the Late Classic basin was ruled by a few entrepreneurial elites perched atop a mass of commoners. The latter might look to their rulers for valued imports but still met their own survival needs largely by themselves. La Sierra's rulers could lure supporters to their cause, using exotic items to pry labor and surpluses from them. They could not, however, threaten the basic existence of the economically self-sufficient households in which the majority of people lived. Lacking this ability, rulers had to mute the demands they made of their followers. Otherwise, subordinates would decide that returns in the form of obsidian blades and painted pottery did not repay long hours tilling fields and building large platforms for elites. As our earlier theoretical position implied, this current formulation resulted in the idea that commoners could then turn their backs on leaders and there was little that the latter could do about it.

Finally, the new formulation continued to emphasize the political importance of imported obsidian and decorated pottery in political processes. Pat had seen these items as goods La Sierra's Late Classic rulers used to secure the loyalty of clients. The difference now was that we hypothesized that the quantities of foreign blades and pots circulating within the Naco Valley were much greater than we had formerly imagined. Their large volume enabled aspiring elites to capture the labor of followers more effectively than when we thought there was only a trickle of such goods down the hierarchy.

Evaluating the Hypothesis

We concentrated our efforts at La Sierra during 1988, based on the assumption that it was the center of long-distance contacts for the Late Classic valley. The entire site was cleared of vegetation and remapped: we could take advantage of the reduced ground cover to record buildings missed during earlier work. An intensive survey within a 1-km radius of the center was also pursued, this zone not having been systematically investigated before. Excavations were also initiated at the capital within 12 patio-focused structure groups, one of which was extensively cleared. Some of our digging continued the work begun in the site core by John Henderson, but most was conducted in the densely settled zone immediately north of the monumental center. Rather than excavating deep probes to obtain information needed to reconstruct the local chronology, efforts were devoted to clearing areas around platforms seen on the surface. Our goal was to maximize the recovery of materials that would contribute to reconstructing ancient behaviors. This meant identifying recurrent associations among artifacts, architecture, and other remains, such as fragments of plants and animals. It was by studying the patterned relations among a wide range of these objects that we hoped to infer the activities pursued by La Sierra's Late Classic inhabitants as well as the importance of trade goods in their daily lives. The limited test trenching conducted in 1975–1979 did not yield this kind of information because only relatively small areas were exposed.

The mapping and survey programs gave rise to the first surprises. La Sierra, it turned out, was far larger than we had imagined. The center held 468 structures crammed within 0.7 km^2 (Figure 7.4). This made La Sierra 10 times the size of the next largest Late Classic valley site. An additional 237 Late Classic constructions were found packed into an area within 1 km of the capital, which we referred to as La Sierra's Near Periphery. It ultimately turned out that slightly less than one-third of all known Late Classic buildings were located within La Sierra and its immediate environs: 29 percent of the buildings were situated in about 2 percent of the valley. Why had so many people chosen to reside so close together? Living within such a densely settled area was probably inconvenient in many ways. Simply finding ways to cope with all the waste material generated by such a large population would have severely challenged the group's ingenuity. A shortage of good farmland would have been equally as pressing. With so much space taken up by buildings, residents of the capital and its immediate vicinity probably traveled several kilometers on foot to reach their fields. Certainly, it would have been more convenient for these farmers to settle closer to their land.

Late Classic Naqueños therefore made some sacrifices when they took up residence in or near La Sierra. What did they hope to get in return? Our first thought was that La Sierra's environs contained a particularly attractive set of resources important to the pursuit of farming, the exploitation of which repaid the travails of living packed together. Conversations with current residents of the area, supported by field observations and later research, confirmed that La Sierra was situated in the midst of well-watered, fertile, river-deposited alluvium that could have reliably supported large crop yields. Broad expanses of arable land, some more productive than La Sierra's soils, were also found near perennial water sources in other parts of the Naco Valley, however. These tracts did not support such concentrated populations. If soil fertility and access to streams were the primary factors determining settlement location, La Sierra should have had building densities not markedly greater than those found in other, equally well-situated valley segments. La Sierra's marked divergence from this expected pattern suggested that other factors were at work attracting people to this spot.

Gradually, we concluded that La Sierra's rulers actively encouraged settlement around their capital. Such actions were taken, we argued, to enhance elite control over subordinates. Remember that all travel within the basin was on foot, so maintaining commoner loyalty may well have depended on keeping them close. Such proximity would have facilitated collecting tribute, conscripting labor for major building projects, and ensuring that subordinates would not be lured away by others seeking to build a following with which to challenge paramount authority. Population concentration implied that valley rulers were far more powerful than we had imagined.

What was the basis of this power? Resettlement benefited a small group of elites but did not offer obvious advantages to those migrating to the capital. It was possible that threats of physical violence moved people to La Sierra and held them there. There was no evidence, in artifacts or artistic representations, that military themes were pronounced in Late Classic Naco Valley culture and society. Threats of coercion may have supported the demands of paramount lords, but it seemed more likely that positive incentives to migration played a larger role in accomplishing elite designs. We had hit a wall. Was control over trade enough to attract and hold supporters at the center? The answer, as is so often the case, came in the form of a surprise.

Here we return to the fragments of shell that we sweated over in March 1988—we talked about them in Chapter 1. These few pieces, it turned out, were part of a deposit that contained 1,256 fragments of marine shell, mostly conch, mixed with 12 pieces of coral (Figure 8.1). Associated with these items was a type of stone tool we had never seen before in the basin (Figure 8.2). These implements stood out because they were made of chert; the majority of stone implements in Late Classic Naco Valley **assemblages**, or artifact collections, were fashioned from imported obsidian. The forms of these chert tools were also distinctive: their long, tapered points had sturdy ends that were well suited for cutting and engraving some resistant material. Shell was the best candidate, since these implements were almost never found in deposits apart from conch fragments. What we had found was a workshop, located a scant 45 m north of La Sierra's site core, in which large pieces of raw shell and, to a lesser extent, coral were shaped into **blanks** from which artifacts, such as beads, could be made. There was no evidence that the last stages of shell artifact manufacture occurred here. Instead, La Sierra's artisans fashioned blanks that were converted into finished goods outside the valley.

This was just the beginning. No other shell workshops were found that year; in fact, very few have come to light in subsequent seasons, and none were as large as this first one. What we did find, however, was significant evidence that some of La Sierra's inhabitants were devoting their time to fashioning blades from imported obsidian cores (Figure 8.3). Up to this point, we had found blades at just about all excavated Late Classic Naco Valley sites but no signs of the nuclei from which they had been struck.

These cores have a distinctive polyhedral (multifaceted) form, rather like an upside-down fireplug with inward-sloping sides continuing to a point. Blades are removed from a nucleus by applying pressure to the edge of the core's flat platform (corresponding to the flat base of a fireplug). A knapper carefully strikes long, thin flakes from the sides, moving concentrically around the perimeter. Core preparation is a demanding job, and fashioning

FIGURE 8.1 Sample of coral and shell recovered at La Sierra in 1988.

IN.

CM

FIGURE 8.2 An example of the distinctive chert tools
found in the shell-and-coral workshop

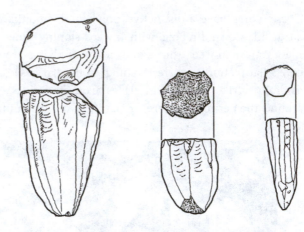

FIGURE 8.3 Polyhedral obsidian cores used in the manufacture of blades.

blades takes considerable skill and practice to conduct successfully. The absence of cores in the valley up through 1979 suggested that Late Classic valley residents lacked these skills and acquired their blades ready-made from producers located elsewhere in Southeast Mesoamerica. The most likely provider was Copan, where obsidian, mostly obtained from the nearby Ixtepeque flows in eastern Guatemala, was plentiful.

The recovery of 14 polyhedral obsidian cores from the same residential compound in La Sierra that yielded all the shell was therefore quite a shock. Here, for the first time, we had clear evidence that the Naco Valley's Late Classic inhabitants were making blades from imported cores. As excavations proceeded throughout 1988, additional cores were retrieved from other household compounds at La Sierra, suggesting that participation in this demanding craft was widespread, but not universal, at the center.

Finds of shell debris and obsidian cores forced us to accept the idea that specialized craft production had been pursued at La Sierra. Our older view, in which all households engaged in the same economic tasks, was no longer tenable. The significance of these findings was yet to sink in.

Digging at La Sierra did yield large quantities of sherds from foreign vessels (about 5% of the pottery fragments analyzed from the 1988 La Sierra excavations were from elaborately decorated imported wares, many of which were painted in three or more colors; Figures 8.4, 8.5). At least something was going according to plan. The Late Classic Naco Valley, it turns out, was not isolated from distant contacts. The concentration of imported pottery at La Sierra confirmed this point, just as it suggested that the transactions by which these vessels were acquired was centrally controlled. Rulers most likely obtained elaborately decorated containers

FIGURE 8.4 Fragment of an elaborately decorated ceramic vessel made in the Naco Valley.

FIGURE 8.5 Example of an imported polychrome ceramic vessel found in the Naco Valley.

from their trading partners in other realms, concentrating this wealth at their capital. Residents of the center, then, received a certain portion of this bounty, possibly as reward for settling so close to the locus of elite power. A few of the valued containers filtered out gradually to those living elsewhere in the valley, thereby accounting for the small number of foreign sherds we had located in excavations pursued during the 1970s.

Our trade hypothesis had been partially right, predicting that further investigations within La Sierra's residential zones would yield substantial evidence of the imported goods that valley rulers used to secure power. On just about every other point, however, we had been wrong. The La Sierra realm was dominated by powerful elites who successfully meddled in the daily lives of their followers, affecting where they chose to live. Our quaint image of economically redundant households was seriously questioned by evidence for production of shell blanks and obsidian artifacts in a few domestic groups at the basin's capital. We can only shudder at how close we had come to writing Naco Valley prehistory based solely on the results obtained through 1979. Had we done so, we would have enshrined some very profound errors in the archaeological literature. This realization encouraged us to shelve plans for future research elsewhere outside of the Naco area. We needed to develop a new theory to account for the valley's new data and test it against a much larger sample of materials. Given how wrong we had been in the past, it was only sensible to make sure that what we thought we were seeing now was an accurate picture of Late Classic Naco Valley society.

A New Theory Rises from the Ashes of the Old

We left the field in 1988 convinced that trade and craft production had important political implications. Why were we so anxious to see blade knapping and shell working in this light? Operating within World Systems theory, we were already predisposed to focus on the strategies elites might have used to acquire power at the expense of others. These machinations, we argued, stimulated changes in Naco Valley society at large, especially the construction of hierarchy and concentration of power. Consequently, we were prone to ask how craft production might have contributed to these processes. Proceeding down a path illuminated by Marxist thought, we were anxious to see where it might lead.

We had some help in imagining the political significance of craft manufacture. Preparing to return to the field in 1990, we forwarded to John Yellen, the director of archaeology at the National Science Foundation, a draft of a grant proposal we were writing. John returned the copy with numerous insightful comments, including one particularly telling question concerning our sources. Why, he asked, were there so few references in our proposal to work conducted outside Mesoamerica? Surely there were other archaeologists investigating relations among power, trade, and craft production besides those we identified in our own world area. It seems obvious now, but as of 1989 we were still very much looking to our colleagues studying in the Maya lowlands and, to a lesser extent, other portions of Mesoamerica, for theoretical inspiration. John's question encouraged us to explore the broader theoretical literature, looking at what people investigating the Scandinavian Bronze Age (1800–500 BC) and the Chalcolithic (copper age) of Mesopotamia (4500–3500 BC), as well as other areas and time periods, had to say on this issue. The result was that we belatedly discovered Prestige Goods theory.

Prestige Goods theory (PGT) is a Marxist-inspired framework that was originally developed to understand political relations among living and historically known West African populations. It posits that centralized control over the acquisition, production, and/or distribution of **social valuables** can be an effective means of fashioning hierarchical political structures. Social valuables are items that are essential to defining, reinforcing, and reproducing relations among people or between people and supernatural entities. Thus, in the West African examples, esteemed items were given to mark and legitimize such life-changing events as births, marriages, and funerals, and were used in mending social ties broken by feuds. These happenings mark major transformations in a person's social identity, their sense of who they are and how they are connected to others. Such conceptual shifts emerge and become tangible through actions, especially those involving the exchange of symbolically charged items. Think of your own social relations. Maintaining ties with others requires work, and part of that work often involves gift-giving. Every time you give a relative or friend a gift, that personal connection is materialized. Every time you leave someone off your gift list, the relationship dwindles in significance. We define ourselves with respect to other important individuals by interacting with them. Gift-giving is one of the most explicit forms of those behaviors by which we define ourselves as social beings.

Prestige Goods theory assumes that such linkages between gifts and social ties are universal, or at least common enough to serve as a starting point for theorizing. Given the importance of gift-giving to virtually everyone's social persona, those who monopolize the flow of social valuables central to a society's gift-giving process can literally control how people define themselves, as well as how effectively they can maintain crucial social connections. The monopolists are in a powerful position to direct the actions of the majority; failure to follow orders could result in exclusion from those goods that are essential to the social processes by which everyone identifies themselves and their place in the world. Living a meaningful existence depends on obeying those who make achieving these basic goals possible. Hence, the prominence of many West African village leaders was, and sometimes is, based in part on their exclusive control over the objects young men need to give in those exchanges through which brides are acquired, disputes resolved, and the births of children legitimated. Anyone who cannot secure the necessary valuables can never become a respected adult. Localized monopolies over the disbursement of certain precious goods, therefore, can be used in strategies to create political structures in which the power of a few is based on their capacity to undercut the social autonomy of the many. The majority, therefore, become dependents of the privileged minority.

The transactions through which social valuables flow from monopolists to their dependents are frequently called *exchanges*. This charade maintains the fiction of equality among the partners. Exchange, however, masks exploitive relationships in which the monopolists receive more than they give. In adopting PGT, therefore, we still viewed political structures as the outcome of struggles among individuals who enjoyed unequal success in pursuing their aims.

The easiest social valuables to control are those that must be imported or that require specialized skills to make. Foreign items are not subject to traditional ownership claims within the recipient society the way that, say, farmland almost certainly is. Elite claims on imports do not run as great a risk of alienating the affections, or the property, of potential followers. Production techniques that are difficult to learn and require considerable practice to maintain can also be monopolized by those able to subsidize manufacturers and thus free them from having to feed and house themselves. The vast majority of the population will simply not have the time to acquire, practice, and perfect such specialized skills. It is also often the case that an object's social value is positively affected by its foreign origin and/or the skilled labor invested in its manufacture. Both factors speak to the amount of effort expended in acquiring the item, effort that frequently involves accomplishing tasks fraught with difficulty, such as crossing territorial boundaries and/or working fragile materials.

Survey in and around La Sierra pointed to the considerable power exercised by its Late Classic rulers as measured by the degree of population aggregation. Excavations suggested that the capital was home to artisans working in at least two media, marine shell and obsidian. Both raw materials had to be imported, and their transformation into finished goods was a demanding process involving several complexly related and technically challenging steps. Concentration of known workshops at La Sierra implied that fashioning blades and marine shell artifacts was controlled by valley overlords. These elites also were the most likely group to have maintained the sorts of far-reaching connections through which shell, coral, and obsidian cores were acquired.

The lack of shell artifacts within the Late Classic Naco Valley meant that they were probably not employed as social valuables here (although we think the coral might have been used to shape the shell, not as a valuable in its own right). Conch artifacts did serve this purpose in other areas, such as the Copan Valley, where they were symbols of leadership and prestige. This patterning suggested to us that the elites' monopolies over the manufacture of shell and, possibly, coral blanks in the basin would have given these notables a decided edge in conducting the inter-societal transactions through which such valuables as obsidian cores and polychrome painted pottery were obtained. Those who could not offer shell blanks to foreign potentates would find it hard, if not impossible, to take part in these politically vital long-distance transfers. By controlling shell-blank manufacture, therefore, La Sierra's rulers ensured that they alone among Late Classic valley residents had access to the imported items used to attract and hold supporters.

Obsidian blades, on the other hand, were widely distributed throughout the Late Classic valley, strongly suggesting that people of every social station needed and used these implements. If, as it then seemed likely, they were only manufactured under elite supervision at La Sierra, members of all ranks were dependent on their rulers for an essential commodity. The concentration of sherds from exotic ceramic containers at the capital further supported the notion that valley rulers were the conduits by which these foreign valuables entered the basin. Just about every Late Classic site, regardless of size, yielded small numbers of foreign pottery fragments along with obsidian blades. Such ubiquity implies that elaborately decorated imported vessels played a significant role in the social lives of all members of the realm. Reliance on La Sierra's rulers for essential pottery containers reinforced dependency relations forged through elite monopolies over obsidian blades.

We were gradually reformulating our vision of the Naco Valley's Late Classic **political economy**—that is, the ways in which issues of power are intertwined with processes of production, consumption, and exchange. Rulers at La Sierra commanded the labor and loyalty of their followers primarily by doling out highly valued foreign pottery and locally made obsidian blades that they alone could provide. To ensure continued access to such generally needed items, subordinates helped feed their leaders and worked on their building projects, including the temples and palaces in the La Sierra site core. Some of the food pouring into La Sierra's coffers was diverted to support a small but very busy force of artisans who made the blades and worked conch and, maybe, coral into artifact blanks. Those blanks, in turn, were traded out of the valley to get more obsidian cores and polychrome pottery. And so this cycle of exchange, production, and consumption continued, to the great benefit of those at the top of the basin's political hierarchy. The elites probably conducted public religious ceremonies at the capital. Some of these, such as rites associated with the ballcourt, were likely modeled on lowland Maya practices. Still, the real source of elite power derived from control over the acquisition, production, and distribution of a limited set of very important commodities.

Note that, in the process of formulating this new hypothesis, we modified some of PGT's basic precepts. Obsidian blades were not, as far as we could tell, purely social valuables. These implements had real economic significance in addition to their social meaning. It seemed likely, given their pervasiveness throughout the valley, that the use of blades as cutting tools was essential to the survival of all residents of the La Sierra realm. The term *social valuable*, therefore, was being stretched to accommodate a good whose circulation was probably not determined primarily by its role in defining interpersonal relations. Imported polychrome pottery, however, did arguably fit more comfortably within the PGT framework. The elaborately painted designs on these vessels almost certainly conveyed important social information, making them stand out from the far more common, simply decorated containers used, most probably, for more purely utilitarian functions. By arguing that centralized control over the distribution of obsidian blades and imported polychrome vessels figured in the domination strategies of La Sierra's elites, we were contending that these two different kinds of goods served similar political purposes (i.e., elevating elites by undermining household autonomy). We did not feel that it was essential to remain true to the details of PGT in order to use it in our investigations. Rather, we drew inspiration from this viewpoint even as we modified it to fit our purposes. Most of us alter some aspects of the theories we use in constructing hypotheses that are meant to apply to particular situations. This is one way in which theories change.

Finally, it all made sense. What had looked out of place and unexpected within the previous theory now seemed like logical outcomes of PGT. Concepts such as Maya and non-Maya were rapidly receding in importance. It did not seem to matter whether goods came from Maya or non-Maya realms. The central issue was how they were used within the valley to create and maintain elite power. The exploitation of commoners by elites that was part of the earlier model now assumed center stage; we saw it as the dominant theme in relations among members of these social categories. Trade still played a role in understanding how one faction came to lord it over another. Our interest, however, had shifted to how imports were integrated in production, consumption, and distribution patterns *within* the Late Classic Naco Valley. The trend toward emphasizing economic factors in our theory of Late Classic Naco Valley society was further developed here.

This was an exciting time for us. New possibilities were becoming apparent as the blinders provided by older theories were forcibly removed. We really thought we were onto something novel. Making sense of Late Classic Naco Valley developments could be done by integrating economics and politics in ways that had not been considered seriously before in Southeast Mesoamerica. All that remained was to test the new hypothesis against more data.

Grappling with Craft Production

Evaluation of the hypothesis derived from PGT occurred during the 1990 and 1991 seasons; the first was largely devoted to field investigations, while three months during 1991 were primarily spent analyzing the massive quantities of artifacts recovered during the preceding year. We primarily looked at La Sierra, where 1,578 m² of prehistoric deposits were excavated across seven different patio-focused structure groups; our aim was to test for the existence of Late Classic workshops. If the hypothesis now being entertained was correct, additional research would uncover evidence of widespread participation in specialized production by La Sierra's residents. Crafts pursued at the capital would, if we were on the right track, have been conducted at high levels of intensity, yielding surpluses beyond the needs of the manufacturers and their immediate households. If we were wrong, continued investigations would unearth no such evidence.

Craft production had not been a concept used in our earlier hypotheses. Active recognition of its potential importance in understanding Late Classic Naco Valley political and economic life meant that we had to take account of it. This is easier said than done. The first step involved defining what we meant by craft production. Subsequent steps were dictated by efforts to come to terms with the implications of that definition. All of these efforts were conducted within the realm of middle-level theory.

Craftworking Defined

Craft production is the fabrication of items by a segment of the total population with the intent of generating surpluses destined for exchange with those outside the producing group. The important point is that people are fashioning items for exchange. Specialized production implies the existence of enduring social and political relations through which manufactured goods are transferred. Without such ties, there is no point in making items for exchange in the first place.

Our identification of craft-producing locales was based, therefore, on the *variable* distribution of debris, tools, and facilities associated with particular manufactures. Those markers of production processes that were universally, or nearly so, distributed among households were not identified as signs of specialized crafts. Grinding stones, used to convert grains such as corn into flour, are consistently found in small numbers within almost every investigated Late Classic Naco Valley patio group. This pattern suggests that all households processed their own food. Such widespread chores were not what elites might exclusively control and manipulate to advance their own interests. Only those manufacturing tasks whose material signatures were localized in a relatively few households were defined as crafts, though all evidence of production was recorded.

Identifying Production

In studies of craft production, as in all archaeological analyses, it really helps to know what you are looking for. Identification of telltale craft residues presupposes some knowledge of the original manufacturing process. Many crafts pursued in antiquity, however, are no longer practiced and cannot be directly observed. This is especially the case in Southeast Mesoamerica, where the indigenous descendants of prehistoric populations were largely wiped out by disease and slaving operations within a century of the Spanish Conquest. Most traces of their original cultures were lost by the 19th century.

We therefore relied heavily on analogies drawn from other culture areas for recognizing crafts archaeologically. As our work progressed, we came to depend especially on the investigations of our colleagues working in middle-range theory (Chapter 2) who had been seeking recurring relations among production processes and their material remains. These investigations involved studies of artisans laboring in the present, analyses of historical accounts of manufacturing tasks, and the conduct of experiments designed to replicate ancient production technologies. Middle-range theory of this sort is essential to research undertaken within all of the high-level theories discussed here; it is one way every one of us can test hypotheses about past behaviors from the physical remains of those actions.

We saw immediately that not all types of manufacturing are easy to identify archaeologically. Those that leave behind large amounts of distinctive, imperishable implements, facilities, and/or debris can be identified with a relatively high degree of assurance. The conch fragments and the locally unusual chert tools found associated with them in 1988 are fairly clear markers of shell-blank fabrication. Similarly, polyhedral obsidian cores and chipping debris signal blade production. Perishable materials, such as feathers, are much harder to identify from surviving remains. Thus, we had to acknowledge that there likely were crafts produced by La Sierra's inhabitants that we had little chance of recognizing.

The Organization of Production

If identifying ancient crafts is difficult, reconstructing the organization of production is even more daunting. Nonetheless, this is a challenge we had to face if we were to figure out the political significance of crafts in the Late Classic Naco Valley. In order to describe ancient manufacturing systems, it is important to identify their **scale** and **intensity** of production. Intensity refers to how much time artisans devote to pursuing their crafts. In general, this variable is mapped out on a continuum stretching from part- to full-time commitment to craftworking. Full-time artisans spend most of their working days practicing their profession, using the output thus produced to obtain goods they need to survive, such as food and tools they do not make. Part-timers fit craftworking around other chores, such as farming. They meet most of their own basic needs by their own efforts, using the exchange of craft goods to supplement what they can get on their own. The more full-time specialists there are in an economy, the more mutual interdependence there is among those participating in that economy.

It is a fairly straightforward task to specify craftworking intensities among living people. Measuring this variable is a bit trickier in prehistoric contexts. Often, archaeologists fall back on lines of evidence that refer to skill levels in distinguishing full- from part-time specialists. If the technology needed to produce a certain good is complicated to learn and requires considerable practice to maintain, then it was probably pursued by full-time specialists. In truth, as noted above, the part-time/full-time distinction is more of a continuum than an either/or proposition. Still, the more complex the production steps in a craft are, the more likely that the individuals or groups performing them are devoting considerable parts of their workdays to these tasks.

Production scale, or the volume of goods made during a certain interval, is often related to craftworking intensity. The more of a good produced in a specified period of time, the more likely it is that its manufacture is being pursued on a full-time basis. But, once again, there is a problem. How do you reconstruct production volume from archaeological remains? To answer this question we relied on the density of manufacturing debris recovered from a particular locale, the quantities of tools specific to the production process found in or near a workshop, and the size of facilities used to fashion the items in question. More and bigger imply greater volumes.

Excavating, as we were, in a variety of contexts at La Sierra only made the situation more complicated. Most of the areas we dug were places where people lived. As we learned, they might have also pursued crafts in their household compounds, but not always. Consider the case where the production tasks generated potentially troublesome debris, such as the sharp fragments of obsidian that flew off cores during the knapping process. Lacking heavy-duty, puncture-proof footwear, people probably found it wise to make the blades away from their living quarters but to store the valuable imported cores at home where they could be protected. As a result, our information was not always sufficient to infer the degree to which households engaged in different crafts. In some cases, as in the obsidian industry, we could quantify the raw materials (those polyhedral cores) that were kept in residences, while in others we had a combination of tools and debris left from the actual manufacturing process (as was the case with shell working). Though we could still use these data to infer the presence and importance of different crafts in the lives of La Sierra's households, we had to bear in mind the differences in the nature of our information.

Given these concerns, it was apparent that as much as we strove to count and weigh debris and tools and measure facilities, the resulting assessments would be subjective estimates of manufacturing volume and intensity, estimates that are difficult to translate into concrete production figures. What does it mean that one patio group yielded 14 obsidian cores while another had only one? These figures could not be translated directly into precise numbers of blades fashioned per year or even clear statements about the full- or part-time status of the artisans involved. We did feel, however, it was possible to say that blade fashioning was more intensively pursued at the locale where 14 cores were found than in its neighbor with only one, assuming that:

1. comparable areas in both locales were excavated;

2. the samples from both were representative (i.e., that the amounts of debris and/or tools found closely approximated the total numbers of tools and debris originally present at those locations);

3. the deposits in question covered comparable time spans.

We controlled for variations in the amount of area excavated by developing ratios of numbers of items found per square meter dug within a patio group. This helped us measure the *relative* importance of the same craft in the economic activities of different households. Say, for example, that in one patio group we cleared 100 m^2 and found 10 obsidian cores, while in another we found 10 cores after uncovering only 50 m^2. The ratio of cores per square meter comes out to 0.1 cores/m^2 and 0.2 cores/m^2, respectively. From this we might say that, if our samples are representative and encompass comparable periods of time, blade knapping was a more significant activity in the second household than in the first. (We are content to use meters squared, rather than the volume of material removed [meters cubed] because clearing operations very seldom removed more than 50 cm of earth and fallen stone; see below.)

It was difficult to control for the amount of time the soil strata containing production debris and tools had accumulated. We could assign deposits to particular phases, such as the Late Classic, based on artifact styles and, when we were lucky, carbon-14 dates. But it was hard to say for how long during the three centuries of the Late Classic the recovered cores had been allowed to sit around. The thickness of deposits containing evidence of craft production can help: the thicker the deposit, the longer it may have accumulated. This is not always the case, however, as some very deep deposits can collect in very short periods, as when people dump a lot of trash after a major feast.

In confronting this very real problem, we made an end run. First, the Late Classic deposits we were dealing with at La Sierra were generally thin: about 0.5 m separated modern ground level from ancient living surfaces associated with the last use of a building. This consistent pattern implied that the tools and debris associated with a craft conducted at the end of a household's occupation had accumulated over relatively short and comparable periods of time. We also concluded that obsidian cores were valuable items and well taken care of until they were no longer useful. Therefore, the nuclei found in a patio group were likely those employed by its last Late Classic occupants over fairly restricted intervals. Detritus produced by shell working, because of its threat to tender human feet, would, we thought, not be allowed to accumulate for long before it became a real danger. Thus, regular removal of sharp shell and coral fragments from domestic areas meant that the debris we found had collected over fairly short spans near the end of a compound's occupation. Since every household involved in these crafts faced the same concerns, the time obsidian cores and shell debris were allowed to collect would be about the same in each case.

Are we sure about this? The short answer is no. The slightly longer answer is that we had to start somewhere, and these assumptions seemed a reasonable place to begin. There is still the problem of how representative our excavated samples were. If the debris, tools, and facilities associated with craft activities were uniformly spread around domestic groups, then digging the same proportions of two compounds would yield precisely comparable results. Unfortunately, the tools, facilities, and detritus of craft production might well be concentrated in a few spots within a patio group and could be missed in even the most thorough excavations. The vast majority of the shell-working debris found in all of La Sierra, for example, was concentrated within the 0.5 m^2 we happened upon in 1988. We could have dug every other part of the compound and missed that one spot. We therefore do not know if our excavations in different patio groups yielded comparable evidence for crafts. The more we dug in a particular building cluster, the more certain we are that the evidence accurately represents the presence, intensity, and scale of craft production conducted in that compound during the Late Classic. Additional excavations in any structure group might change the picture derived from completed studies. Archaeology is always a work in progress.

Summary of Our Efforts to Reconstruct the Structure of Ancient Craft Production

We were fairly confident that we could infer what crafts were being pursued at Late Classic La Sierra, assuming that those manufacturing processes left behind material remains. Specifying exactly how much product was generated by artisans in any given period or where precisely along the full- to part-time continuum these craftworkers fell was beyond us. Instead, we opted to compare the *relative* intensities and scales of craft production across households in Late Classic La Sierra, distinguishing different degrees of commitment to craft production among domestic units. The more debris and/or tools found per excavated m^2 within a household compound, and the higher the skill requirements of the crafts in question, the more heavily committed a domestic unit was to a specific craft. The result is a sliding scale of manufacturing volume and intensity.

After pondering the nature of crafts and puzzling out ways to assess manufacturing intensity and scale using multiple lines of evidence, we felt ready to evaluate the latest hypothesis. We were, in fact, prepared to look for evidence of shell-blank and obsidian-blade production. But there was more at La Sierra than our theory led us to expect.

Evaluating the Hypothesis, 1990–1991

By the conclusion of the 1991 season we were truly surprised. Not only had we encountered additional evidence of obsidian blade knapping at La Sierra, but it seemed that the occupants of just about every patio group at the capital, outside the site core, were engaged in this craft. Commitment to blade fabrication varied. Excavations at one structure group in southern La Sierra yielded 70 polyhedral nuclei, pointing to the presence of artisans fashioning large quantities of blades here (0.4 cores/m^2). Investigation of an additional five La Sierra compounds (70% of those extensively cleared at the capital from 1988 to 1990) yielded between 2 to 14 nuclei, suggestive of a more moderate involvement in the craft ($0.01–0.1$ cores/m^2). Despite these differences in production scales, La Sierra was emerging as a center whose business was obsidian. As only one polyhedral core was then known from rural portions of the valley, households residing beyond the capital were shaping up as consumers of blades fashioned under elite control.

Since blade knapping takes considerable skill, we reasoned that at least some of La Sierra's households harbored specialists who devoted most of their productive efforts to working obsidian. They may not have been full-time specialists, but making blades seems to have been very significant in ensuring their livelihoods. On the other hand, patio groups where relatively few cores were found may have included people who were less committed to, and not as economically dependent on, this trade. Once again, there was apparently a sliding scale in both production intensity and volume across La Sierra's Late Classic domestic groups. Similarly, just because there was a very productive knapper in a household did not mean that all members of the domestic group were involved in this task to equal degrees, if at all. In fact, it became clear that participants in several households were pursuing multiple specialties. This, too, took us unawares.

Evidence for the working of marine shell and coral was localized at the patio group where it was first identified in 1988 (0.5 shell and coral fragments/m^2). Such quantities of debris and implements, coupled with the skill required to cut shell and coral, led us to believe that this was a task pursued by full-time artisans who generated considerable quantities of blanks. They were largely alone in this pursuit, as similar implements and shell detritus were rarely found elsewhere: the second largest shell deposit was dated to an earlier period in the same household, while a third, smaller deposit was buried under the floor of a building at La Sierra that dated to late in the Late Classic. This pattern contrasts starkly with the widespread dispersion of raw materials and skills needed to pursue other crafts at Late Classic La Sierra. Much as we had expected, therefore, fabrication of shell blanks was seemingly kept under strict centralized control.

Obsidian cores, marine shell, and coral all came from distant sources; most likely, the last two were obtained from residents of the Caribbean coast 35 km to the north, while the majority of the obsidian derived from the Ixtepeque flows in eastern Guatemala, roughly 200 km to the southwest. In keeping with the earlier trade model, we presumed that valley rulers acquired these goods. What we had not imagined prior to 1988 was that these acquisitions were used to fuel a thriving craft economy in the basin.

Evidence for cloth decoration and the fashioning of fired clay figurines and musical instruments also came to light in excavated La Sierra compounds. Textiles, especially elaborately decorated examples, frequently served as social valuables in many societies throughout antiquity. For example, in Mesopotamia from at least 3500 BC onward, the finest cloth was given as gifts to the gods and used as a badge of high rank. We were therefore alert to the possibility that well-made garments served the same purposes in the Naco Valley. One artifact we think was associated with cloth decoration is the ceramic stamp (Figure 8.6). The flat face of each stamp bears motifs that were deeply engraved or molded into its surface prior to firing. Traces of paint are sometimes preserved in the design's deep recesses. Recognized motifs include everything from naturalistic renditions of animals to figures composed of human and non-human elements to purely geometric designs. The stamp's back usually bears a conical protrusion that was grasped while using the implement. Available evidence suggests that stamps were dipped into paint and used to decorate clothing. Limited variation in the frequency of stamps across several excavated compounds (0.05–0.08 stamps/m^2) implies that domestic groups differed relatively little in their commitment to tasks involving this implement. Based on historic and ethnographic analogies, it did not seem that this craft was particularly time-consuming or required considerable skill. Cloth stamping therefore seemed to fall at the part-time end of the intensity continuum and was characterized by modest production scales.

Figure 8.6 Examples of ceramic stamps likely used in cloth decoration.

The presence of ceramic spindle whorls in deposits indicated partici- pation in a different aspect of textile production. Whorls are, in our area, round objects either made purposefully for the task or fashioned from broken pottery vessels. The holes in their centers are used to hold a stick, called the *spindle*. Thread is produced by gathering raw cotton in a ball, attaching one end to the spindle, twisting the fiber to start the thread, and then dropping the weighted spindle, making sure it is turning so that the raw cotton is twisted into thread. The whorl is the weight. Spindle whorls are spread throughout households, so this might also be a task that was pursued on a part-time basis.

Ceramic figurines, whistles, and ocarinas are miniature renditions of humans, animals, or some combination of the two (Figures 8.7, 8.8). Whistles and ocarinas are musical instruments distinguished from fig- urines by the one or more sounding chambers added to the back of the figurative portion. Whistles sound a single note when blown into, but the multiple holes in ocarinas afford a greater musical range. Figurines, whis- tles, and ocarinas are generally thought to be paraphernalia employed in the conduct of small-scale rituals pursued within ancient households. All three of these artifacts were made using fired clay molds into which the wet clay was pressed during the manufacturing process (Figure 8.9). Re- covery of these molds from specific locations signaled involvement of a household in fashioning figurines, whistles, and/or ocarinas.

FIGURE 8.7 Example of a ceramic figurine.

Variations in mold frequencies among patio groups at La Sierra were noted (0.004–0.01 pieces/m^2), suggesting, once again, that households were differentially involved in this craft. As to skill level, making figurines

FIGURE 8.8 Example of a ceramic ocarina; the rear sounding chamber has broken off.

FIGURE 8.9 Example of a mold used to make figurines.

is fairly easy. At minimum, fashioning a figurine mold requires taking an existing figurine, pressing the decorated part into wet clay, and then letting the new mold dry. The mold can then be fired. Making a new design is more difficult. The artisan first needs to sculpt the form, using the fabricated piece to make the mold.

Whistles and ocarinas are another matter. In making a whistle, shaping the sounding chamber and attaching it to the figurative element adds at least two extra steps. Creating ocarinas is a much more complex process. Simple ocarinas have a single chamber, and a mouthpiece like a whistle, and the artisan must puncture the sounding chamber to make playing holes. The several playing holes make it possible to produce the multiple notes, as the holes can be covered and exposed in sequence while blowing into the mouthpiece. Multiple-chamber ocarinas are even more difficult to make. These have several interconnected sounding chambers with one or two fingering holes per chamber. The mouthpieces are also different: whereas whistles and single-chamber ocarinas have mouthpieces like modern whistles, multi-chamber ocarinas are played by blowing over an open mouthpiece much like that of a modern flute. To make the more complex ocarinas requires more technical knowledge as well as a fair amount of coordinated effort by several people. In no case, however, would much time be needed in fashioning any of these items. Manufacturing figurines, whistles, and ocarinas probably could also be pursued on a parttime basis. The skills seem to be easy to learn and could be maintained with relatively little practice. This is especially true for figurines, and somewhat less so for whistles and ocarinas.

The biggest surprise, however, was the identification of large-scale facilities for making ceramic vessels on La Sierra's northern outskirts. There was nothing in our previous experience in Southeast Mesoamerica that prepared us for this discovery. In large part, this was because most Precolumbian pottery manufacture was thought to have been a low-volume domestic affair, individuals casually fabricating a few pots as these were needed, using simple technologies that left few archaeological traces. This had been the experience of just about all investigators working in southern Mesoamerica, including scholars doing research in the Maya lowlands where ceramic production facilities, relevant tools, and manufacturing debris had rarely been recovered by this time. A prehistoric ceramic kiln was unearthed in the Sula Plain on Honduras's north coast in the early 20th century, but no comparable remains were found in the five decades since that discovery. Like most finds that do not match prevailing expectations, this information was so out of step with generally accepted theoretical positions that it was ignored and largely forgotten. Consequently, our clearing of an unprepossessing platform on La Sierra's northern margin took on the nature of farce.

Chosen for study because it represented the small end of the structure size continuum in this area, the building in question posed problems from the start. The quantities of pottery sherds found during the initial digging seemed unusually large by local standards (354 sherds/m^2 were unearthed here). To make matters worse, the building's **facings**—walls designed to retain platform fill—failed to run straight and had a maddening tendency to curve. The large quantities of burnt **daub**—clay used in constructing super-structures—unearthed within the structure had unusual forms, indicating that the perishable structure raised atop the platform was dome-shaped. After a week of denial, we admitted that what we had mapped during survey as a low, rectangular platform was, in fact, a stone-lined circle whose massive (1.5–2 m thick) walls enclosed a central open space with a diameter of 2.8 m (Figure 8.10). A domed superstructure built of clay applied over a stick framework was raised above these circular foundations. Evidence of considerable burning within the structure's core, the presence of two stone-lined vents piercing opposite sides of the rock-walled circle, the large quantities of pottery fragments recovered off its flanks, and the ash deposits inside the circle and outside the circular facings strongly implied that this was not a residence. Instead, it looked like a very large pottery kiln, similar to firing facilities reported from other parts of the world but not found in recent investigations within Southeast Mesoamerica. The building did, however, resemble that earlier kiln reported from the Sula Plain, in form if not in size.

Recognition of the kiln did not come easily to us. As much as we had anticipated finding evidence of craft production at La Sierra, we did not expect this kind of firing facility. Discovery of the kiln did, however, open up whole new vistas. One of La Sierra's distinctive features that we had long noted was its position on top of an extensive clay deposit lying just below ground surface. We had often passed by a small factory southwest of the center where people were busily mining this clay to make roof tiles. We had driven into, and cursed at, the sticky clay that entrapped our vehicles after heavy rains. In short, we knew that the clay was there but thought little of it except when we had to extricate the truck from its clutches. The discovery of the kiln changed all that. Suddenly it was terribly significant that La Sierra was sitting on so much clay. Test pits were dug along transects emanating from La Sierra's center to evaluate the deposit's extent, this work eventually determining that the clay spread out in all directions for roughly 220 m beyond the capital's constructions.

Why all this concern with clay? If La Sierra was a center of high-volume pottery production, as implied by the recovery of the kiln, then its residents would likely choose to live and work near the bulkiest, hardest-to-move component in the ceramic-making process—namely, clay. Now we could see why La Sierra was situated where it was: not only could its fertile soils support large numbers of people, but the easily accessible clay surrounding the capital could fuel the pottery industry. In addition, a small stream had once coursed through the site, making water easy to get—and potting requires lots of water.

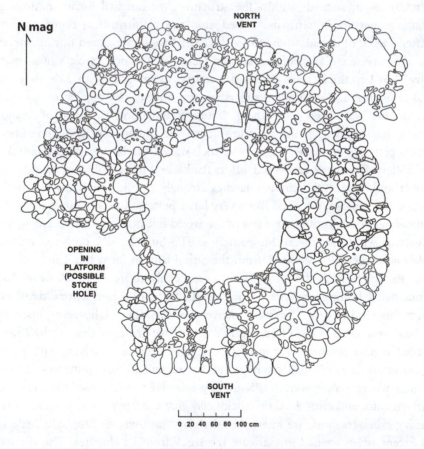

LA SIERRA OP 31 KILN

FIGURE **8.10** Plan drawing of the pottery kiln unearthed at La Sierra during 1990.

Our attention also fixed on five extensive depressions that we had mapped but otherwise ignored within La Sierra. One of these basin-shaped areas lay within 70 m southwest of the newly discovered kiln. What had previously seemed inconsequential features of the landscape now started to look like the partially filled-in remains of holes dug to extract clay for pottery manufacture. By the time all of this registered, the 1990 field season was drawing to a close and money was becoming more precious as its quantity diminished daily. We were only able, therefore, to dig a series of 18 test pits across the depression closest to the kiln to try to determine its original size and when it was excavated. The results suggested a Late Classic date for clay mining.

This extended discussion of the kiln is meant to demonstrate a very simple point: there is a lot to see at any archaeological site, but we assign meaning to, and so truly perceive, only that which makes sense. What we genuinely observe are those entities that conform to what we expect to find, and these expectations derive, in part, from the theories we bring with us to the work. Ceramic firing facilities, especially those designed to turn out large quantities of vessels, were not supposed to be found in prehistoric Southeast Mesoamerican sites. Despite all the changes in our guiding theory, we still unconsciously clung to this belief rooted in Culture Historical notions concerning the nature of indigenous ceramic production in southern Mesoamerica. The significance of the curved stone walls, domed superstructure, proximity of La Sierra to clay, and all those odd depressions were therefore not initially recognized. Once one element in this puzzle finally muscled its way into our consciousness, however, the others started demanding attention. Sites are full of material patterns, many of which remain implicit until we are forced to look at and acknowledge them. These formerly invisible arrangements are often important sources of new information. Theories can help us see and make sense of such patterns or hide them from view.

The new insights were exciting, but we still faced a major problem. There was relatively little information available on the kiln firing of ceramics in southern Mesoamerica. Lacking a body of studies comparable to those dealing with fashioning obsidian blades and shell artifacts, we needed to establish a firmer base for interpreting La Sierra's ceramic industry. This would depend on tapping new lines of evidence to infer the importance and structure of pottery manufacture within the political economy focused on Late Classic La Sierra.

The extent to which La Sierra's artisans blanketed the Late Classic Naco Valley pottery market was in part addressed through **instrumental**

neutron activation analysis (INAA) of ceramic and clay samples drawn from Late Classic sites throughout the basin, including the capital. Clays from different deposits sometimes contain varying amounts of particular minerals and chemical elements. Pottery vessels made from these materials retain the distinctive mineral-chemical signatures of their parent sources. INAA reveals these mineral-chemical profiles, allowing researchers to match particular vessels, or sherds, to known clay deposits.

To progress further, we pursued our own investigations within middle-range theory. Ethnoarchaeological studies were initiated during 1991 to facilitate recognition of ancient pottery-producing areas and enhance assessments of manufacturing scales and skills. A survey was conducted among contemporary potters in the Naco Valley as part of this effort. The research involved observing and talking with people who worked in large-scale concerns turning out roof tiles and figurines. In addition, we interviewed members of that fast-dwindling portion of the population who still fashioned pottery vessels in small numbers for their own use and sale. Evaluations of local clay qualities, and the appropriateness of different clays for fabricating diverse finished products, were elicited in the course of these investigations. Detailed information on the material remains left behind by pottery production conducted at different scales was also gathered. The ethnoarchaeological work was supplemented by a survey designed to look for clay deposits; from this we know that there are dozens of good deposits scattered across the valley, but none is as large or of as high quality as that underlying La Sierra.

We do not assume that modern potters are direct cultural heirs of Late Classic Naco Valley artisans. There have been too many disjunctions during the valley's long prehistory and history to make such a claim. Contemporary behaviors, therefore, are examined because certain features involved in fashioning pottery vessels by hand are so thoroughly conditioned by technology and the nature of the raw materials used that they transcend cultural and temporal differences. Potters working in the Naco Valley during all periods would, by this argument, have assessed the quality of available clays and structured their production activities in much the same ways.

Subsequent work in 1996 built on this foundation and focused on constructing replicas of Late Classic kilns. Here the goal was to get a rough idea of the effort invested in raising these facilities, temperatures achievable within them, production volumes of kilns with different dimensions, and the material remains left after a kiln collapses. These efforts have gone a long way toward establishing a foundation for identifying ceramic production locales and reconstructing manufacturing volumes. They have also helped us make sense of material patterns seen in the archaeological record and to predict better where additional pottery-producing sites might be found. This research would never have been pursued if we had not come across that initial kiln.

By the end of the 1991 field season, we knew that people were making pottery at Late Classic La Sierra. The size of the kiln, coupled with the large quantities of sherds unearthed in its vicinity, hinted at the production of vessels on a large scale. This inference was supported by later replicative studies in which we learned that a kiln of this size could have been used to fire, minimally, 150 sizable ceramic containers at one time. Pottery making need not require great technological sophistication, but building and using a kiln indicates significant knowledge about the firing process and skill in controlling firing temperatures and oxygen flows. In fact, La Sierra's Late Classic potters seemed to be making a relatively simple job of ceramic firing into a complex process. We presumed that they did this to increase production quality and scale to provide a wide array of pots to all residents of the Late Classic Naco Valley.

Where We Stood in 1991

We were very happy at the conclusion of the 1991 field season. Our new theory worked. Based on its premises, we had successfully predicted the existence of large-scale workshops at La Sierra. The valley's paramount lords, it seemed, used their exclusive control over the acquisition, production, and local distribution of a wide range of locally made and foreign products to capture the rest of the population in webs of dependency. By manipulating economic relations, La Sierra's rulers acquired the power manifest in the comparatively great size of their capital. Supporters were enticed, or compelled, to move to the center by the prospect of enhancing their access to valued commodities obtainable only from elites. Once there, commoners could take advantage of the opportunity to pursue a craft supported by the patronage of powerful nobles, the ultimate suppliers of such valuable raw materials as obsidian cores. Threat of exclusion from the network by which foreign pottery, obsidian blades, decorated cloth, ceramic figurines, whistles, ocarinas, and locally made pottery vessels moved from elites to subordinates within the valley was probably enough to keep most people in line.

It is important to bear in mind that we arrived at this latest of our inferences to the best explanation through a process in which changes in theory and the accumulation of new data were tightly related. Experiences we had conducting research within the middle Ulua drainage led us to reconsider the relevance of WST to our work. Applying hypotheses based on this conceptual framework during the 1988 investigations at La Sierra generated findings that did not fit comfortably within a WST -based approach. With the help of others, we identified PGT as a more promising source of hypotheses that could explain events within the Late Classic Naco Valley. Data that we collected during 1990 and 1991 seemingly confirmed those hypotheses, resulting in the inference to the best explanation outlined here. Evaluating the utility of hypotheses in understanding the past, therefore, involves the interplay among:

■ the data found;

■ the theories available for generating testable explanations about that data;

■ what the researcher thinks about the relevance of specific theories to particular data sets.

Changes in any one of these factors can lead to shifts in what investigators see as a "best explanation" of the past.

The Naco Valley, AD 825—As of the Early 1990s

Life in the Late Classic Naco Valley looked quite different in 1991 than it had in 1979. The serenity of a valley whose members lived peacefully with one another and where differences in rank were muted by the ability of each household to meet its own economic needs by its own efforts was now shattered. In its place, we perceived a situation where ruler and ruled were pitted against each other in an ongoing battle for dominance. Paramount elites moved effectively to exclude other valley denizens from participation in inter-societal transactions by making sure that they alone controlled the acquisition and fashioning of commodities (such as shell blanks) prized by social leaders in other realms. In return for processed exotic shell (and, presumably, other items), La Sierra's aristocrats secured imports that were highly esteemed within the basin. Some of these goods arrived in finished form (elaborately decorated pottery vessels) while others required additional, highly skilled work to complete (obsidian blades). In the latter case, rulers concentrated craftworkers possessing the needed talents at the capital, where they knapped blades under elite supervision, supported by elite patronage. Imported pottery containers and obsidian blades were widely distributed among people of all ranks within the Naco Valley but were available only from La Sierra's power-holders. These patterns strongly suggested that Late Classic valley residents relied on their rulers for goods that they needed (or thought they did) but could not produce themselves. Such dependency put the majority at the mercy of the minority.

Not content with monopolizing the flow of imports into and within the valley, La Sierra's leaders also moved to control the production of decorated cloth and ceramic artifacts, the latter using locally abundant clays and a sophisticated firing procedure involving at least one large kiln. Both prosaic goods (pottery vessels) and those associated with the sacred realm (figurines, whistles, and ocarinas) were fabricated at the center for dispersal throughout the basin (we were not sure where stamped cloth fit into this sacred/profane continuum). Local raw materials and the technologies needed to transform them into finished items at large volumes were also part of elite domination strategies.

Importantly, all of the goods made at La Sierra were fragile. That is, they were likely to wear out or break in a relatively short period of time. Obsidian blades dulled from frequent use, pots and figurines fractured, and cloth frayed. This fragility ensured a constant, fairly high demand for the output of La Sierra's workshops. Commoners could not easily hoard blades, dragging their feet in meeting elite demands until their stash of tools ran low. They were compelled, instead, to react smartly to decrees from rulers, as there was always a shortage of essential items made under the auspices of paramount lords.

Commoners, trapped in a web of economic obligations centered on their rulers, were constrained to obey orders or lose access to basic items. They gave up some of their crops and agreed to labor on construction projects in La Sierra's site core in return for these objects. Many also left their natal homes and resettled at the capital, lured there by the prospect of enhanced opportunities to accumulate more valuables. Once at the center, subordinates were subject to heightened supervision and were less able to avoid meeting their obligations to La Sierra's notables than they had been in rural areas.

Representatives of distant lands were regular visitors to La Sierra. They brought with them gifts of pottery, obsidian, and, presumably, other (perishable) goods, and left laden with shell, perhaps some coral, and, maybe, cloth decorated by artisans using Naco's distinctive line of stamps. Figurines, whistles, and ocarinas also may have been of interest to outsiders. Potentates from such lowland Maya centers as Copan and, possibly, Quiriguá would have recognized La Sierra's ballcourt as an appropriate symbol of elite power. Otherwise, they found little that reminded them of their home capitals. Such discrepancies might have given rise to the occasional snide comment about the sophistication of the Naco Valley's denizens and their leaders. Visitors from other areas would likely have been careful to keep such observations to themselves, however, for fear of offending an important trade partner. As powerful as the lords of Copan and Quiriguá might have been, they did not dictate terms of exchange to ancient Naqueños. Leaders of all these realms brought to their interactions something(s) that the others needed, and everyone was forced to deal with one another as equals whenever they met to trade.

The Late Classic Naco Valley was, therefore, a vital place where competing interests met on a daily basis whenever rulers gave gifts to followers and followers went to work for, pledged loyalty and surrendered food to, rulers. Foreign nobles, if not a common sight at the capital, were regular visitors, the goods they brought and received fueling an economy that served the political ambitions of La Sierra's elites. This place was anything but boring.

Further Reading

Archaeology, Settlement Survey

De Montmollin, O.
   1989   *The Archaeology of Political Structure: Settlement Analysis in a Classic Maya Polity*. Cambridge: Cambridge University Press.
         De Montmollin's review of how political structure can be read from settlement patterns was influential in our own work and that of many others.

Naco Valley

Connell, S.
   2002   Getting Closer to the Source: Using Ethnoarchaeology to Find Ancient Pottery Making in the Naco Valley, Honduras. *Latin American Antiquity* 13:401–417.

This article reports on Connell's research into modern pottery-making processes in the Naco Valley and their relations to understanding the ancient ceramics industry there.

Southeast Mesoamerica, General Discussions

Robinson, E., ed.
1987 *Interaction on the Southeast Mesoamerican Frontier: Prehistoric and Historic Honduras and El Salvador*. Oxford: British Archaeological Reports International Series 327.

Though a bit dated now, this collection of essays recounts general trends in Southeast Mesoamerican prehistory as they were understood in the middle 1980s.

Schortman, E., P. Urban, W. Ashmore, and J. Benyo
1986 Interregional Interaction in the Southeast Maya Periphery: The Santa Barbara Archaeological Project 1983–1984 Seasons. *Journal of Field Archaeology* 13:259–272.

This article provides a brief synopsis of the investigations we conducted with our colleagues after 1979. These investigations informed our approach to Naco Valley studies in 1988.

Theory, Crafts

Arnold, P.
1991 *Domestic Ceramic Production and Spatial Organization: A Mexican Case Study in Ethnoarchaeology*. Cambridge: Cambridge University Press.

Arnold considers how ethnoarchaeology, a form of middle-range theory, can be used to infer aspects of ceramic production.

Bey, G., III, and C. Poole, eds.
1992 *Ceramic Production and Distribution: An Integrated Approach*. Boulder, CO: Westview Press.

The authors represented in this collection of essays were striving to define a systematic approach to linking processes of manufacture, consumption, and distribution within ancient pottery industries.

Brumfiel, E., and T. Earle, eds.
1987 *Specialization, Exchange, and Complex Societies*. Cambridge: Cambridge University Press.

This collection of essays conveys a sense of how craft production studies can be integrated within the archaeological examination of ancient political economies. Prestige-goods models are stressed in a number of these contributions.

Clark, J., and W. Parry
  1990   Craft Specialization and Cultural Complexity. *Economic Anthropology* 12:289–346.
          This overview deals with the ways in which specialized manufacture might figure in ancient political economies.

Costin, C.
  1991   Craft Specialization: Issues in Defining, Documenting, and Explaining the Organization of Production. In *Archaeological Method and Theory,* Volume 3, ed. M. Schiffer, pp. 1–56. Tucson: University of Arizona Press.
          This is a thoroughgoing review of the craft production literature that is still widely cited.

  2001   Craft Production Systems. In *Archaeology at the Millennium: A Sourcebook,* ed. G. Feinman and T. Price, pp. 273–327. New York: Kluwer Academic/Plenum Publishers.
          Costin provides here an updated version of her 1991 essay, together with a wealth of references as well as insights into the organization of craft production.

Rice, P.
  2006   *Pottery Analysis: A Sourcebook.* Chicago: University of Chicago Press.
          This is an essential resource for analyzing pottery making in all periods and world areas.

Schortman, E., and P. Urban
  2004   Modeling the Roles of Craft Production in Ancient Political Economies. *Journal of Archaeological Research* 12:185–226.
          This take on craft production stresses the various ways specialized manufacture has been understood to function in ancient political economies. The article provides an extensive list of references useful for those who want to investigate the various ways craft production has been understood by archaeologists.

Tosi, M.
  1984   The Notion of Craft Specialization and Its Representation in the Archaeological Records of Early States. In *Marxist Perspectives in Archaeology,* ed. M. Spriggs, pp. 22–52. Cambridge: Cambridge University Press.
          Tosi's account of how craft production might have figured in ancient political economies is from a strong Marxist perspective.

Wailes, B., ed.
  1996   *Craft Specialization and Social Evolution: In Memory of V. Gordon Childe.* Philadelphia: University Museum, University of Pennsylvania.

The essays included here review the various ways craft production may have been integrated within the political economies of a wide array of ancient societies.

Theory, Inter-Societal Interaction and Trade

Adams, R.
  1974 Anthropological Perspectives on Ancient Trade. *Current Anthropology* 15:239–258.
       Adams provides here a classic summary of the problems with, and potentials of, trade studies in archaeology.

Cusick, J., ed.
  1998 *Studies in Culture Contact: Interaction, Culture Change, and Archaeology.* Carbondale: Center for Archaeological Investigations, Southern Illinois University.
       The essays in Cusick's volume review different approaches to interregional interaction research, including cases from prehistoric and historic contexts.

Earle, T., and J. Ericson, eds.
  1977 *Exchange Systems in Prehistory.* New York: Academic Press.
       Like the Sabloff and Lamberg-Karlovsky volume listed below (this section), this collection contains some of the most widely read essays published on trade and its relation to long-term political processes.

Gosden, C.
  2004 *Archaeology and Colonialism: Cultural Contact from 5000 BC to the Present.* Cambridge: Cambridge University Press.
       Gosden stresses in this book the variety of intercultural interaction processes that do not all rely on distinctions between cores and peripheries.

Green, S., and S. Perleman, eds.
  1985 *The Archaeology of Frontiers and Boundaries.* New York: Academic Press.
       This collection of essays deals with inter-societal interaction, especially in the relatively recent past.

Helms, M.
  1976 *Ancient Panama: Chiefs in Search of Power.* Austin: University of Texas Press.
  1988 *Ulysses' Sail: An Ethnographic Odyssey of Power, Knowledge, and Geographical Distance.* Princeton, NJ: Princeton University Press.
  1993 *Art and the Kingly Ideal: Art, Trade, and Power.* Austin: University of Texas Press.

Helms is one of the leading figures in discussions of how ideological and political factors intersect in the context of long-distance interchanges. These books summarize and, in *Ulysses' Sail*, refine her position on this topic. *Art and the Kingly Ideal* also highlights the political and conceptual significance of specialized production in creating and sustaining hierarchy.

Mauss, M.
1990   *The Gift: The Form and Reason for Exchange in Archaic Societies.* London: Routledge.

Originally published in 1923, this classic text remains an influential example of how the exchange of material items instantiates (makes tangible) social relations. Practitioners of Prestige Goods theory and Practice theory draw inspiration from Mauss's work.

Renfrew, C., and J. F. Cherry, eds.
1986   *Peer Polity Interaction and Socio-political Change.* Cambridge: Cambridge University Press.

Contributors to this influential volume draw on their experiences working in different world areas to construct an approach to the political consequences of interregional interaction that is an alternative to World Systems theory and other perspectives based on trade.

Rowlands, M., M. Larsen, and K. Kristiansen, eds.
1987   *Centre and Periphery in the Ancient World.* Cambridge: Cambridge University Press.

Essays in this volume helped shape thinking about the political, economic, and social consequences of relations among polities of varying sizes within interregional exchange networks. Several of the articles employ elements of Prestige Goods theory.

Sabloff, J., and C. C. Lamberg-Karlovsky, eds.
1975   *Ancient Civilization and Trade.* Albuquerque: University of New Mexico Press.

These essays summarize approaches to the archaeological study of trade at the point when interest in the topic was near its peak. See, especially, Renfrew's article, "Trade as Action at a Distance"; it remained influential in trade research for many years after its publication.

Schortman, E., and P. Urban
1987   Modeling Interregional Interaction in Prehistory. *Advances in Archaeological Method and Theory* 11:37–95.

This article summarizes our understanding of World Systems theory and its utility in archaeology. Written just prior to the 1988 field season, it gives you some idea of what we thought about this approach and how it might be applied to non-capitalist situations.

Schortman, E. and P. Urban, eds.

1992   *Resources, Power, and Interregional Interaction.* New York: Plenum Press.

The essays in this volume review various approaches to inter-societal interaction, focusing on Prestige Goods theory (Part III) and World Systems theory (Part II).

Stein, G.

2002   From Passive Periphery to Active Agents: Emerging Perspectives in the Archaeology of Interregional Interaction. *American Anthropologist* 104:903–916.

Stein reviews intercultural interaction processes in antiquity, emphasizing the importance of treating so-called peripheral populations as active shapers of these developments.

Wells, P.

1980   *Culture Contact and Culture Change: Early Iron Age Central Europe and the Mediterranean World.* Cambridge: Cambridge University Press.

This case study of interactions among agents of classical Mediterranean civilizations and their "barbarian" neighbors emphasizes the political impact of cultural knowledge flowing along the social networks that linked these very different societies. Wells provides a discussion of cores and peripheries that does not marginalize the latter in favor of the former.

Wright, H.

1972   A Consideration of Interregional Exchange in Greater Mesopotamia: 4000–3000 BC. In *Social Exchange and Interaction*, ed. E. Wilmsen, pp. 95–105. Ann Arbor: Anthropological Papers, Museum of Anthropology, University of Michigan, No. 46.

Wright provides an example of one of the ways in which trade was being used to explain the appearance of cultural complexity.

Theory, Prestige Goods

D'Altroy, T., and T. Earle

1985   Staple Finance, Wealth Finance, and Staple Storage in the Inka Political Economy. *Current Anthropology* 26:187–206.

The concept of "wealth finance" discussed here closely parallels the idea of prestige goods in both the nature of the items involved and their use in political strategies of domination.

Ekholm, K.

1972   *Power and Prestige: The Rise and Fall of the Kongo Kingdom.* Uppsala: SKRIV Service AB.

This is one of the earliest summaries of Prestige Goods theory.

Friedman, J., and M. Rowlands
1977 Notes towards an Epigenetic Model of the Evolution of Civilization. In *The Evolution of Social Systems*, ed. J. Friedman and M. Rowlands, pp. 201–276. Pittsburgh: University of Pittsburgh Press.

This essay includes a detailed, early exposition of Prestige Goods theory as it applies to archaeology.

Meillassoux, C.
1981 *Maidens, Meals, and Money*. Cambridge: Cambridge University Press.

Meillassoux's book constitutes one of the most influential early applications of Prestige Goods theory in anthropology.

Shennan, S.
1982 Exchange and Ranking: The Role of Amber in the Early Bronze Age of Europe. In *Ranking, Resources, and Exchange*, ed. C. Renfrew and S. Shennan, pp. 33–45. Cambridge: Cambridge University Press.

Referred to here as "prestige good ranking systems," this article lays out the precepts of Prestige Goods theory.

Theory, World Systems

Chase-Dunn, C., and T. Hall, eds.
1991 *Core-Periphery Relations in Pre-Capitalist Worlds*. Boulder, CO: Westview Press.

Though not available to us when we conducted our research in 1988, this volume conveys how applications of World System theory to archaeological cases continued to evolve into the 1990s.

Schneider, J.
1977 Was There a Pre-Capitalist World System? *Peasant Studies* 6:20–29.

This is one of the first attempts to apply World Systems theory to anthropological cases. It was instrumental in introducing this theory to archaeologists.

CHAPTER 9

PRACTICING POWER OVER TIME

Introduction

THE 1992–1996 INVESTIGATIONS WERE DESIGNED to evaluate our evolving theory concerning relations among power, wealth, and craft production in the Late Classic Naco Valley. Pursuing this topic raised several important issues that we had not appreciated earlier. Specifically, the 1992–1996 research highlighted questions of:

1. rural commoner participation in specialized manufacture;

2. changes over time among measures of wealth, power, and craft production at all sites;

3. the ways in which political structures can arise from the ground up out of numerous interpersonal interactions.

In previous field seasons, we thought of ancient political economies as having been shaped by broad, rather impersonal, processes of domination. After 1996, we began to wonder if ancient life in the Naco Valley had really been that simple. This disquiet depended on three major developments:

1. evidence for craftworking was found outside La Sierra;

2. we realized that the "long Late Classic" was, in fact, divisible into two periods, over which political and economic relations changed dramatically;

3. we became aware of the relevance of Practice theory to our work.

These "epiphanies" and their consequences for the conduct of our studies are outlined here.

Hypothesis Testing Continues

Everything was clear and fine by the end of the 1991 field season. Maybe it was time to move on to a new area. Nagging doubts still plagued us, however. Our understanding of rural material and behavior patterns was largely based on limited excavations. These probes were in no way comparable to the more extensive exposures cleared at La Sierra and sites in its immediate environs. Fully 2,729 m^2 had been dug at La Sierra by 1990, and an additional 1,151 m^2 of Late Classic deposits were unearthed in that center's Near Periphery, but only 592 m^2 were exposed in all of the rural zone. At the very least, we had to admit that our chances of identifying evidence of craft production were much greater at La Sierra than anywhere else in the valley, if only because we had cleared so much more of the capital. Such research biases might have made La Sierra look like an industrial center. Happy as we were with the Prestige Goods theory–based hypothesis, therefore, we had to test it against data gathered from comparably broad exposures dug at sites elsewhere in the Naco Valley. That is what we set out to do in 1992 and 1995–1996.

Operating under our guiding theory, we expected that more work among rural settlements would unearth evidence that their residents used goods made at La Sierra and did not manufacture these items themselves. To ensure that our excavated sample of hinterland sites was as representative of general rural behavioral and material patterns as possible, we chose to investigate Late Classic settlements of all sizes and locations within the valley. Variations in the numbers and dimensions of buildings at settlements might relate significantly to differences in the types of crafts pursued by their residents and the scales at which these were conducted. Along the same lines, artisans likely chose to live near those raw materials that were essential to the pursuit of their craft. Sites located in different portions of the valley, near different sets of resources, could therefore have been home to distinct sets of craftworkers. Frankly, we did not think that either of these considerations would prove to be significant. They were possibilities that had to be considered, if only to be rejected. Overall, 5,717 m^2 were dug in and around Late Classic structures distributed among 26 rural sites during 1992–1996. An additional 2,608 m^2 were excavated at La Sierra during 1995–1996 to gain a clearer sense of manufacturing processes there.

Crafting in the Hinterland

It did not take long for our hypothesis to fall victim to an influx of data. No sooner had we begun excavations in 1992 than evidence for craft production began coming out of Late Classic rural settlements of all sizes. We initially tried consoling ourselves with the notion that artisans outside the capital fashioned goods at very low volumes. Maybe a few people occasionally turned their hands to fabricating a couple of figurines, but they still had to depend on La Sierra's workshops to make up the difference between what they could make and what they needed. That hopeful fiction did not survive confrontation with the 29 figurine molds retrieved from excavations at Site 337 in the northwestern valley (0.2 mold fragments/m^2). It was highly unlikely that the occupants of the three low platforms found at this settlement used all of the objects produced in these molds. No other patio group within or outside La Sierra came close to yielding this many molds. Clearly, Site 337's residents were generating fairly large surpluses that were being exchanged with others. There was no evidence that either the manufacturing process or the transactions by which the goods left Site 337 were under paramount elite control (La Sierra is 7.3 km southeast of this settlement).

We eventually acknowledged that almost all of the extensively cleared hinterland settlements investigated during 1992–1996 yielded some evidence of craft production, strongly suggesting widespread participation in specialized manufacture. Commitment to these tasks was not uniform, however. Site 337's occupants, for example, apparently put together figurines, and/or ocarinas and whistles, in numbers far beyond those needed to meet their own requirements. Digging at Site 335, a settlement comparable in size to (and 250 m southeast of) Site 337, revealed no hint of figurine production. There was evidence here, in the form of several unfinished examples, that people were making stone adze blades (Figure 9.1). These implements, found in small numbers at Late Classic sites throughout the valley, were an important part of tool kits used in woodworking. Such complementarity in production may have been the basis for economic relations among residents of different Late Classic Naco Valley households. In this view, members of particular domestic units specialized in fashioning certain goods that were then exchanged with others engaged in different economic pursuits. Most of these transactions seem to have occurred outside the view of La Sierra's rulers. Instead, they were apparently handled on the local level through arrangements worked out among members of individual households. Commoners, in short, were meeting at least

FIGURE 9.1 A sample of stone adze blades, or *hachas*.

some of their own needs through their own efforts. Those they could not satisfy by themselves were addressed through exchanges with their peers. What were the implications of these findings for our understanding of the Naco Valley's Late Classic political economy? Addressing that question required that we deal with another interpretive wrinkle, this one in time.

Change Over Time and a Return to Chronology

The temporal sequence we had been working with since the 1970s outlined large blocks of years based on perceived changes in material styles, primarily the decoration of pottery vessels. Every subsequent field season saw refinement in that chronology. The time span most seriously modified by these efforts is the Late Classic. Originally defined as a single interval spanning three centuries, the 1995–1996 studies helped us to subdivide it into two segments: the Late Classic (AD 600–800) and the Terminal Classic (AD 800–1000). This distinction results from our greater appreciation of subtle shifts in artifact styles occurring within a general framework of persistent occupation at sites spanning these 400 years.

As we noted before, ancient Naqueños frequently recycled trash deposits, using them as fill in later platforms. Consequently, the deep middens covering long time periods that are so dear to the hearts of chronology-builders continued to elude us. What we did encounter, however, were more and more examples of building reuse and renovation. Some of these modifications buried artifact deposits associated with earlier versions of a construction. It was possible, therefore, to identify artifact styles linked to different periods of a structure's use. In this way, we finally recognized the distinction between the Late and Terminal Classic. Because the stylistic shifts between these two intervals are subtle, their importance did not become apparent until we had analyzed quite a few artifacts associated with different periods of occupation at many buildings. This division, based on changes in artifact styles and stratigraphic relations, was confirmed by carbon-14 assays of burnt organic material occasionally found with the analyzed artifacts.

Our inferences were also encouraged and supported by the work of colleagues in neighboring areas. **Rosemary Joyce** (see sidebar), for example, had identified a Terminal Classic phase in the Sula Plain, about 15 km northeast of where we were working. The artifact styles that mark the Terminal Classic in the Sula Plain are different from Naco Valley styles. Still, Joyce's definition of this phase alerted us to the possible existence of a Terminal Classic period in the Naco Valley. The Terminal Classic phase

Rosemary Joyce

Rosemary Joyce began conducting research in Southeast Mesoamerica in 1977 and continues to do so now. She has directed investigations dealing with time periods ranging from 1600 BC to the colonial period throughout northern Honduras. Joyce, in fact, worked with John Henderson and the authors in the Naco Valley in 1977, contributing to the early survey and excavation program in rural portions of the basin. She is also one of the leading proponents in Mesoamerica of an Interpretivist approach to the past, stressing in particular the ways in which people actively deployed material culture in efforts to establish a sense of themselves and their relations with others. In the process of developing these ideas, Joyce has promoted a vision of past societies as internally heterogeneous. She has paid special, though not exclusive, attention to how gender contributes to the varied ways people use material items in understanding and taking part in their cultures. Consequently, Joyce's writings have significantly challenged Culture Historical and Processual views of cultures as homogeneous, or at least internally balanced wholes unmarred by internal dissension. Her influence extends well beyond Mesoamerica.

was also emerging from studies at sites in the adjacent Maya lowlands. All of this work pointed out that earlier understandings of the Late Classic in southern Mesoamerica were oversimplified. Instead, significant changes marked this interval, especially during the 9th through 10th centuries. These developments further strengthened our appreciation for a comparable period of major change in the Naco Valley.

How did such chronological shifts affect our interpretations of political and economic processes? We had earlier succumbed to the tendency, common in archaeology, to view every site or deposit assigned to a particular phase as precisely contemporary. All settlements dated to the Late Classic in the basin were thus treated as though they had been occupied simultaneously. Every part of a large site, like La Sierra, that was assigned to the Late Classic was also thought to have been in use at the same moment and throughout roughly 300 years. This was much the same problem faced by early students of Stonehenge before changes in the arrangement of features at that monument were recognized (Chapter 6). Such propositions in all cases convey an improbably static view of the past. According to this perspective, major cultural changes are concentrated during the relatively brief transitions that mark the boundaries between phases. Once these shifts have occurred, the political and economic structures they produce remain more or less constant until the next major period. The point is that we had compressed a variety of different events strung out over long spans of time into one static image.

Changing Power Relations at La Sierra

As with all such realizations (for us), the recognition that something was amiss took a while. Earlier work in La Sierra's site core (Figure 7.5) suggested that some of the largest edifices, those located in the westernmost plaza along with constructions making up the ballcourt, had been systematically stripped of their masonry facings in antiquity. Cut blocks survived in these cases only on the bottom-most terraces, where they were probably accidentally hidden from vandals by rockfall and soil accumulation. We knew this was the case for several large platforms. What we did not realize was how widespread the pattern was. Excavation in 1995–1996 of four massive constructions in La Sierra's western site core revealed similar results. Now we had evidence that eight of the eleven investigated buildings from the same area were missing large portions of their facades. Digging throughout La Sierra in 1995–1996 revealed that the recycled

cut block

FIGURE 9.2 Examples of faced stone blocks reused in
Terminal Classic constructions at La Sierra.

blocks showed up in buildings of all sizes, often mixed with the more
commonly used river cobbles in platform facings (Figure 9.2). Again, we
had seen these cut blocks in structure facades before but had not linked
their appearance to the dismantling of site core platforms.

What we finally came to realize was that there had been a sequence of activities at La Sierra that went something like this:

1. the monumental edifices of the western site core were raised, probably in the 7th century;

2. those buildings were abandoned around AD 800;

3. large portions of most western site core platforms were dismantled;

4. stones from those constructions were recycled into structures of all sizes built in the rest of the center.

We were forced to recognize, therefore, that a good deal of the architecture at La Sierra was erected *after* the large buildings in the western site core were abandoned. This does not mean that all of La Sierra was built following the western site core's demise. Many of the reused blocks were incorporated into late additions appended onto preexisting platforms, the same additions that had been so helpful in our recognition of Terminal Classic ceramic styles. Most of these constructions were probably first raised in the Late Classic, when La Sierra's lords still ruled from their large residences, worshiped at their massive temples, and played ball in their court. In the subsequent Terminal Classic, people of all ranks continued to live at the capital after those monuments to elite power had been abandoned.

Even as the above observations were being made, investigations of smaller La Sierra structures were reinforcing our appreciation for the changing face of the capital. For example, in 1995 when we cleared three platforms that seemed, on the surface, to belong to the same patio group, we learned that one had been in an advanced state of decay while the other two were still occupied and being maintained. In another part of the capital, a fairly substantial platform raised during the Late Classic was converted into a firing facility, possibly for making ceramics, during the Terminal Classic. All of these shifts indicated that centers of power, people, and production moved around within La Sierra during what had previously been seen as a single period.

La Sierra, therefore, was not all that different from most towns and cities. At any moment, some parts of it were thriving centers of commerce, politics, and population while others were falling into decline. We had come perilously close to ignoring that simple truism. Just as the changes in Stonehenge's form discussed in Chapter 6 challenged archaeologists to account for shifts in the activities conducted there, our view of La Sierra and its history was altered when we realized how complex its history had been.

The site clearly did not assume in one short period the shape and size we discerned on the surface and then retain those basic features unmodified for centuries. Most importantly from our perspective, the transformations that were coming to light were related to changes in how power was wielded and by whom. If such volatility characterized the form and governance of La Sierra, what changes had we missed in rural areas?

Changing Power Relations among Rural Populations

Up to 1991, we had assumed that people in the Late Classic Naco Valley occupied different positions in a single structure of inequality. Most were downtrodden while a few, those who monopolized certain crafts, did the treading. This may have been the case during the 7th and 8th centuries, and PGT still seemed to provide a good basis for explaining these developments. The abandonment and dismantling of La Sierra's western core, however, suggested that in the Terminal Classic something different succeeded this monolithic hierarchical arrangement.

There were several possibilities. Perhaps the majority of commoners rose up, threw off their oppressors, and then moved out of the capital. We knew this was not the case, as La Sierra remained a major population center right through the Terminal Classic. In fact, not only were there still people at the old capital, but they raised 13 large constructions around a sizable plaza immediately east of the Late Classic site core (Figure 7.5). Somebody still exercised power at La Sierra. In contrast to the Late Classic, however (when La Sierra's rulers reigned supreme), in the Terminal Classic there were 12 other centers with monumental edifices. Three of these areas were within sight of La Sierra's Late Classic monumental core and in its Near Periphery. We had previously seen such locales as homes to members of a lesser nobility who were subservient to paramount lords at the valley's capital. But now, armed with the newly won ability to distinguish Late from Terminal Classic, we could see in the archaeological record at these sites and in parts of La Sierra that most had risen to prominence in the latter period as La Sierra's rulers were losing some of their power. Those who lived at these small centers were looking more and more like challengers to centralized rule rather than agents of it.

La Sierra's elites during the Terminal Classic, therefore, shared the political stage with other members of the aristocracy. What had been a hierarchy in which all valley residents owed allegiance to La Sierra's overlords became, during the Terminal Classic, a **heterarchy** wherein a variety

---

Carole Crumley

Carole Crumley is a pioneer in the archaeological study of ancient landscapes, or the many ways political, cultural, social, economic, and ecological variables are interrelated in shaping people's relations to, and understandings of, the places where they live. Her more than three decades of research in Burgundy, France, focuses on the interplay of these factors in affecting settlement forms and distributions, along with land use patterns, dating from the last centuries BC to the present. The importance of state intervention in influencing the decisions Burgundians have made concerning their use of, and relations to, the land has been an especially important theme pursued by members of this multidisciplinary project. Crumley's highly influential notion of heterarchy was developed as a way of imagining sociopolitical formations and their environmental relations in ways that did not presuppose a single, regional ordering of all people and institutions within one overarching hierarchy. Since first articulated by Crumley, the utility of heterarchy in describing variably decentralized political formations has been much debated. Today the term is finding increasing acceptance among researchers working in diverse world areas and time periods.

---

of political leaders had more or less equivalent power. Heterarchy, an idea originally advanced by **Carole Crumley** (see sidebar), generally defines situations where interpersonal relations are not organized within a single, overarching structure composed of clear, vertically arranged ranked divisions, such as elite and commoner classes. Instead, there may be multiple hierarchies operating according to different principles and/or a network of horizontally structured relations of interdependence and competition. This does not mean that everyone is equal. It does mean that people cannot be placed strictly in one structure of domination and subordination. We increasingly suspected that the Late Classic basin-wide hierarchy was succeeded in the Terminal Classic by shifting alliances and competitions among valley notables, no one of whom held absolute dominion over the others. Understanding these changes required a shift in theory away from PGT.

How was craft production implicated in this volatile situation? The widespread distribution of crafts attested to in our excavations seemed to signal a dispersal of specialized manufacture over time. During the Late Classic, La Sierra residents specialized in the manufacture of obsidian blades, ceramic vessels, figurines, whistles, ocarinas, *hachas* (the adze blades mentioned earlier), cloth, and blanks of conch and coral, as anticipated under the premises of PGT. Outside the capital, there is some evidence at this time for weaving, cloth decoration, and the fashioning of figurines, whistles, and ocarinas, as well as the shaping of grinding stones.

By the Terminal Classic, crafts were more widely distributed throughout the basin, though they were still strongly represented within La Sierra. For example, pottery kilns remained concentrated at the old capital, and at least the one found in 1990 on the north edge of the center was used throughout the Terminal Classic. Nonetheless, ceramic vessels were now also being made at five other sites scattered throughout the basin. In addition, evidence for obsidian blade knapping, formerly restricted primarily to La Sierra, was recovered from seven Terminal Classic rural sites. There is no sign of declining participation in this craft at La Sierra or in its Near Periphery from the Late to Terminal Classic. The nuclei were still acquired from great distances, most likely by elites. Notables residing at different valley centers, however, may now have competed to obtain cores rather than relying on La Sierra's rulers, who had formerly monopolized such exchange networks.

The number of sites with evidence for producing figurines, whistles, and ocarinas also rose, in this case from 6 (including La Sierra) in the Late Classic to 16 in the Terminal Classic. Variation in production scales grew as well: nowhere were more than 4 molds found at any one site or patio group in the Late Classic, whereas in the Terminal Classic the numbers range from 1 to 21, the largest concentration coming from outside La Sierra at Site 337 (now dated to the Terminal Classic). Working cloth, marked by the distribution of spindle whorls used to spin thread, shows up at eight Terminal Classic settlements, up from four in the Late Classic. Manufacturing volumes and intensities everywhere seem low for this craft. Cloth decoration using ceramic stamps occurred at five sites in the Late Classic; the vast majority of stamps come from patio groups at La Sierra. By the Terminal Classic, residents of 14 sites were participating in cloth decoration, some at considerable scales (21 stamps were recovered from Terminal Classic Site 128 northwest of La Sierra; this number is surpassed only by the 26 examples from a La Sierra patio group).

As power diffused from La Sierra, so too, it seems, did crafting. It may be that artisans were initially encouraged by Late Classic lords to take up production specialties and settle at the capital as a means of establishing a valley-wide hierarchy of political control, as specified in PGT. This strategy could have had the unintended consequence of encouraging some valley residents to pursue manufacturing tasks for which they had the necessary raw materials and skills. Using La Sierra's workshops as models, different families might then have incorporated craft production into their daily rounds as a way of meeting their own needs and of obtaining goods from others engaged in different economic pursuits. Households at La Sierra were the most fully committed to this economic strategy during the Late Classic and continued to pursue it in the Terminal Classic. With the decline of centralized rule, any restrictions limiting households from participating in crafts were lifted. Specialized manufacturing then spread widely, to the point that nearly every household was engaged in at least one craft by the Terminal Classic's conclusion. How this system of production and exchange operated and what relations it might have had to contests over power are questions with which we are increasingly concerned. We will review how they are being addressed shortly.

The Naco Valley in a Regional Context

What we have reconstructed for the Naco Valley parallels developments seen in other parts of Southeast Mesoamerica from the 8th through 10th centuries. Around AD 800, for example, the Copan dynasty had fallen, and the land its kings ruled was divided among what had been the lesser nobility. Similar patterns of political decentralization are also coming to light in areas bordering the Naco and Copan valleys. This suggests that the political perturbations experienced in the former area were part of a more general phenomenon. Remember that two of the three possible foundations of paramount power in the Late Classic Naco Valley—elite control over the local distribution of decorated pottery vessels and obsidian cores—depended on imports. Any events that undermined the ability of exchange partners to provide elaborately decorated ceramics and obsidian nuclei threatened the very foundations of the Naco Valley hierarchy. It may not be the case that the quantities of valuables passing among Southeast Mesoamerican polities dropped initially during the Terminal Classic. The fall of powerful dynasties, however, likely made it difficult to restrict these transactions to small groups of elites who could monopolize the local disbursement of esteemed items to their clients. Imported valuables may now have been accessible to a wider range of people who could employ them in their own bids for supporters and power. Thus, political decentralization and the dispersion of crafts across the Naco Valley were related to developments occurring throughout large parts of southern Mesoamerica.

Shifting Relations among Power, Production, and People

Changes in the organization of power and the distribution of people and crafts within La Sierra were apparently related to comparable developments throughout the Naco Valley. Before 1992, we saw a single, basin-wide hierarchy that endured for three centuries and was based, in part, on centralized control over craft production. Now we recognized that this picture was faulty, the result of combining evidence from different points in a long period of political and economic development into one unchanging image. Equipped with the ability to distinguish at least some moments in that sequence from each other, we were forced to recognize just how dynamic life in the Naco Valley had been from the 7th through 10th centuries. We also became increasingly aware of how events in surrounding areas were implicated in the basin's history.

These discoveries raised new questions. In particular, how were political and economic relations reconstituted during the Terminal Classic? It was shifts in these variables that posed the greatest challenges to our guiding PGT. We had not expected to see power and crafts flowing out from La Sierra during the 9th and 10th centuries, creating a mosaic of political centers variably related to a complex arrangement of manufacturing locales. Prestige Goods theory, as we were employing it, encouraged us to see craft production as a firm basis of centralized power. That connection may have applied in the Late Classic, but it did not describe the Terminal Classic political economy. We are trying now to understand how specialized manufacture might have figured in the strategies of those seeking political preeminence during a period of political decentralization.

In the section that follows, we outline some of what we learned as a result of that inquiry. In order to make sense of the complex relations among power, crafts, and changes in both over time, we increasingly turned for inspiration to Practice theory (PT). The interpretive structure we developed based on the intersection of PT and the Naco data is summarized at the chapter's end.

Coping with Diversity

A major surprise was the subtle variation among rural settlements in the ways in which power and crafts were woven into people's daily lives during the Terminal Classic. Detailed analyses of material patterning suggested that one consequence of the devolution of power during the Terminal

Classic was increased variation within and among sites in the ways in which political economies were structured on very local levels. What follows are several examples that illustrate this diversity.

Variation within Sites

Site 128, a political center composed of 28 structures situated 5 km northwest of La Sierra, was originally interpreted as an administrative node subordinate to the valley's Late Classic rulers (Figure 9.3). Excavations here during 1996, however, indicated that all of the visible buildings, including the six monumental platforms, reached their final form during the Terminal Clas-

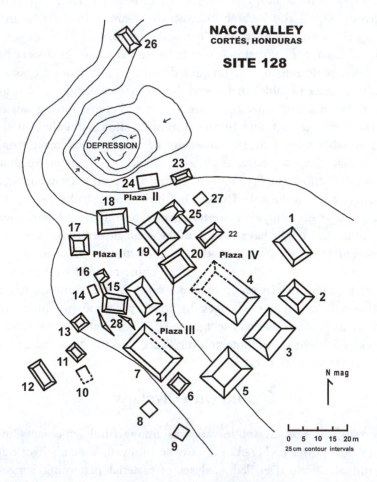

FIGURE 9.3 Map of Site 128.

sic, when centralized power was waning at La Sierra. These studies also indicated that Site 128 was anything but a homogeneous community. Instead, there is evidence that it was home to artisans engaged in a variety of crafts and contained at least two factions whose members contested for power.

In brief, it appears that Site 128's competing political leaders used the same resources—imported ceramics and obsidian blades—to attract and hold supporters. These goods were concentrated at specific buildings associated with each faction, from which we hypothesize the goods were doled out to attract the labor and loyalty of the center's residents. Contests among notables for these valuables must have been intense. That neither side won out completely implies that the resulting political structure was unstable and intergroup relations were tense.

Aside from the fashioning of obsidian blades, craft production does not seem to have figured in elite efforts to gain power over others. Specialized manufacture may, however, have been instrumental in protecting the power of individual households to preserve some level of independence from their leaders. Tools used in and debris generated by fabricating ceramic figurines, pottery vessels, and cloth decoration are widespread, suggesting that perhaps all of the site's residents pursued some crafts. It looks as though non-elites were successfully meeting most of their needs by their own efforts. Such relative self-sufficiency would have frustrated any efforts to create the sort of dependency relations on which stable political hierarchies might be created. Consequently, it looks as though Site 128's political economy was marked by unresolved contests among two elite factions and the commoners they sought to lead, all of the participants using craft goods to assert and question power relations. Unlike in the Late Classic, craft manufacture may have served the political objectives of commoners as well as elites.

Behavioral Variation among Sites

Ongoing analyses suggest that residents of even neighboring Terminal Classic sites significantly diverged in the kinds of crafts they pursued. The case cited earlier of the complementary manufacturing activities recorded for Terminal Classic Sites 337 and 335 exemplifies this process. Additional excavations in 1995–1996 yielded other comparable situations. For example, Sites 175, 470, and 471 are located within 275 m of one another on the southern edge of the Naco Valley, about 3 km southwest of La Sierra. Each was home to a household, though the one utilizing 12 buildings at

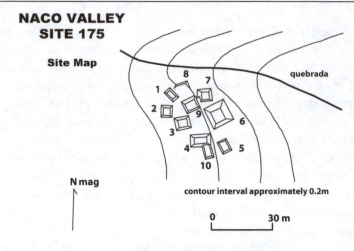

FIGURE 9.4 Map of Site 175.

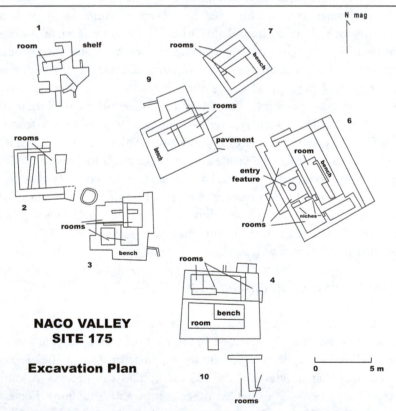

FIGURE 9.5 Plan of the excavations at Site 175. Structures 3, 4, 6, 7, and 9 were residences; Structures 2 and 10 were storerooms; Structure 1 was a raised work station with associated storage compartments.

Site 175 was larger than those who raised the three small structures found at each of its immediate neighbors (Figures 9.4, 9.5). All were occupied primarily in the Terminal Classic and yielded evidence of significant variations in the activities performed within them, especially crafts. Site 470, for example, seems to have been a place where the household stored figurine molds and incense burners (ceramic vessels used to heat smoke- and scent-generating resins during rituals). Fragments of both materials are far more common here than at Sites 471 and 175. On the other hand, it seems likely that the residents at Site 471 fired pottery vessels, probably including incense burners, and figurines, as attested by a stone-lined oven found associated with tools used in fashioning ceramics (Figures 9.6, 9.7). Apparently, tasks involved in the making of figurines and incense burners were divided among several close-by sites, some tools and product being stored at Site 470 but with the firing done at Site 471. Meanwhile, grinding stones employed in processing such staples as corn into flour are heavily concentrated at Site 175 and are much less common at the other two neighboring settlements. That several of the grinding stones retrieved from Site 175 were unfinished points to their manufacture there.

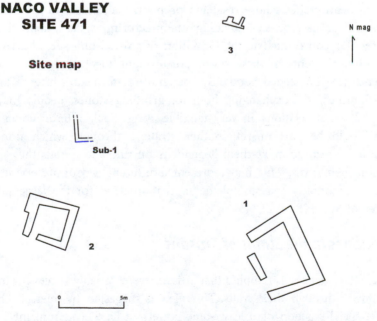

NACO VALLEY
SITE 471

Site map

3

N mag

Sub-1

2

1

0   5m

FIGURE 9.6 Plan of excavations at Site 471. Structure 3 on the settlement's north edge is the oven used in firing ceramics.

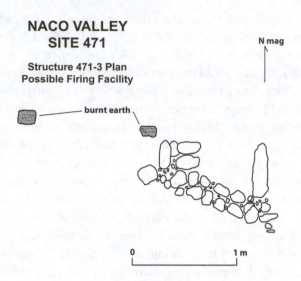

NACO VALLEY
SITE 471

N mag

Structure 471-3 Plan
Possible Firing Facility

burnt earth

0   1 m

FIGURE **9.7** Plan of Structure 3, the oven found at Site 471.

We were surprised to find such variation in craft-related activities among nearby sites whose residents probably had access to the same raw materials. It may be that dividing manufacturing tasks among different households contributed to the formation of a social unit spread across several sites; residents of these sites were brought together by their mutual dependence for needed goods. By cooperating in making incense burners and figurines, and exchanging both for grinding stones, people may have enacted social relations in very tangible ways. Such interdependence, in turn, could be part of yet another strategy through which non-elites thwarted efforts to make them dependent on rulers for goods they did not fashion themselves. This may represent a different way of preserving some level of autonomy that complements that inferred for the large political center of Site 128.

Variations in the Status of Artisans

Available evidence also implies that artisans were variably successful in seeking power through their crafts. This view is suggested by inferred changes in the social position of at least some potters at La Sierra from the Late to Terminal Classic. During the former period, those working at the several kilns situated on the capital's northern and southern margins lived in relatively humble accommodations close by firing facilities. The scale of the kilns themselves was modest, their designs apparently determined primarily by functional considerations. The one known kiln dating to the Terminal Classic differs considerably from its predecessors in its scale, nature of construction, and position within the built environment. This is the circular structure that we had so much trouble identifying during the 1990 field season (Figure 8.10). Its diameter of roughly 6 m makes it one of the largest kilns known anywhere in prehistoric southern Mesoamerica. Not only is the oven big, everything about the construction seems outsized. Its stone walls are 1.5–2.0 m thick, the air vents on the north and south are lined with cut blocks, and the surviving portion of the building is 0.6 m tall. When the domed *bajareque* (clay daub on wood) superstructure was added, the kiln probably stood about 2 m high, making it one of the tallest constructions at Terminal Classic La Sierra. This was an impressive manufacturing facility made all the more so by its setting on the edge of a 2-m-high natural rise.

The kiln's importance was reinforced by the construction of an extensive staircase, at least 8.4 m wide, that ascends this rise immediately northwest of the firing facility (Figure 9.8). The lower four steps are fashioned of cut blocks that were likely obtained from monumental buildings in the Late

FIGURE **9.8** Photo of the basal steps that make up part of the staircase that ascends the natural rise immediately northwest of the Terminal Classic pottery kiln at La Sierra. Note the prevalence of cut blocks in the construction.

Classic site core. The use of shaped masonry here hints at the importance the builders attributed to this entry feature. The residences lying just east of the kiln are also some of the larger domiciles found outside the Terminal Classic site core. Their occupants may well have commanded more labor than most Naco Valley householders, but less than that exercised by the high-ranking elites who survived the fall of the capital's Late Classic rulers.

In short, La Sierra's Terminal Classic kiln seems to have been a monument to the importance of this group of potters within Terminal Classic Naco Valley society. There were good, practical reasons for situating a workshop that generates such noxious by-products as high heat, smoke, and sharp ceramic fragments away from most residences on the edge of the settlement. By carefully orchestrating the placement of the kiln and its architectural setting, however, potters could convert their marginal location into a position of preeminence. Their homes and kiln rising majestically above a stone staircase, La Sierra's pottery workers seem to have moved beyond protecting their autonomy and succeeded in converting craft production into a source of some preeminence.

Wealth Variations among Households

Far from being divided into clear socioeconomic classes, Terminal Classic Naco Valley households were arrayed along a continuum of varying degrees of **wealth**. Wealth is a relative measure of material well-being that can be hard to define in non-capitalist contexts where there are no obvious shared standards of value against which everyone's standing can be explicitly evaluated. If, minimally, being wealthy involves accumulating objects of high value, how is that crucial concept of "value" to be inferred from archaeological remains? In answering that question we pursued the idea, suggested by others, that an item's value is directly related to the time and effort required to make and/or acquire it. There are certainly other considerations that define value. Nevertheless, we felt that the time and effort expended in fashioning and obtaining an item stood a good chance of being universal components of value and had the advantage of being measurable archaeologically .

The Naco Valley data class that exhibits the greatest variation in these factors is pottery vessels. Sherds from locally made containers exhibit significant differences in degrees of decoration, from those lacking designs to others embellished with motifs that required as many as four steps to complete. Similarly, excavations throughout the valley had encountered varying numbers of ceramic fragments that came from imports. These exotic pots were frequently also adorned with complexly painted, incised, and/or engraved designs. The time spent in decorating such foreign vessels would have increased their value above that based on the effort required to secure them from distant realms. The scenes portrayed on many local and foreign containers almost certainly conveyed important social information that would have further enhanced local appreciation for these jars and bowls. Imported and locally made decorated pots are, at the least, prehistoric equivalents of the "good china" many of us have in our homes today. The obvious high quality of these plates, bowls, and cups, brought out only on special occasions, conveys our economic standing (we had the resources to acquire the set) and social refinement (we know how to use them in hosting honored guests). Simpler, less expensive plates are used when reheating leftovers for a quiet dinner at which only immediate family members are present.

Based on these assumptions, we computed the proportion that sherds from high-value containers made up of all Terminal Classic ceramics recovered from excavations in different patio groups. Variations in these figures pointed to the contrasting abilities of households to acquire valuables and to distinctions in wealth among them. A patio cluster at Site 391, where only 1.9 percent of the 1,775 analyzed sherds fell within the high-value class, was therefore home to a household that was "poorer" than the household of comparable size represented by Site 418, where 3.4 percent of the 1,959 studied fragments belonged to this category.

Wealth, it turns out, correlates roughly with craft activities, in that the better-off households within and outside La Sierra tended to be those whose members engaged to the greatest degree in the widest range of specialized production. One factor contributing to the material well-being of a domestic group was, seemingly, participation in crafts generating surpluses that could be exchanged for valuables. This relationship was hardly perfect. In some settlements, residents producing considerable surpluses were not richly rewarded for their efforts. The figurine manufacturers of Site 337, for example, did not enjoy wealth measures appreciably higher than the people living at Site 391, who did not engage to any great extent in a craft.

Still, it looked as though people might choose to engage in specialized manufacturing to enhance their ability to accumulate valuables. Such decisions, however, were made within structural constraints that included considerations of:

1. what raw materials a household had access to;

2. the manufacturing skills they possessed;

3. the number of people who could be recruited to fashion goods;

4. what other producers were making in different parts of the basin.

Successful households mobilized labor, knowledge, and resources to meet their own requirements and to exchange for esteemed items, including high-value ceramics. The more desirable vessels ultimately, if not directly, came from the elites who imported them. Less advantaged social units could meet fewer of their material needs through their own work. Thus, they had to "spend" a proportionately greater amount of their total assets to get what they required, and less was left over with which to acquire valuables.

Assets, therefore, flowed toward those who could produce the most, and widest range of, goods, and away from those who could make the least and fewest. The result was a Terminal Classic political economy that was *not* characterized by a rigid division between wealthy elites and impoverished commoners. Rather, there was a continuum of wealth that was shaped by choices, made within structural constraints, to engage in certain manufacturing streams.

Political Structure and Individual Action

We are coming to realize that the broad processes of political change on which we had focused through 1991 arose from a complex array of mini-processes operating between and within Terminal Classic sites. Macro-processes, such as political decentralization, describe the outcomes of decisions made by a host of people of all ranks as they sought to adapt to the changing circumstances precipitated by the collapse of dynastic rule at La Sierra around AD 800. The Terminal Classic Naco Valley political economy, therefore, was not the product of a centrally conceived design imposed by elites. Rather, it was an unstable outcome of numerous daily interactions in the course of which valley residents of all ranks defined their goals and developed strategies to achieve them. It was in these contexts that people decided what, if any, crafts they wished to take up, the scale and intensity at which they would pursue them, and with whom they would ally within and across settlements. Committing to any craft depended on a person's assessment of what her/his compatriots living throughout the basin were doing, including what manufacturing tasks they were pursuing and what political and economic rewards were likely to result from fashioning vessels, molding figurines, or working obsidian.

Crafts, in short, were among the ways in which people navigated a dynamic political landscape. Pursuing certain manufacturing tasks offered opportunities for advancement for those who could successfully calculate the risks and advantages of using different strategies. It was out of this give-and-take that the heterarchical structure of multiple political centers and factional contests for power (seen at places such as Site 128) emerged. Prestige Goods theory directed us to look for the genesis of power differentials in elite-inspired domination schemes. We needed some way of conceiving how political formations might have risen instead from the bottom up.

Practice Theory

Inspiration for our reimagining of power and economic relations was provided by Practice theory. This body of thought, associated with social scientists such as **Pierre Bourdieu**, **Sir Anthony Giddens**, and **Sherry**

Pierre Bourdieu

Pierre Bourdieu, a French sociologist and anthropologist, was one of the most influential social scientists of the late 20th century. He challenged traditional approaches to the study of human behavior that stressed the power of economic, social, political, and ideological structures to determine human actions. In his *Theory of Practice* (English translation, 1977) and later works, Bourdieu argues that there is a reflexive relationship between structure and action such that structural principles (for example, hierarchy and class) only take shape and influence human behavior when they are internalized and put into practice by individuals. Central to his formulation is the notion of *habitus*, the set of durable, largely unconscious dispositions to action that we learn as children and which guide our behaviors throughout life. These habitus (the word takes the same form in the singular and plural) are strategies by which agents deploy the tangible and conceptual resources (also called "capital" by Bourdieu) available to them in pursuit of the power to achieve their own goals and dominion over others. Access to these assets within a society is unequally distributed, depending on a person's social position. Any society, therefore, accommodates multiple habitus yielding variable behaviors and degrees of success in political struggles. Bourdieu's formulations have been challenged, but his central insight that structures of inequality are regularly enacted in a wide array of contexts by diverse sets of people employing varied resources has helped open new vistas into the causes of human behavior. It has also clarified how inequality can persist despite its deleterious consequences for the majority.

Sir Anthony Giddens

British sociologist Sir Anthony Giddens is engaged in a lifelong effort to reform sociology by critically examining classic works in the field; promote an approach, which he calls "structuration theory," to the study of modern social life; and, most recently, assess how broad processes such as globalization affect the lives of individuals. His work on structuration theory, especially as it is described in *The Constitution of Society: Outline of the Theory of Structuration* (1984), has had a profound influence on anthropological and archaeological thought. A form of Practice theory, Giddens's formulation hinges on what he calls "the duality of structure." This phrase conveys the important notion that structure and agency are not opposed to each other, as they have traditionally been described in social theory. Instead, they exist in a recursive relationship. The former consists of a set of conceptual and physical resources along with the rules by which they are allocated to people occupying different positions within that structure. Those positions might be defined by the intersection of such variables as age, gender, and class. Structure preexists those born into it and both constrains and enables the exercise of individual agency. Nonetheless, structure only comes to life when agents use the available rules and resources to define and achieve their objectives. Hence, structure does not exist above and apart from the behaviors of agents. Most actions reinforce and reproduce the structure in which they are carried out. Still, because structure exists in and through the behaviors of agents, the latter can change structure if they act to modify the distribution of its resources and the nature of its rules. Understanding social change and continuity, therefore, requires grasping the crucial nexus among resources, rules, and the ways people employ both in their daily lives.

Ortner (see sidebars), was not new in 1995–1996. Discussions of the approach began to appear in print with some frequency in the late 1970s, and some anthropologists were embracing PT by the middle 1980s. Content with PGT , we had not paid these developments much heed. Things were different by 1996.

Practice theory loosely unites researchers who are committed to finding a middle path between explanations founded on structural principles and those that rely heavily on the enlightened actions of motivated individuals. We reviewed the nature of structural theories and their relation to issues of agency in Chapter 3. In essence, structural theories see human behavior as an outcome of forces that are largely beyond individual control. We do what we do because we are constrained to act in certain ways by those social, political, ideological, and/or physical environmental

---

Sherry Ortner

Sherry Ortner is an anthropologist who has done extensive research among the Sherpas of Nepal and, more recently, on class relations in the United States. She played a large role in introducing the precepts of Practice theory, as championed by social scientists such as Pierre Bourdieu and Sir Anthony Giddens, into U.S. anthropology. Her 1984 article "Theory in Anthropology since the Sixties," in particular, has done much to make the principles of Practice theory part of mainstream theoretical debates among U.S. anthropologists. Much of Ortner's work within Practice theory has focused on questions of how people resist overarching social rules and try to transform those rules in the course of daily interactions. As with Bourdieu and Giddens, social structures for Ortner do not exist apart from, nor do they totally dominate, the individuals who operate within them. Instead, these frameworks may set boundaries to action within which people maneuver with varying success to define and obtain their objectives. In the process of these maneuverings, social structures may change, though not always in the directions that those initiating the transformation may have intended.

---

forces that define our lives. Theories that give pride of place to agency—the potential people have to define and achieve objectives—take the opposite position. Here it is the goal-driven actions of rational agents that determine cultural forms and patterns of change.

The structure/agency distinction defines two poles on a continuum of thought. Few theorists propose that people are unreflective automatons incapable of understanding their place in the world or what causes them to act in certain ways. Similarly, views of culture dominated by the exercise of unbridled free will in the pursuit of individual aims represent an extreme position to which few would subscribe. Nevertheless, social science theories tend to gravitate toward one or the other of the structure/agency poles. Practice theorists are distinguished by their insistence on exploring how structure and agency are combined in the genesis and reproduction of patterned human behavior. The notion that structure does not exist apart from agency is essential to most investigations conducted along these lines. The two are inextricably melded: structural principles underlying, say, political relations, only have social significance when enacted by people in the course of their daily lives. Agency, in turn, cannot be initiated without resources, in the form of ideas, social relations, and actual goods, provided by structure. Nevertheless, structures that are never enacted in regularly recurring events have no social reality. Written works that imagine utopian communities may outline structures of interpersonal interaction. If these plans never inspire action, however, their social significance is negligible, even if their importance as literature may be great.

Many Practice theorists are concerned with actions taken in the political sphere. Here attention often centers on how inequality is created within modern nation-states. According to Practice theorists, such odious distinctions are not solely the outcome of government bureaucracies enforcing explicit policies. These political processes are part of the framework that defines the limits of individual advancement. They do not, however, dictate how people will understand those limits and work within them to accomplish their own objectives. What is of particular interest to Practice theorists are the ways in which political structures are insinuated within, and thus come alive through, the habitual behaviors of goal-seeking individuals.

The link between structure and action is often mediated through the concept of a strategy. In essence, people are variably aware of the conditions, including power relations, within which they live. However conscious they are of these circumstances, they have to make do within them. They must get on with life in ways that offer at least some physical and conceptual rewards. To do so, they formulate strategies that are adjusted to the social, political, economic, and environmental conditions into which they are born. Drawing on the physical and conceptual resources available to them by virtue of their position within a structure, they define goals that are attainable and develop the means to reach them. Successful strategies survive and are adopted by many of those living within the same general structural circumstances. In this way, patterns of behavior develop and are transmitted across generations. Since any one society is composed of people who occupy different structural positions—say, of class, gender, and/or ethnicity—it is likely to encompass a variety of strategies. Practice theorists, therefore, subscribe to the Postmodernist position that societies are fragmented along different, variably intersecting lines of interest and experience.

There are several important points to keep in mind about these strategies. First, there is rarely only one way to cope with a given structure from a certain position within it. Structures define the parameters of action; they do not dictate the forms those actions will take. This leads to the second point: structures are both constraining and enabling. The ways in which resources are distributed within these frameworks preclude some possible strategies while making others both imaginable and doable.

If people are born into a low social group whose members are denied education beyond the sixth grade, then they cannot reasonably develop a strategy aimed at becoming a lawyer or doctor. If jobs such as blacksmithing, sheep shearing, and cattle herding are deemed appropriate for members of this social unit, and they are provided with the resources to pursue those careers, then low-status individuals can choose from among such options in developing a strategy to support themselves. In this way, people exercise their creativity within limits as they make a life for themselves within a specific structure.

Third, once established, strategies tend to be practiced habitually— that is, they are rarely subject to conscious, critical evaluation. Strategies are part of life and of the world views that make that life intelligible (see the discussion of world views in Chapter 1). Such generally unreflective acceptance of these ways of making do leads to the fourth point: these procedures powerfully enact structural principles, however indirectly. If, as a lower-status member, you decide to be a blacksmith, you are reinforcing a structure that subordinates you and your peers by denying all of you education and other resources, thus limiting your life chances. On some level you may know this. But if the blacksmithing strategy works, if it gets you through life with a certain amount of personal security and satisfaction, then you will pursue it. Should you challenge the system and insist on getting the schooling you need to be a lawyer, you will be instituting a new strategy, or appropriating one used by others but previously denied you. This has system-changing possibilities. And that is the last point we wish to highlight: social change occurs through the intended and unintended consequences of shifts made in the strategies people employ to cope with specific structures. This follows from the observation that it is through patterned actions in the form of strategies that structure exists as a social force. A change in strategies means a change in the structure on which they are based. The trick is to get new strategies accepted. Just wanting to be a lawyer is not enough. You have to know what a lawyer is, how to become one, have the resources to support this quest, and then convince others that they should let you try. Achieving these goals is never easy, as the history of efforts made by women and minorities in the United States to become doctors and lawyers bears out.

Practice theorists thus look for the causes of human behavior in the mundane practices that give life to overarching structures, as behavior is shaped through the conditional agency of goal-directed individuals. It is at the intersection of structure and agency that human action is born.

Our Version of Practice Theory

What we took from this approach is a formulation inspired by the writings of numerous scholars but not precisely based on the work of any one of them. In adapting PT to our emerging appreciation of data patterns in the Terminal Classic Naco Valley, we arrived at the following conceptual framework.

People seek to accomplish a variety of goals in life. Among those objectives is the ability to live their lives as they choose and to get others to help them in that process. People, in short, seek *power to* define and meet their own needs and *power over* others whose labor and support can be harnessed to achieve those aims. Since individuals are all seeking the power to protect their own labor while siphoning off the productive efforts of their neighbors, political contests are an important part of many, but not all, human interactions. This is the aspect of life on which our theory concentrates.

To be successful in political competitions, it is necessary to acquire regular and predictable control over assets essential to gaining power in all its senses. These resources range from tangible features of the physical environment—say, arable land and the food harvested from it—to such intangible elements as conceptions of supernatural beings and the knowledge needed to conduct rituals to appease them. Assets composed of ideas and things are equally important to achieving power in both senses used here. Insofar as people can sustain themselves physically and define their place within the world of human and supernatural forces, they are in an excellent position to lead their own lives as they choose. To the extent that a few can monopolize some set of these resources, they can exert power over all those who must turn to that small group for the means to feed themselves and/or establish their position within the world, broadly defined. The wider the array of resources controlled by a privileged minority, the greater their ability to dictate what others must surrender in labor and loyalty in return for access to those goods and ideas. The fewer such assets under central control, the weaker the position of would-be elites.

People rarely engage in power contests alone. Instead, the successful acquisition, distribution, and use of resources depend on cooperation with others, organized in social networks, in pursuit of similar political projects. Cooperation in these webs is often founded on their members sharing a social identity, or persona, a socially constructed sense of self in relation to others, marked by distinctive symbols. Networks are, therefore, socially constructed means for coordinating the actions of groups of people who deploy resources in support of common projects designed to exert power over others and in their own lives.

Individuals can, and often do, belong to multiple networks, each with its own identity and geared to accomplishing certain goals using the distinct set of resources controlled by members of that web. Any one society, like that which existed in the Terminal Classic Naco Valley, consists of a dense network made up of smaller networks among which people move with variable ease. Some of these webs extend beyond a society's boundaries, linking members in different realms who cooperate in the pursuit of common political projects (for example, those involving the exchange of obsidian cores and decorated pottery). Others are highly localized, such as nets that tie together members of a single household. Still other nets unite all members of a specific polity. This is just a skeletal outline of the complex web of interconnections in which people may have participated. Archaeologists can only identify those networks that were distinguished by long-surviving and prominent material symbols. We can console ourselves with the thought that whereas we may never be able to describe all the social connections people might have activated, we should be able to identify the most significant of such linkages. These are the ones that probably played the largest roles in structuring interpersonal interactions and determining the results of political contests.

Political webs are created and reproduced within structural constraints. These latter features—combining physical characteristics of the environment with social, political, and economic relations and variably shared world views—define how material and conceptual resources are distributed among all participants taking part in social networks and, hence, what political projects are possible. They do not determine how those potentials are translated into action. Rather, what shapes power structures is the manner in which individuals, as members of social nets, take advantage of the opportunities offered by existing arrangements of structural features to secure assets by allying with some in opposition to others.

Agency, in this formulation, is not exercised solely by willful individuals. It is a feature of groups who operate with variable degrees of freedom and success to claim the tangible and intangible resources offered within particular structures. An element of creativity is inherent in this process: people's actions are not dictated by the resource framework into which they are born. Nor is there ever an infinite array of possible ways assets can be harnessed through networks in seeking political goals—but there is usually

286 ■ Archaeological Theory in Practice

more than one. How nets and resources are combined determines the manner in which political structures will remain the same and change.

We are now in the process of applying the theory sketched above to Terminal Classic data that have been gathered over all field seasons. Specifically, we are looking at craft production as part of the strategies that people adopted to deal with a political structure that was in the process of undergoing dramatic transformations. We want to answer such questions as:

1. How was craft manufacture used as a resource by networks of people seeking some form of power at varying spatial and temporal scales?

2. In what ways did the production, exchange, and use of items instantiate these social webs?

3. How can we evaluate the success of such efforts in the form of control over labor or the ability of artisans to accumulate valued items?

In the course of these studies, we have to acknowledge that different crafts had varying political significance in different periods and that their relevance to power struggles changed over time. Thus, while artisans may have manufactured pottery in their role as clients of Late Classic elites at La Sierra, at least some potters seemingly used their craft as the basis for claims to increasing preeminence after their patrons' fall. That is, the production and distribution of ceramic vessels were among the actions by which social webs of different sorts came alive in the dealings of craftworkers and those who consumed their output. Similarly, at Site 128, the strategic distribution of obsidian blades that were made at the center may have been one way that several factions of elites competed to create hierarchically structured networks that they dominated. At the same time, commoners at Site 128 seemingly tried to lessen their reliance on these would-be rulers by fashioning their own social webs, made tangible through the creation, use, and exchange of other goods. Crafts may also have been used to unite social networks composed of commoners residing at multiple sites. This seems to have been the case at Sites 175, 470, and 471, where mutual dependence was enacted in daily practices of manufacture, storage, and exchange that transcended settlement boundaries. Distinctions in household wealth may be one symptom of the varying degrees of success enjoyed by members of these and other networks as they sought valued goods. Such success, in turn, apparently depended partly on the ability of people working within different webs to mobilize the skills and raw materials needed to engage in various crafts.

The resulting political economy is thus one in which power and wealth did not neatly covary within a single valley-wide hierarchy. Instead, the variably coordinated, rarely harmonious actions of numerous protagonists organized in overlapping networks yielded a dynamic, heterarchical structure in which people of diverse ranks actively participated. This framework was a joint project whose form was constantly shifting, as decisions made in one quarter altered the distribution of resources that everyone else needed to define and accomplish their goals. The Terminal Classic Naco Valley political economy was, paraphrasing Sir Anthony Giddens, the product of intentional action, but not an intended product.

We are no longer using PGT to explain events that transpired in the Naco Valley from the 7th through 10th centuries. This theory may still yield insights into political relations during the first two centuries of that span but has given way to PT in understanding what happened in the succeeding Terminal Classic. The shift was made not because the latter approach is better than its predecessor in any absolute sense. Practice theory just helps us to make sense of the detailed data now available for the Terminal Classic in ways that PGT did not; using PT we can see relations we had never perceived before and are less mystified by what had heretofore been baffling. Our inferences to the best explanation have again changed. This transformation is driven by the recovery of new data, the availability of hypotheses based on theories with which to account for those finds, and our newfound appreciation for how the latter can be successfully applied to the former.

We will not be testing hypotheses derived from PT against new data unearthed from the Naco Valley. Instead, we will offer interpretations of existing material patterns based on our PT-inspired framework for others to evaluate. Hopefully, some will find them useful and apply their own version of our interpretive structure in their work, just as other people's investigations in other places spurred our research. The refinements made in the course of such applications will inevitably yield the fresh insights out of which knowledge emerges, honed in the application of theory to data.

The Naco Valley, AD 825—As of 2011

By AD 825, the newly ensconced elites at La Sierra must have worn their preeminence uneasily. They were precariously balanced atop a political structure whose form was continually up for negotiation. The usurpers had literally driven their predecessors from memory, abandoning and vandalizing the buildings in which the latter had lived and worshiped. Nevertheless, there was some charisma still attached to those old monarchs, and raising the new site core adjoining its Late Classic antecedent allowed the successors to draw on that aura. They would need all the help they could get. Challengers had set themselves up in political capitals of their own within the basin and were avidly competing for those imports essential to securing and exhibiting power differences. La Sierra's new lords might have been slightly ahead in these contests, but not by much. Every new leader was forging the networks that tied him or her to foreign suppliers of obsidian cores and decorated pottery. They then used these valuables to create webs of dependents who owed them labor and loyalty in return for precious gifts. It behooved every aspirant to power to be generous with their clients, however, as there were several potential benefactors to choose from. Power was a fragile commodity, and while La Sierra's notables might hold their heads high, they and all their counterparts had to keep their feet firmly planted on the ground, aware of what each subordinate wanted and what they were being offered by competitors.

As elites saw the situation, a big part of the problem was the annoying capacity of their underlings to shield themselves from demands issuing from on high. The collapse of the Late Classic dynasty opened up new opportunities for households to assert control over their own destinies. The skills needed to pursue crafts that had formerly been limited primarily to La Sierra were now available to many. Commoners were not slow to seize this opportunity. Taking advantage of raw materials easily secured from their immediate surroundings, these new artisans started fashioning goods for their own use and exchange. In some cases, several households banded together to make a wide array of items, sharing responsibility for the work and any goods obtained through exchange. The result was an increasingly complex economy linking households in overlapping networks of mutual dependence. This system largely operated outside elite control and could be used to sustain commoners physically as well as spiritually; the paraphernalia, such as figurines, whistles, ocarinas, and incense burners, needed to approach supernatural forces were obtained through interhousehold transactions, as were such prosaic items as ground stone tools essential to processing food. Making this strategy work required that all participants devote time and energy to building their own social webs instantiated, in part, through the exchange of craft products. Once established, the participants had to work hard to hold the loyalty of their peers who were themselves calculating the advantages and disadvantages of allying with some households and not others.

The resulting system was far from stable, as elites sought supporters among commoners who were simultaneously courting allies in exchange relations on which everyone was coming to depend. A wide range of imports and local goods moved through the valley among equals and between elites and clients, but slight perturbations in such a complex, decentralized network of networks could spell its doom. Those enmeshed in the system were probably too busy acquiring, making, and distributing goods, as well as negotiating social relations, to note its fragility. It would catch up with them eventually. In AD 825, however, the future may well have looked bright, especially for those commoners who were emerging from under the shadow of La Sierra's Late Classic dynasty.

The Naco Valley of AD 825, as seen from 2011, bears little resemblance to how the valley looked to us in 1979. The peaceful earlier vision is superseded by the hustle and bustle of people trying to create their own futures through their own efforts. Is this version true? That is a very difficult question to answer. What we can say with confidence is that the above reconstruction is almost certainly closer to the messy, shifting reality that all residents of the Naco Valley faced in AD 825 than the earlier scenarios we have outlined here. That is progress we can believe in.

Further Reading

Archaeology, Households

Hendon, J.
  1996 Archaeological Approaches to the Organization of Domestic Labor: Household Practice and Domestic Relations. *Annual Review of Anthropology* 25:45–61.

  Hendon's review of household studies offers a fresh perspective on these crucial units of analysis.

Santley, R., and K. Hirth, eds.
  1993 *Prehispanic Domestic Units in Western Mesoamerica*. Boca Raton, FL: CRC Press.

  This is a much-cited contribution to the literature on ancient households in Mesoamerica; the contribution by Santley and Kneebone was especially important to us as we strove to understand how crafts and domestic activities might be accommodated within Late and Terminal Classic Naco Valley households.

Schwartz, G., and S. Falconer, eds.
1994 *Archaeological Views from the Countryside: Village Communities in Early Complex Societies.* Washington, DC: Smithsonian Institution Press.
These essays convey the growing recognition of the varied ways commoners and elites, rural and urban populations, together create the political and economic systems in which they live. The collection also argues against a top-down view of culture change.

Wattenmaker, P.
1998 *Household and State in Upper Mesopotamia.* Washington, DC: Smithsonian Institution Press.
Wattenmaker's case study highlights the complex interrelations between power and craft production in one of the world's earliest states.

Wilk, R., and W. Ashmore, eds.
1988 *Household and Community in the Mesoamerican Past.* Albuquerque: University of New Mexico Press.
This influential collection of essays, focused primarily on studies of the Maya lowlands, deals with the structure and organization of ancient Mesoamerican domestic groups.

Mesoamerica, General Discussions

Demarest, A., P. Rice, and D. Rice, eds.
2004 *The Terminal Classic in the Maya Lowlands: Collapse, Transition, and Transformation.* Boulder: University of Colorado Press.
The papers in this collection summarize research on Terminal Classic developments across the Maya lowlands.

Naco Valley

Douglass, J.
2002 *Hinterland Households: Rural Agrarian Household Diversity in Northwest Honduras.* Boulder: University of Colorado Press.
Douglass conducted research with us in 1996 that was inspired by Processual theory. This case study provides a good example of how the same data (settlement forms and distributions) can be successfully approached in several different ways.

Schortman, E., and P. Urban
1994 Living on the Edge: Core/Periphery Relations in Ancient Southeast Mesoamerica. *Current Anthropology* 35:401–430.
This paper gives you an idea of where we stood on questions of inter-societal interaction at the end of the 1992 field season.

2011   *Networks of Power: Political Relations in the Late Postclassic Naco Valley, Honduras.* Boulder: University of Colorado Press.

In this book we apply our version of Practice theory to the study of late prehistoric developments (AD 1300–1532) in the Naco Valley.

Schortman, E., P. Urban, and M. Ausec

2001   Politics with Style: Identity Formation in Prehispanic Southeastern Mesoamerica. *American Anthropologist* 103:1–19.

Here we elaborate our ideas about relations among social identities, social networks, political centralization, and the material means by which these phenomena are linked. We did not discuss the above issues in the text but refer you to the article if you are interested in this aspect of our studies.

Urban, P., and E. Schortman

2004   Opportunities for Advancement: Intra-Community Power Contests in the Midst of Political Decentralization in Terminal Classic Southeastern Mesoamerica. *Latin American Antiquity* 15:251–272.

This paper applies some of the ideas concerning changing political arrangements discussed in the present chapter to the study of Naco Valley Site 128.

Southeast Mesoamerica, General Discussions

Joyce, R.

1988   The Ulua Valley and the Coastal Maya Lowlands: The View from Cerro Palenque. In *The Southeast Classic Maya Zone*, ed. E. Boone and G. Willey, pp. 269–295. Washington, DC: Dumbarton Oaks.

1991   *Cerro Palenque: Power and Identity on the Maya Periphery.* Austin: University of Texas Press.

This book and article by a leading researcher in Southeast Mesoamerica summarize her research in the Sula Plain on Honduras's north coast. Joyce's investigations comprise some of the work to which we referred when discussing the diverse trajectories followed by Southeast Mesoamerican societies during the Late-to-Terminal Classic transition.

Sheets, P.

2005   *The Ceren Site: An Ancient Village Buried by Volcanic Ash.* New York: Wadsworth Publishing.

Sheets, P., ed.

2002   *Before the Volcano Erupted: The Ancient Ceren Village in Central America.* Austin: University of Texas Press.

In both sources, Sheets and his colleagues describe the extraordinarily well-preserved 7th-century AD households they uncovered at the Ceren site in El Salvador. This project has established a baseline for household studies in Southeast Mesoamerica.

Theory, Feminist

Hays-Gilpin, K.

2000 Feminist Scholarship in Archaeology. *Annals of the American Academy of Political and Social Science* 571:89–106.

Hays-Gilpin summarizes here feminist approaches in archaeology as of the end of the 20th century. Much of the current discussion of social identities in archaeology is inspired by feminist studies, and this is a good source to consult as you try to understand relations between gender and social affiliation.

Theory, General Discussions

Brumfiel, E., and J. Fox, eds.

1994 *Factional Competition and Political Development in the New World.* Cambridge: Cambridge University Press.

The authors contributing to this volume treat political processes, such as power centralization and hierarchy building, as products of contests for preeminence occurring within social formations. These essays run counter to many Processualist approaches to the study of political developments.

Carr, C., and J. Neitzel, eds.

1995 *Style, Society, and Person.* New York: Plenum Press.

This collection of essays deals with the various ways in which style is understood in archaeological research and was used by ancient people to achieve their ends.

Crumley, C.

1979 Three Locational Models: An Epistemological Assessment of Anthropology and Archaeology. *Advances in Archaeological Method and Theory* 2:141–173.

This is Crumley's original discussion of heterarchy. See Ehrenreich et al. 1995 (below, this section) for examples of heterarchy's application to particular research cases.

DeMarrais, E., L. Castillo, and T. Earle

1996 Ideology, Materialization, and Power Strategies. *Current Anthropology* 37:15–31.

This article discusses the strategic links between political processes, especially power centralization and hierarchy building, and the material symbols by which they are tangibly expressed.

Earle, T.
  1997 *How Chiefs Come to Power: The Political Economy of Prehistory.* Stanford,
        CA: Stanford University Press.
          Earle reviews the various political, ideological, and economic re-
        sources elites use in their efforts to gain political advantages. He fa-
        vors explanations of hierarchy building founded on centralized con-
        trol over economic assets, though you need not agree with his
        conclusions to appreciate the argument.

Ehrenreich, R., C. Crumley, and J. Levy, eds.
  1995 *Heterarchy and the Analysis of Complex Societies.* Arlington, VA: Archaeo-
        logical Papers of the American Anthropological Association, No. 6.
          Crumley's introductory essay defines heterarchy, while the subse-
        quent articles explore different ways this concept can be employed in
        archaeological analyses.

Feinman, G., and J. Neitzel
  1984 Too Many Types: An Overview of Sedentary Pre-State Societies in the
        Americas. *Advances in Archaeological Method and Theory* 7:39–102.
          Along with the McGuire (1983) reference cited below (this section),
        this essay challenged archaeologists to measure social complexity along
        continuums of variation rather than using a typological approach.

Foucault, M.
  1982 *The Archaeology of Power.* New York: Pantheon Books.
          Foucault's notion that power is not some "thing" that is adminis-
        tered from the top down but is inherent and imminent in all social
        relations influenced archaeologists who were trying to imagine how
        people of all ranks contributed actively to the creation of socio-
        political structures.

Gailey, C.
  1987 Culture Wars: Resistance to State Formation. In *Power Relations and
        State Formation,* ed. T. Patterson and C. Gailey, pp. 35–56. Washing-
        ton, DC: American Anthropological Association.
          This is an early statement about the importance of accounting, in
        analyses of political change, for the reluctance of commoners to par-
        ticipate in the schemes of elite aggrandizers.

Goffman, E.
  1974 *Frame Analysis.* Cambridge, MA: Harvard University Press.
          Goffman draws our attention to the detailed study of how people
        enact structure through the seemingly mundane interactions in
        which they engage with one another and their culturally structured
        environments. His work cast a bright light on how microprocesses of

the everyday are crucial to understanding the broad forces that shape history. Goffman's work remains influential in some forms of Practice theory, especially the version promoted by Giddens.

Hirth, K. G.

1993   Identifying Rank and Socioeconomic Status in Domestic Contexts: An Example from Central Mexico. In *Prehispanic Domestic Units in Western Mesoamerica*, ed. R. Santley and K. G. Hirth, pp. 121–146. Boca Raton, FL: CRC Press.

   Hirth considers here how household wealth can be assessed using archaeological data.

Mann, M.

1986   *The Sources of Social Power,* Volume 1: *A History of Power from the Beginning to A.D. 1760.* Cambridge: Cambridge University Press.

   Mann's broad overview of human history and the creation of inequality is often cited by archaeologists dealing with questions of power. Especially important from our perspective is the distinction Mann makes among different sources of power (political, ideological, social, and economic) and the various roles they can play in strategies of elite domination.

McGuire, R.

1983   Breaking Down Cultural Complexity: Inequality and Heterogeneity . *Advances in Archaeological Method and Theory* 7:91–142.

   This is an early call to reimagine cultural complexity as a continuum of variation rather than as a domain neatly divided into clear, discrete categories. Many of our ideas on the interplay among power, wealth, and craft production were ultimately inspired by this essay.

Price, T., and G. Feinman, eds.

1995   *Foundations of Social Inequality.* New York: Plenum Press.

   The authors here express a diverse set of perspectives on how power is manipulated at a variety of spatial scales, from households to states.

Scott, J.

1985   *Weapons of the Weak: Everyday Forms of Peasant Resistance.* New Haven, CT: Yale University Press.

   Scott describes how peasants resist the demands of their overlords. His formulation has been influential in discussions among archaeologists about how free subordinates might have been to question the demands of rulers.

Smith, M.

1987   Household Possessions and Wealth in Agrarian States: Implications for Archaeology. *Journal of Anthropological Archaeology* 6:297–335.

This is a much-referenced review of how wealth differences can be recognized archaeologically.

Theory, Marxism

Miller, D., M. Rowlands, and C. Tilley, eds.
  1989 *Domination and Resistance*. London: Unwin Hyman.

  Contributors to this volume consider the various strategies by which elites seek to achieve power and their erstwhile subordinates maneuver to undermine the pretensions of their "social betters." The authors, in general, espouse variations of Marxist principles in their interpretations.

Paynter, R., and R. McGuire
  1991 The Archaeology of Inequality: Culture, Domination, and Resistance. In *The Archaeology of Inequality*, ed. R. McGuire and R. Paynter, pp. 1–27. Oxford: Blackwell.

  This essay reviews issues relating to the ways in which political centralization is challenged by those in society's lower echelons.

Theory, Practice

Bourdieu, P.
  1977 *Outline of a Theory of Practice*. Translated by R. Nice. Cambridge: Cambridge University Press.

  This is one of the foundational texts of Practice theory. You might try reading the Ortner article (see below, this section) first, as it will help you decode some of Bourdieu's more complexly phrased arguments. Pay special attention to the idea of habitus outlined here; it roughly translates as Bourdieu's version of "strategy" discussed in this chapter.

Dobres, M., and J. Robb, eds.
  2000 *Agency in Archaeology*. Routledge: London.

  Reading this collection of essays will give you a good sense of how agency has been incorporated in archaeological research.

Dornan, J.
  2002 Agency and Archaeology: Past, Present, and Future Directions. *Journal of Archaeological Method and Theory* 9:303–329.

  Dornan provides a helpful review of how Agency theory was applied in archaeology at the turn of the 21st century.

Giddens, A.
  1984 *The Constitution of Society: Outline of the Theory of Structuration*. Berkeley: University of California Press.

  This is another seminal text that sets the foundation for Practice theory. Giddens's ideas converge to some extent with those of

Bourdieu, but he arrives at them from a very different basis. We were especially influenced by the ways in which Giddens integrates the concept of resources and rules into his understanding of human interaction.

Ortner, S.
  1984 Theory in Anthropology since the Sixties. *Comparative Studies in Society and History* 26:126–166.

   This overview of changes in anthropological thought appeared during a crucial interval in theory development; the essay also provides a clear introduction to Practice theory.

Sewell, W.
  1992 A Theory of Structure: Duality, Agency, and Transformation. *American Journal of Sociology* 98:1–29.

   Sewell critiques Giddens's theory of structuration, stressing the importance of resources in understanding the relationship between structure and agency. Sewell's essay has been frequently cited by archaeologists who are attempting to use Practice theory's precepts in studying the past.

CHAPTER 10

CONCLUSIONS

Introduction

THIS FINAL CHAPTER DRAWS ON ARGUMENTS articulated throughout the book to examine how archaeological knowledge emerges from a conjunction of recovered data, the theories available for interpreting those materials, and the researcher's appreciation for the utility of those theories. This knowledge structure both enables and constrains further investigations. It enables them in that the intersection of data and theory, mediated through hypothesis testing, can yield fresh insights into past actions that suggest new questions to be asked. The structure is constraining in that theories are focusing mechanisms, directing our attention to particular sets of factors and their relations while ignoring others. The intersection of theory and data, therefore, inevitably raises specific queries while obscuring others. The knowledge that results from applying theory to data is also dynamic, shifting as new findings come to light, new theories are developed, and our experiences with both change. These fluid relations guarantee that what we know about the past, our evaluations of what constitutes an inference to the best explanation, are forever changing.

What Have We Learned about Naco Valley Prehistory?

The short answer to that question might be, The more you dig, the less you know. This glib remark states a fundamental truth. After the 1975–1979 field seasons, we were fairly certain that Late Classic Naco Valley society was moderate in size and organized within a relatively simple hierarchy headed by notables who ruled by virtue of their privileged connections with Copan's lowland Maya lords. Everyone in the valley lived similar lives, though those in the ruling class drew on the tribute and labor of their subordinates to support a relatively leisured, if not sumptuous, lifestyle. By 1991, much of that supposed knowledge had been challenged. Not only were La Sierra's rulers far more powerful than we had imagined, but their preeminence was underwritten by centralized monopolies over the production and distribution of essential commodities. Connections with neighboring areas, including the Copan realm, remained important; they were the source for some of the valuables used to create the bonds of dependency that underwrote elite power. These foreign contacts were nonetheless diverse, and Naco Valley's lords exercised considerable freedom in using imported raw materials (such as obsidian cores), finished goods (especially decorated pottery vessels), and ideas (materialized by such structures as the ballcourt) to meet their own objectives.

The 1992–1996 field seasons successfully questioned this newly won understanding of the past. What had been a static image of a La Sierra polity that had endured for three centuries became a more dynamic landscape in which relations among power, wealth, and crafts were anything but stable. Successful efforts to centralize control over the valley by La Sierra's Late Classic elites were possibly facilitated by their encouragement of craft production at the capital. Though they may never have fully monopolized all manufacturing tasks, these magnates seemingly did benefit from their control over large-scale pottery production, shell working, obsidian blade knapping, and the distribution of esteemed foreign ceramic containers. The fall of these dynasts in the 9th century changed the political, cultural, and economic structure of the basin. Though some potentates remained ensconced at the old capital, 12 other political centers were founded, each one home to elites who exercised some control over their segment of the former unified realm. Throughout the Naco Valley, people of all ranks took advantage of changing political relations to engage in crafts that generated surpluses given in return for prosaic goods and for imported valuables still circulating within local exchange networks. Power now seems to have arisen out of intense, and intensely complex, interactions among people of all ranks, occupations, and places of residence.

This sequence illustrates the shifting nature of what constitutes an inference to the best explanation. What we thought was a "best explanation" of Naco Valley prehistory at any one point was a product of the theories available in the literature, which of them we chose to use, and the data gathered in the course of fieldwork guided by theory. Unexpected finds would challenge the assumptions of our guiding theory, leading us to search the extant array of conceptual structures for those that helped us make sense of these discoveries. Hence, when we started work in the Naco Valley in 1975, Culture History's prevalence in Southeast Mesoamerican studies and Processualism's dominance of theoretical debate within archaeology strongly predisposed us to adopt these perspectives in our work. Such approaches as Prestige Goods theory and Practice theory were not accessible to us and so could not inform our search for, and interpretation of, data at the project's inception. Changing assessments of Naco Valley prehistory were thus enabled and constrained by the research structure in which we worked, a framework that was contingent on the state of theory development, data gathering, and our shifting understandings of both at any moment.

The same case can be made for the longer-term research efforts outlined in Chapters 5 and 6. Archaeologists working in southern Mesopotamia and at Stonehenge in 1950 operated within a different research structure than those who studied this area and site in 2000. Changes in archaeological theory during those five decades opened up new interpretive possibilities, the pursuit of which generated novel data that encouraged the application of additional conceptual schemes. What we knew of life in southern Mesopotamia during the 5th–3rd millennia BC changed over this span in large part because of the dynamic interplay among theory, data, and the perceptions of researchers. Similarly, the results of the Riverside Project on Salisbury Plain were motivated by Interpretivist approaches that sought to place Stonehenge in its ancient landscape. The new information generated by this work, in turn, required archaeologists of all theoretical persuasions to reformulate their understandings of the monument.

What Does This Tell Us about the Nature of Archaeological Research?

In Chapters 1 and 2, we stressed that theories are essential research tools that focus attention on certain aspects of reality. Investigations are not possible without these conceptual structures, but all studies are inevitably biased by the theories that guide them. As discussed in Chapter 2, such observations raise significant questions concerning how we come to learn about the world. Are theory and data so firmly wedded that the former determines what we see? If so, then what can be said about past people depends less on how they lived and more on what our conceptual frameworks tell us should be the case. Alternatively, do data exist apart from theory such that judicious testing of ideas against findings will reveal which explanations are best? As we have tried to indicate throughout Chapters 5–9, the truth lies somewhere between these extremes. But what have our examples taught us about the relation among theory, data, methods, and knowledge?

Seeing What You Expect to See

First, theory does condition us to look at the world in certain ways. Researchers pursuing investigations guided by Processualist and Marxist premises in southern Mesopotamia, for example, saw evidence of cities, hierarchy, and centralized control of land in different lights. What comprised an inference to the best explanation differed among them. To Processualists, cities, hierarchy, and centralized control over land were seen as outgrowths of behaviors that promoted adaptation. To Marxists, they were the means by which a few gained advantages over many. Similarly, where some Processualists saw a monument to a particular form of communal power at Stonehenge, some Interpretivists perceived a symbolic structure that conditioned experiences in ways that promoted culturally constructed understandings of difference among the living, and between them and the revered dead. We saw time and again in our Naco Valley studies how difficult it was for us to perceive aspects of the archaeological record that were not highlighted in the theory we were employing at the time. When operating under Prestige Goods theory, for example, we were reluctant to accept evidence for specialized production in rural settlements. Further, our difficulty identifying the pottery kiln found at La Sierra in 1990 resulted in large part from long-standing assumptions about the nature of craft manufacture in Southeast Mesoamerica, assumptions that have deep roots in the Culture Historical perspective. Theory does predispose us to view the world from a certain perspective, making it relatively easy to observe certain things but not others.

Seeing beyond Theory's Expectations

Second, theory's dominion over perception is not absolute. It is possible to observe what our conceptual structures obscure, though it is never easy. Diffusionist accounts of Stonehenge's origins were thus countered by carbon-14 analyses that were not intended to undermine this view. In our own work, we had trouble identifying that pottery kiln but eventually did so. Along the same lines, we did not want to recognize at first that a wide array of goods were fashioned at diverse scales and levels of intensity throughout the Naco Valley but did come to acknowledge that fact. A conceptual framework may guide you down a relatively narrow research path, but that route need not be a rut you are fated to follow because of your theoretical perspective.

Obstacles to Vision

Third, some research topics are precluded in specific cases because the data are insufficient, the theories for their study are unavailable, and/or the researcher does not choose to recognize certain questions and approaches as interesting. An example drawn from our own work concerns our inability to address questions of gender in Naco Valley prehistory. There is no lack of theory dealing with this topic in archaeology, and methods based on these conceptual frameworks have been available for quite some time. Still, we consistently failed to find, for example, the sorts of evidence Pollock drew on to identify gender-based hierarchies in early southern Mesopotamia (Chapter 5). Accounts describing how gender helped shape the lives of Southeast Mesoamerica's current and historically known indigenous people are very few. Archaeological data often used to address such topics, such as the patterned relations among interments of different sexes and the goods buried with them, were not recovered for any period in the Naco Valley. The few representations of clear male and female bodies that we found— especially on ceramic figurines, whistles, and ocarinas—also do not offer a clear picture of how gender was defined and affected human interactions. We therefore regretfully conclude that *in this particular case* we cannot successfully investigate questions of gender. Some of our colleagues, such as Rosemary Joyce, have fruitfully dealt with the issue in nearby areas but usually in situations where there are texts and/or solid information derived from archaeological contexts that speak to gender issues. Gender is an important topic and there is no lack of theory that facilitates its study. Our experience in the Naco Valley indicates, however, that theory alone does not determine what issues will be examined; the nature of the data may well enable some investigations while making others difficult to consider.

Sharing Information across Theoretical Divides

Fourth, information gathered under the aegis of one theory can be used by researchers operating within other conceptual structures. We saw this in Chapter 5, where investigators working from one perspective in southern Mesopotamia freely drew on information provided by those pursuing research guided by different premises. Culture Historians, Processualists, Marxists, and Interpretivists may well differ profoundly on the political significance of those institutions that controlled land, water, and labor in southern Mesopotamia by 3200 BC. Nonetheless, they all used information gathered by their colleagues who espoused different theoretical positions. The detailed stratigraphic analyses conducted by Culture Historians at Stonehenge revealed the site's complex history, a history that researchers of different schools have to take into account when discerning astronomical alignments or shifts in meaningful structures. In a similar vein, as we chose among varied theories throughout the course of our Naco Valley investigations, information that was accumulated under earlier conceptual structures was incorporated into interpretations developed from different vantage points. In fact, it was often data collected under one theory that led us to question the utility of that approach and to consider another. Not only are data *not* determined by theory, they can be used to challenge the conceptual structure within which they were gathered and contribute to the research of those guided by different premises.

Theory and Methods

Fifth, the methods used to gather data are strongly influenced by theory but are transferable among investigators working from diverse theoretical positions. Hence, we saw in southern Mesopotamia and at Stonehenge that the techniques pioneered by Culture Historians to create chronologies were adopted by those who subscribed to other schools of thought. Similarly, as discussed in Chapter 5, survey methods crucial to Processualists in measuring connections among population numbers, natural resources, and administrative structures were employed by Marxists and Interpretivists in their studies. Throughout the Naco Valley investigations, we also used methods drawn from diverse schools. In fact, it was in the course of using principles of seriation and stratigraphy developed by Culture Historians that the Terminal Classic was eventually distinguished from the Late Classic. This revelation, in turn, encouraged us to adopt a new theory, Practice theory, as we rethought developments dating to the 9th through 10th centuries in the basin. Methods founded on venerable precedents can thus inspire novel interpretations.

How Real Are Schools of Thought?

Sixth, we should be cautious about ascribing too much significance to the schools of thought discussed in Chapter 4. Like all models, the depiction of conceptual variety presented in that section simplified a complex reality to make it intelligible. The examples of research guided by theory provided in Chapters 5–9 suggest that the insights, methods, and data derived from numerous theories are regularly combined in archaeological practice. We are, for example, all Culture Historians in our fieldwork insofar as we chart culture change. Similarly, in attending to human–environment relations, we rely on the work of Processualists, just as considerations of power often lead us to review what Marxists have said on this topic.

Rather than seeing the domain of archaeological thought divided among clear schools, therefore, it might be best to view these more or less coherent bodies of theory as representing tendencies within a dense web of interpretive possibilities responding to the questions raised in Chapter 3:

1. How widely can we generalize cause-and-effect relations?

2. What is the balance of structure and agency in explaining human action?

3. Which factors are causally significant in channeling human behavior?

Some archaeologists respond to these queries in the same ways throughout their careers; many shift perspectives and/or combine the insights of several viewpoints in their own unique syntheses. The question is not which approach is right, but which one most benefits your research.

In short, theory comes alive as it is applied to investigations; and yet that complex intersection of data, methods, and thought rarely conforms to the neat categorical distinctions made in Chapter 4. Schools of thought thus have permeable boundaries, across which methods, findings, and researchers move over time. This process is on display in our Naco Valley investigations and can be seen in the work of multiple scholars pursuing research dealing with southern Mesopotamia and late Neolithic Britain.

How We Learn and What We Know

These six points suggest that we might usefully draw a distinction between how we learn about the past and what we know about it. The learning process involves focusing attention on a manageable topic and using specific methods to gather certain kinds of data relevant to that topic, all guided by theory. The result is frequently a set of novel insights into a specific set of variables and their relationships (say, between craft production and political power, cities and storage, materials and meaning). What we know in the aggregate about the people who lived in any area at certain points in time, however, is built on a complex amalgam of diverse data gathered using multiple methods under the guidance of different theories. No one theory, therefore, determines what we come to apprehend about our object of study; that knowledge is the outcome of many studies guided by diverse conceptual structures.

Why So Many Theories?

Why do we need so many theories? This returns us to some of the issues raised in Chapter 2. Human behavior, in any era, is conditioned by so wide an array of variables that no one theory could usefully address them all. Trying to do so would undermine theory's greatest advantage: its power to focus attention on important components of human actions and their causes. If this is the case, then there will always be valid reasons for people of good faith to espouse and elaborate different conceptual frameworks that highlight specific facets of human behavior while inevitably leaving some other, equally interesting features of those behaviors in the shadows. Grasping the richness of past lives requires drawing insights from multiple approaches. There is no reason to think that archaeology will ever be characterized by one overarching conceptual scheme. In fact, fragmentation, rather than unity, will probably always characterize archaeological theory. Learning to appreciate the value of others' views, and the inevitable limitations of our own, may well help us advance the common cause of understanding the lives of past people in all their complexity.

Do Not Be Afraid to Fail

One message that comes through our research in the Naco Valley is that there is something to be said for failure. As you have seen, every year that we returned to the basin we were confronted with stark evidence that our interpretations of that basin's prehistory were flawed. As we hope you also saw, it was in the course of confronting these limitations that we learned something. Finding out how wrong we were about La Sierra's size made us aware of how powerful its Late Classic rulers had been. Realizing how misguided we were about the persistence of centralized craft monopolies opened the door to considering how people might have used specialized manufacture in strategies to secure power during the Terminal Classic. The examples go on and on. Learning in general often involves challenging our assumptions about the world and undermining our complacency about how things work. The archaeological record has the capacity to surprise us at every turn. Staying alert for these surprises, and learning from them, requires that we pay close attention to theory.

Theory and Communication

Theory also plays a role in promoting communication among investigators. Throughout the history of Naco Valley studies, our search for new conceptual frameworks constantly forced us to look outside Southeast Mesoamerica, and sometimes outside archaeology, to find inspiration. This meant that we had to be aware of the various ways World Systems, Prestige Goods, and Practice theory were applied in a variety of prehistoric, historic, and modern contexts. In the process, we certainly learned something about capitalist expansion from the 15th century onward and about the importance of metallurgy in defining political hierarchies in Bronze Age Scandinavia. More importantly, we became aware of what our colleagues working in other world areas were thinking, and were sensitized to the various ways such broad processes as political centralization might act everywhere, but nowhere in exactly the same ways. Paying attention to theory, therefore, broadened our vision of archaeology and of human behavior.

When engaged in this borrowing, it is important to understand in some detail the contexts in which the theory from which you draw inspiration are used. Without knowing that context, you will be borrowing blindly, running the risk of misusing methods, concepts, and findings in your own work. Such misapplications sow confusion in the literature, as concepts with one set of meanings in a specific theory are employed differently in new interpretive settings. For example, fruitful applications of World Systems theory to prehistoric cases require careful and explicit redefinition of such key terms as *core*, *periphery*, and *semi-periphery*, which originally were used to describe the spread of capitalism and explain that economic system's effects on political economies around the globe. Failure to make this translation only muddies discussions of long-distance interactions, as readers wonder how Researcher #1 is using *core* in his or her analysis and how it relates to its original meaning in World Systems theory and to the way it is employed by Researcher #2.

Learning about diverse theories and their applications also alerts you to the implications your data may have for debates in the social sciences and to the relevance those discussions may have for what your findings might mean. Such tacking back and forth between the abstract and the concrete helps ensure that what we learn from our studies does not remain locked up within them, accessible only to ourselves and other specialists who have the detailed knowledge of local events needed to decode our remarks and intuit their meanings. All theories give you the vocabulary to translate specific observations into statements that others working in diverse domains of study can understand, applaud, or challenge. By using theory to communicate, you contribute to the broad discourse about what it means to be human. Such conversations are impossible without theory.

Theory both constrains and enables these conversations. It is relatively easy to talk with people with whom you share the same perspectives, who employ the same, or similar, conceptual structures in their work. Theory's tendency to channel conversation along certain lines, and among particular scholars, is an unintended consequence of what theory does best—that is, concentrate attention on selected aspects of a complex reality. We do not need, however, to treat theory's blinkers as natural obstacles to communication. Those scholars drawing inspiration across conceptual divides in southern Mesopotamia and at Stonehenge, for example, are clearly bridging such gaps. We best serve ourselves, the field, and those we study when we acknowledge the limitations, as well as advantages, of all conceptual schemes and familiarize ourselves with the premises underlying different viewpoints. Not only are we thus well prepared to adopt new theories as our research directions change, but we are also better able to benefit from what colleagues pursuing other investigations guided by different principles have to say. Like those who are able to speak multiple languages, we can talk with people from diverse backgrounds and grasp the points they are making.

What Is Archaeological Truth?

As noted above, archaeological knowledge is unstable. What we think happened and why it occurred are constantly shifting as:

1. new theories are developed;

2. novel methods based on those constructs are deployed;

3. data generated by these studies are published;

4. researchers' views of said theories, methods, and data shift.

Such dynamism raises the problem of reliability: If the structure of archaeological knowledge is changeable, why should we trust it? Could it be undermined by more data and new theories? The answer to the second question is yes. We are thus well advised to accept any inference to the best explanation of past events as the best one available given the state of theory, methods, and data at the time it was made. What we can say now about southern Mesopotamian political developments, relations among crafts and power in the Naco Valley, and the meaning of Stonehenge are certainly far more nuanced and probably come closer to capturing the complex reality of ancient lives than anything that could have been offered earlier. At the same time, some very wrong interpretations of the past have been eliminated from consideration. We are, for example, no longer looking to Sumerians as the bringers of civilization or to the Mycenaeans as inspiration for Stonehenge's creation; nor is La Sierra seen as the capital of a simply structured polity in thrall to Copan. There is comfort in those negative conclusions. Years of fieldwork have narrowed the range of possible interpretations, excluding some as highly unlikely.

Saying that the truth of human prehistory is contingent on theories, methods, data, and investigators' perceptions of all three does not detract from the validity of what we can say about the past. It just indicates that those truths are incomplete. This partial quality of our findings poses for us a constant challenge to fill in gaps and evaluate existing claims that future generations may take up as they build on the knowledge structures their predecessors created. Archaeological truths, therefore, are always emerging and rarely definitive. In that sense, research never ends.

Truth for Whom?

The above remarks, and those made throughout this book, apply primarily to the ways archaeologists employ theory to understand data. The past is of interest to more than just archaeologists, however. As discussed in Chapter 6, there are a number of parties who are variably concerned with how our finds are treated and interpreted. Pressure from these groups impinges to various degrees on archaeologists working in different areas of the world and in different time periods. In our case, very few Hondurans have expressed to us more than a passing interest in what we have found. Similarly, though the Honduran government continues to oversee our work, its agents have never encouraged us to cant our results in a particular direction. We thus have been relatively free to pursue the Naco Valley studies described here as we saw fit. The situation is fraught with greater uncertainty and anxiety at places like Stonehenge, where more individuals and groups have vested interests in how that site and its past are studied and understood.

It might be fair to say, therefore, that the interpretive structure in which archaeologists operate is composed of theories, data, methods, and the perspectives of those various actors who also have a stake in the archaeological record. How much influence the latter people and groups have on the conduct of investigations depends, in part, on their power to impose their views, as well as the openness of archaeologists to the interests of these stakeholders. In any case, it is fairly certain that the varied lay audiences with whom we deal will be motivated by concerns that are different from our own, just as the criteria they use to evaluate what constitutes a "best explanation" of that past will diverge from those we employ. It is almost certainly a mistake to try to rank the legitimacy of these approaches according to some universal set of standards. Do archaeologists make better statements about antiquity than members of religious congregations? Than do government agents? What criteria could be used to evaluate the relative worth of such different claims?

The main point, as we understand the matter, is that in negotiating among such diverse interest groups we are probably best advised to be clear in our goals and truthful in our statements about what we know and how we know it. In doing so, we have a right to insist that all other parties to the discussion be equally explicit on both counts. It is only through such frankness that we can all find something to say to one another and learn the limits of our own knowledge.

A Few Final Words

Here we return to where we started in the preface—specifically , to the question of how archaeological thought is related to archaeological practice, and what roles you have to play in making that connection. Theory is always a means to an end, its goal being to help describe and understand the significance of past behaviors. Abstracted from the research process, at best theory runs the risk of seeming to be tangential to the project of archaeology . As we hope we have demonstrated in the argument developed over the preceding pages, theory is essential to the practice of archaeology and is creatively entwined with everything we say about the past. This is not to claim that theories determine in some absolute sense what we see in the archaeological record and how we interpret it. As noted above, the physical remains we encounter in the course of fieldwork are critical to the research structure that limits as well as enables our interpretations of ancient actions and their significance. But theory is another major feature of that framework, and it is through the use of theory that data make sense. Theory is woven into anything you read about the past. Understanding those accounts requires being aware of theory's presence within them.

At the worst, considering theories in isolation from data gathering sometimes tempts scholars to compare conceptual structures in order to identify one as best in some absolute sense. We have already laid out our case for believing that such an effort is fruitless. It was just this sort of search for unassailable verities on the part of Modernists that led some Postmodernists to reject the existence of any knowable truth. We think that such strong relativism is as misguided as the robust **positivism**, or explanation by recourse to universal laws, that it was designed to counter. There are many things we can learn about the past, and, just as importantly, there are many presuppositions about that past we can challenge effectively. Theory is essential to both intellectual projects. The value of a theory lies in how well it helps in this process. The synergism of theory, data, and the manner in which you apply the former to the latter enables you to learn about the past and contribute to knowledge. As long as the conceptual structure you are using encourages you to ask questions that lead to new insights and yet more questions, then it is a valuable tool. When a theory no longer helps clarify what happened and ceases to spur you to perceive what you never thought to observe, then it has lost its utility *as far as your investigations at that particular moment are concerned*. Just because a theory no longer works for you does not mean that you should reject it forever or criticize others for espousing it.

The relevance of any tool—and that is what theory is—depends on the context in which it is employed. That context consists of the data you are confronting, the state of theory development at the moment of confrontation, and your understanding and evaluation of both. As these variables shift, so too will your perceptions of a conceptual framework's productivity and fruitfulness. Losing track of the contingent utility of theory can lead to pointless arguments about the absolute superiority or inferiority of different schemes. Not only are such disagreements unresolvable, they discourage intelligent searching by archaeologists for the inspiration that different theories can provide. Ignoring the various theories developed by diverse scholars can only slow our understanding of the past and the complex lives of those who shaped it. We owe the people whose remains we study our best efforts at recapturing the vibrancy of their lived experiences, and this means being open to the different insights promised by different theories.

Finally, we return to another problem encouraged by treating theory independently of archaeological practice—that is, the tendency to treat theory's creators as specialists skilled in conceptual matters. Much of the way in which theory is taught encourages this viewpoint, especially when we single out specific thinkers for their work in developing particular schools of thought. There is no denying the powerful contributions certain archaeologists have made to framing how we think. What is misleading in this characterization, and what is difficult to convey in any theory course, is the simple fact that everyone who conducts research into the past shapes the theoretical framework in which we all come to operate. Those of us participating in the Naco Valley Archaeological Project changed the conceptual schemes we derived from our readings of the literature to match better what we were finding. In this way, we modified PGT as well as aspects of PT. Similarly, Adams's and Renfrew's takes on Processualism, Diakonoff's and Algaze's applications of Marxism, and Pollock's, Thomas's, and Parker Pearson's uses of Interpretivism are not slavish replications of established theories, but creative modifications of those frameworks in novel situations. These transformations, in turn, become part of the general discourse on archaeological theory through publications and conversations with students and colleagues. Now, multiply these experiences by the number of archaeologists working throughout the world and you see that theory changes less through a particular individual's inspirations and more through the concerted efforts of numerous scholars, each of whom changes and enriches our communal conceptual framework as they apply ideas to data in their work.

Archaeological theory, in this vision, constitutes a dynamic and democratic field that is constantly being transformed. Every student of the past has a role to play in shaping this conceptual domain; in fact, making such contributions is an inevitable consequence of doing research. We are most effective in developing archaeological theory when we are alert to the various ways that it figures in all aspects of our studies. By sensitizing ourselves to theory's pervasive influence, we can be aware of how these frameworks are inevitably shaped through our actions. We very much hope that this book helps awaken in you a sense of your own role as a theoretician and of the contributions you can make to our increasingly rich understanding of the human past.

GLOSSARY

Acropolis: As the term is used in Mesoamerica, it refers to a massive, artificial platform that supports at least one other building. Acropolises usually reached their final forms through many stages of sequent construction. In the course of this buildup, earlier edifices were covered by their successors, ultimately resulting in huge constructions.

Adze: In this case, a finely polished stone blade that was probably hafted at an acute angle to a wooden handle. Adzes were most likely woodworking implements.

Agency: The potential that people have to define and achieve their objectives.

Antiquary: Individuals, generally Europeans living during the 17th through 19th centuries, who relied, in part, on the study of ancient objects to answer questions about the past. Unlike archaeologists, antiquaries usually focused on the presumed significance of objects treated in isolation and less on their contexts of recovery.

Archaeoastronomer: A student of the past who is primarily interested in ancient understandings of celestial phenomena, such as the movement of stars and planets, and the relation of those conceptions to the organization of material remains, such as the arrangement of buildings in sites.

Archaeological culture: Distinctive material patterns that characterize a group of sites located within a spatially delimited area. These recurring associations are thought to materialize the distinctive shared beliefs and practices of the culture in which residents of the sites in question participated.

Artifact blank: An unfinished object that is roughly shaped to approximate its final form.

Assemblage: A collection of artifacts recovered from a particular component.

Attribute: Any identifiable feature of an artifact. A stylistic attribute of a pottery vessel might be the color of the paint used in its decoration. A container's shape might be an attribute related to its function.

Ballcourt: In Mesoamerica, a venue, usually delimited by two parallel platforms, in which two individuals or teams attempted to score points by knocking a hard rubber ball into the opponent's end of the alley and/or through rings mounted on the court's flanking walls. Use of the hands was generally prohibited. Though these games could sometimes be held for entertainment, they were often important parts of rituals engaged in by elites.

Carbon-14 dating: A radiometric dating procedure based on the regular decay in organic materials of naturally occurring, unstable, radioactive carbon-14 to its stable state.

Chiefdom: A form of sociopolitical organization characterized by moderately large populations, social ranking, and a modest degree of both political centralization and social differentiation. It was thought by many Processualists to represent an intermediate stage of development between small-scale egalitarian societies and those organized as large, highly centralized states.

Component: All deposits identified at an archaeological site that date to roughly the same time period.

Concept: Refers to an idea or principle embedded within a theory. Concepts are often named variables thought to be significant in describing and explaining a particular phenomenon or process.

Context: Describes the horizontal and vertical relations among objects, including the soil in which materials are found, as revealed in archaeological investigations. It is from studying patterns in these relations among things that ancient behaviors and chronologies are reconstructed.

Craft specialization: Production processes engaged in by a segment of an entire population that generate surpluses for exchange (*see* **Scale of production** and **Intensity of production**).

Culture: A set of beliefs, values, and assumptions shared by a group of people that gives rise to a coherent and predictable body of behavior.

Daub: Clay that was originally used to make the walls of buildings. The clay was applied over a woven stick framework; impressions of this wooden structure sometimes were preserved in burnt fragments of daub.

Deconstruction: A process by which the basic, often unconscious assumptions and values underlying any act (including the writing of texts) are exposed and their essential contradictions highlighted.

Dependent variable: A factor, the form or nature of which is specified within a theory as being determined by the operation of another process or factor (the latter being the *independent variable*).

Description: A statement that specifies the nature, form, and/or quality of something.

Development of underdevelopment: Originally articulated by development theorists, this concept was later used by proponents of World Systems theory to express the process by which societies in peripheries are systematically impoverished due to unrelenting exploitation by cores.

Diffusion: The spread of ideas or goods without the permanent or long-term migration of people.

Elite: Those members of a society who enjoy privileged access to resources, including the power to direct the actions of others. Also called *monarchs, nobility, paramount lords, potentates, scions,* and *magnates* in this text.

Emic: A study that seeks to understand patterned human behavior from the perspective of the people engaged in those actions. Generally associated with inferring the meanings actors attribute to their behaviors.

Ethnoarchaeology: Conduct of research in the present for the insights it can provide into ancient behaviors. Considerable attention in these investigations is devoted to chronicling the material signatures of past behaviors.

Etic: A study that seeks to determine the significance and causes of patterned human behavior by reference to concepts and theories judged relevant by outside observers. These terms and processes may well not be recognized or understood by the people being studied.

Explanation: A set of statements that specify a causal relationship(s) among a set of variables operating under a specific set of conditions.

Evolutionists: As used in this text, the term refers to a loosely connected group of social thinkers of the late 19th and early 20th centuries in Europe and the United States. They proposed that all human behavior could be explained by ascertaining where within their universal, unilineal, and progressive schemes of culture change those actions fell. Taking modern Europe and the U.S. as the current end points of this evolutionary progression, they arranged all known human societies within stages of increasing complexity that recapitulated the supposed course of human history.

Facing: The stone retaining walls that bound a platform's perimeter and contain the fill that makes up the building's core.

Gender: Culturally defined expectations of behaviors and dispositions appropriate to people with certain sexual characteristics.

Heterarchy: A situation in which people and groups are not organized within a single political hierarchy (see below) but can be ranked in various hierarchies according to different principles and/or criteria.

Hierarchy: A situation in which people and groups can be arranged within a single, overarching system of inequality based on differential access to essential political, social, ideological, and/or economic resources.

Historically contingent: To say that a behavior is "historically contingent" is to claim that it is the result of interactions among variables the nature of, and relations among, which are the product of conditions that pertain at a specific moment in time. This phrase and the ideas it conveys are central to Culture Historical and Interpretivist arguments that cultural developments are largely the unpredictable outcomes of events that are not subject to general laws but are the consequences of unique historical circumstances.

Household: An enduring group of people who reside together and cooperate in tasks crucial to meeting their members' needs of physical and social reproduction. Household members may or may not acknowledge kinship connections with one another.

Hypotheses: A set of propositions about the causal relations among a collection of variables that applies directly to a particular set of spatially and temporally delimited circumstances. Hypotheses transform the abstract propositions of a theory into terms specific to a particular context. This grounding of the abstract in the prosaic facilitates evaluating a theory's utility in accounting for a given set of observations. *See also* **Theory, middle-level**.

Ideology: As used here, a body of beliefs, values, and assumptions that rationalizes, naturalizes, and/or legitimizes existing social and political relations.

Identity: *See* **Social identity**.

INAA: Instrumental neutron activation analysis is a method for describing the chemical and mineral composition of materials based on examining the reactions of the atoms comprising these items to bombardment with neutrons.

Independent variable: A factor that, according to the principles of a specific theory, causes the form and nature of other factors (called the *dependent variables*).

Inference to the best explanation: The notion that estimations of a hypothesis's ability to explain observed material patterns in terms of human behavior are always subject to change as new data come to light or new hypotheses, possibly based on novel theories, are developed.

Instantiate: To make manifest in a tangible form. This term is often used in Interpretivist approaches to refer to processes by which abstract cultural principles are expressed in physical actions.

Intensity of production: Describes the relative time an artisan invests in fashioning craft items. Measures of production intensity are usually ranged from full- to part-time.

Intertextuality: The notion that any event is so thoroughly conditioned by a wide range of events and processes that precede and are contemporary with it that (1) it cannot be understood in isolation from this rich context; and

(2) it cannot be predicted or explained by reference to general laws, as these broad prescriptions strip the event of its dense network of historically contingent, causally significant interconnections.

Kiln: An enclosed structure designed for firing pottery at controlled temperatures. Kilns are usually associated with the high-volume manufacture of ceramics.

Landscape archaeology: Refers to the study of the meanings attributed by ancient populations to constructed and natural features of their environment.

Materialism: A general term for theories that privilege people's interactions with the physical conditions of their existence in explaining human behavior. In this view, ideas are secondary to, and determined by, interactions between people and tangible features of their physical environments. Processualism and most forms of Marxism are materialist perspectives.

Maya lowlands: The adjoining portions of Mexico, Belize, Guatemala, and Honduras that are of moderate elevation and witnessed the flowering of Maya civilization from at least the 4th century BC through the 10th century AD.

Mesoamerica: A culture area stretching from central Mexico through Guatemala, western Honduras, Belize, and western El Salvador. The zone is distinguished culturally by shared general features of prehistoric beliefs and practices as well as by relatively intense interactions among members of its component societies.

Migration: The long-term resettlement of sizable numbers of people in a locale at some distance from their original home. This process often involves the transfer of cultural information.

Model: A schematic, simplified representation of the phenomenon under study that includes only those variables thought to be important in understanding that phenomenon. There are fine distinctions among *model*, *hypothesis*, and *theory*, and definitions of each differ somewhat among sources. In this volume, we have focused on theory and hypothesis, largely treating models as equivalent to theories.

Modernism: The general intellectual movement whose members espoused the notion that all aspects of human behavior are best understood by employing scientific procedures based on models developed in the natural sciences. Human action is therefore knowable and can be explained using universally applicable general laws. Ultimately, many Modernists believed that these investigations would form the basis for reorganizing society along supposed rational lines in accord with clear scientific principles.

Norm: Refers to a rule of behavior. Normative views of society posit that all members of the group share much the same views of the world and conform to the same rules.

Observation: The selective registering, and organization into a coherent structure, of data through various senses.

Obsidian: Volcanic ejecta that has rapidly cooled after exposure to the air. This stone is so fine-grained that it is often referred to as "volcanic glass." It was used throughout prehispanic Mesoamerica for making tools. Obsidian flows are highly localized in Mesoamerica, each source having a distinct mineral-chemical signature by which its products can be traced.

Palace: Term given to long structures, set atop tall platforms, the rooms of which were home to high-ranking members of ancient Mesoamerican societies. Palaces often doubled as administrative offices for the ruling elite.

Paradigm: A body of concepts, assumptions, associated methods, and criteria for evaluating research, shared by members of a scientific community, that guides and informs the investigations of its members.

Phase: Refers to all **components** at sites within a region that date to the same period and pertain to the same **archaeological culture**.

Political centralization: The process by which power is concentrated into ever fewer hands.

Political economy: A flexible concept that for our purposes is understood as the manner in which issues of power, on the one hand, and processes of production, consumption, and distribution, on the other, are entwined.

Polychrome pottery: Ceramic vessels decorated with designs painted in three or more colors.

Polysemous: Refers to the multiple meanings a symbol can have for the various persons, operating from different structural positions within a society, who interact with that symbol.

Positivism: Describes an approach to explanation based on a hierarchy of laws, hypotheses, and operating conditions. Specific events are explained as manifestations of general principles, expressed as laws, thought to operate universally under specifiable conditions. These explanations are tested through proposing hypotheses, based on the overarching laws, that are structured to fit the circumstances in question, and deducing from those hypotheses what should be found in the study if the hypotheses are correct.

Postmodernism: A broad intellectual movement that developed in opposition to **Modernism**. This perspective encompasses a wide array of different viewpoints generally united by their (1) distrust of broad theory that purports to account for phenomena by the operation of universal principles; (2) belief that, as far as human behavior is concerned, action is **historically contingent** and culturally constructed (i.e., it derives from a context shaped by the convergence of unique cultural and historical forces); and (3) a commitment to highlighting the diverse ways in which people understand their world and negotiate their place within it.

Postprocessualism: Generally used as a synonym for Interpretivist archaeology.

Power: The ability to define and achieve one's goals (= power to) and to direct the actions of others (= power over). Power need not be associated with physical coercion, nor must it be invested in formal political offices. Rather, power is an attribute of all social relations, permeating most interactions in which we engage. Power is also expressed at many levels, from individual actions to the economic, political, and ideological structures in which those initiatives are taken. In general, social scientists are primarily interested in how these structural variables condition the choices made by individuals. Recent trends in theory question this emphasis and, instead, consider the recursive relation between individual actions and the structures in which those behaviors occur.

Recursive: A relationship among two or more variables in which the form of one is strongly affected by the form of the other(s).

Reductionist: A mode of explanation in which a phenomenon is accounted for by reference to factors and relations thought to operate on a more basic level than the phenomenon in question. Accounting for cultural features by the operation of such non-cultural forces as adaptation to the physical environment is a form of reductionist explanation.

Relative/relativism: The view that a set of human behaviors can only be understood within the context of the cultural system in which they are performed. Taken to its extreme, relativism can also mean that all truth claims are only supportable within the conceptual system that inspires them. Truth, in this view, is relative to the perspective of the observer.

Representative sample: A set of observations that is thought to capture the full range of variation within the total universe of possible observations from which it is drawn.

Romanticism: An intellectual tradition opposed to analytical and generalizing approaches to knowledge. Its adherents stress understanding phenomena within the unique cultural and historical conditions in which they arose and operate.

Sampling: Selecting a set of observations from the total universe of potential observations within a specific domain. The sample is the basis for statements made about features of the domain from which the sample was drawn.

Scale of production: Describes the volume of goods produced within a certain craft or by a particular set of artisans within a specified unit of time.

School of thought: A very general, abstract body of principles and concepts employed in explaining a set of processes, such as human behavior, out of which specific high-level theories are created. The precepts and principles of a school of thought are less clearly articulated, and are less widely shared within an academic discipline, than are those of a paradigm.

See: Introduced here to contrast with **observe**. Seeing involves registering visual stimuli though not necessarily organizing those stimuli into coherent images of the world.

Seriation: Arranging deposits within a chronological sequence based on variations in the proportions of artifacts characterized by particular styles found within these units.

Settlement pattern: The distribution of sites located during survey across the landscape.

Site: Any spatially discrete evidence of occupation; also referred to here as *settlement*.

Social fact: A recurring pattern of behavior that is guided by a shared body of underlying assumptions and values. Social facts are not the result solely or primarily of an individual's wishes or inclinations. Rather, those desires and dispositions are shaped by the cultural principles pertaining in a particular place at a specific moment in time. It is these patterned actions and their underlying premises that make up the basic subject matter of the social sciences.

Social identity: A sense of self established in relation to others. Each individual has multiple social identities to draw on, depending in part on who they are interacting with, in which contexts, and with what goals in mind. Social identities are often distinguished by behaviors and material markers. *Persona* is used as a synonym for social identity here.

Social valuables: Items that play an important role in producing and reproducing important interpersonal relationships through their exchange and use.

Southeast Mesoamerica: The adjacent portions of Honduras, El Salvador, and Guatemala; sometimes called the Southeast Maya Periphery.

Spindle whorls: These are weights attached to a spindle (usually a wooden rod) that together enable the production of thread for weaving. Loose, unspun material, such as wool or cotton, is attached to the spindle rod. When the rod is rotated, the spinner draws out the raw material. This, in turn, is twisted into thread by the spinning.

Stratigraphy: The principle that, in cases where earth levels are relatively undisturbed, materials found deeper down are older than those found higher up in the sequence. It is through the study of temporal changes in material styles, as revealed in stratigraphic sequences, that we can reconstruct the **phases** through which cultures in a region have passed.

Structure: That concatenation of ecological, political, economic, ideological, social, and demographic forces that constrain and enable people's actions.

Style: Attributes of an action or object that are not strongly constrained by technological and/or functional considerations and are thus relatively free to convey social information and vary through time.

Sui generis: As used here, this is an approach to the study of human behavior in which explanations are phrased in purely cultural terms.

Survey: Systematic search of the ground surface in an effort to locate, record, and describe ancient sites.

Swidden: A form of agriculture in which fields are cleared by cutting and burning. Tracts are then used for varying numbers of years before being allowed to lie fallow. The fallow interval, during which natural vegetation encroaches on the plot, allows the soil to regain fertility. Also called *slash-and-burn* agriculture, this farming practice requires large amounts of land per person to be effective.

Symbols: Any thing or action to which is attached an arbitrary meaning. "Arbitrary" in this sense refers to a meaning that is culturally determined and is not inherent in the object or action comprising the symbol.

Systems theory: A perspective, often linked to Processualism, that at its most general posits such close interrelations among behaviors within a culture that no action can be fully understood without specifying its connection to other behaviors enacted within that culture.

Techno-environmental determinism: Refers to explanations that view culture as a system in which the overall form is determined by causally significant interrelations among variables of technology, demography, and those aspects of the physical environment to which a group of people is adapting. This notion is usually associated with Processualism.

Theory, high-level: A body of interrelated statements that specify concepts, and relations among those concepts, used to describe and explain some aspect of the world. *Conceptual structure, conceptual framework*, and *conceptual scheme* are used synonymously with high-level theory here.

Theory, low-level: Observed recurring patterns noted among two or more variables.

Theory, middle-level: Propositions that explain relations among two or more variables by reference to principles derived from high-level theory. These propositions should be stated in ways that they can be proven to be false. *See also* **Hypotheses**.

Theory, middle-range: Propositions that account for patterns noted in archaeologically uncovered material remains by reference to the behaviors that caused those patterns. Middle-range theory often draws on some form of analogy in identifying these relationships.

Time-space systematics: Shorthand for defining the basic units of material variation by means of which ancient cultures and their histories are described. These units include **archaeological cultures**, **components**, and **phases**.

Totalizing narrative: This refers to an account of human behavior based on general principles thought to apply to a wide range of societies.

Trait: Any aspect of human behavior that is thought to be isolable; the rough behavioral equivalent of an attribute in an artifact.

Valuables: Refers to items held in high esteem by the people who made and/or used them.

Variable: An entity that can have more than one value.

Wealth: A measure of a person's or group's ability to accumulate valuable items. The objects collected may be esteemed for their economic, social, political, and/or ideological significance.

World view: A body of concepts shared by a group of people who use those ideas to understand themselves, others, and the world around them. Unlike theories, world views are not subject to systematic testing.

BIBLIOGRAPHY

Adams, R.
2005   *Prehistoric Mesoamerica*. Norman: University of Oklahoma Press.
Adams, R. McC.
1965   *The Land behind Baghdad: A History of Settlement on the Diyala Plain.* Chicago: University of Chicago Press.
1966   *The Evolution of Urban Society: Early Mesopotamia and Prehispanic Mexico.* Chicago: University of Chicago Press.
1974   Anthropological Perspectives on Ancient Trade. *Current Anthropology* 15:239–258.
1981   *Heartland of Cities: Surveys of Ancient Settlement and Land Use of the Central Floodplain of the Euphrates.* Chicago: University of Chicago Press.
Adams, R. McC., and H. Nissen
1972   *Uruk Countryside: Natural Setting of Urban Societies.* Chicago: University of Chicago Press.
Algaze, G.
1989   The Uruk Expansion: Cross-Cultural Exchange in Early Mesopotamian Civilization. *Current Anthropology* 30:571–608.
1993   *The Uruk World System: The Dynamics of Expansion of Early Mesopotamian Civilization.* Chicago: University of Chicago Press.
2008   *Ancient Mesopotamia at the Dawn of Civilization: The Evolution of an Urban Landscape.* Chicago: University of Chicago Press.
Arnold, P.
1991   *Domestic Ceramic Production and Spatial Organization: A Mexican Case Study in Ethnoarchaeology.* Cambridge: Cambridge University Press.
Aronson, M., ed.
2010   *If Stones Could Speak: Unlocking the Secrets of Stonehenge.* Washington, DC: National Geographic.
Ashmore, W.
1991   Site Planning Principles and Concepts of Directionality among the Ancient Maya. *Latin American Antiquity* 2:199–226.

321

Ashmore, W., and J. Sabloff
  2002   Spatial Orders in Maya Civic Plans. *Latin American Antiquity* 13:201–215.
Barton, C., and G. Clark
  1997   Evolutionary Theory in Archaeological Explanation. In *Rediscovering Darwin: Evolutionary Theory and Archaeological Explanation*, ed. C. Barton and G. Clark, pp. 3–15. Arlington, VA: American Anthropological Association, Archaeological Papers of the American Anthropological Association, No. 7.
Becker, M.
  1979   Priests, Peasants and Ceremonial Centers: The Intellectual History of a Model. In *Maya Archaeology and Ethnohistory*, ed. N. Hammond and G. Willey, pp. 3–20. Austin: University of Texas Press.
Bey, G., III, and C. Poole, eds.
  1992   *Ceramic Production and Distribution: An Integrated Approach*. Boulder, CO: Westview Press.
Binford, L.
  1981   *Bones: Ancient Men and Modern Myths*. New York: Academic Press.
Binford, L., and S. Binford, eds.
  1968   *New Perspectives in Archaeology*. Chicago: Aldine.
Boone, E., and G. Willey, eds.
  1988   *The Southeast Classic Maya Zone*. Washington, DC: Dumbarton Oaks.
Bourdieu, P.
  1977   *Outline of a Theory of Practice*. Translated by R. Nice. Cambridge: Cambridge University Press.
Bradley, R.
  1998   *The Significance of Monuments: On the Shaping of Human Experience in Neolithic and Bronze Age Europe*. New York: Routledge.
Brainerd, G.
  1951   The Place of Chronological Ordering in Archaeological Analysis. *American Antiquity* 16:301–313.
Brumfiel, E.
  1992   Distinguished Lecture in Archaeology: Breaking and Entering the Ecosystem: Gender, Class, and Faction Steal the Show. *American Anthropologist* 94:551–567.
Brumfiel, E., and J. Fox, eds.
  1994   *Factional Competition and Political Development in the New World*. Cambridge: Cambridge University Press.
Brumfiel, E., and T. Earle, eds.
  1987   *Specialization, Exchange, and Complex Societies*. Cambridge: Cambridge University Press.
Burl, A.
  2007   *Stonehenge: A Complete History and Archaeology of the World's Most Enigmatic Stone Circle*. New York: Carroll and Graf Publishers.

Carr, C., and J. Neitzel, eds.

1995   *Style, Society, and Person.* New York: Plenum Press.

Chase-Dunn, C., and T. Hall, eds.

1991   *Core-Periphery Relations in Pre-Capitalist Worlds.* Boulder, CO: Westview Press.

Childe, V. G.

1925   *The Dawn of European Civilization.* London: Keagan, Paul.

1936   *Man Makes Himself.* New York: Mentor Books.

1951   *Social Evolution.* New York: Schuman.

Chippindale, C.

2004   *Stonehenge Complete.* 3rd edition. New York: Thames and Hudson.

Clark, J., and W. Parry

1990   Craft Specialization and Cultural Complexity. *Economic Anthropology* 12: 289–346.

Clarke, D.

1968   *Analytical Archaeology.* London: Methuen and Co.

1972   Models and Paradigms in Contemporary Archaeology. In *Models in Archaeology*, ed. D. Clarke, pp. 1–60. London: Methuen.

1973   Archaeology: The Loss of Innocence. *Antiquity* 47:6–18.

Cleal, R., and M. Allen

1995   Stonehenge in Its Landscape. In *Stonehenge in Its Landscape: Twentieth Century Excavations*, by R. Cleal, K. Walker, and R. Montague, pp. 464–491. London: English Heritage.

Cleal, R., K. Walker, and R. Montague

1995   *Stonehenge in Its Landscape: Twentieth Century Excavations.* London: English Heritage.

Cohen, M.

1977   *The Food Crisis in Prehistory.* New Haven, CT: Yale University Press.

Conkey, M., and J. Gero

1997   Programme to Practice: Gender and Feminism in Archaeology. *Annual Review of Anthropology* 26:411–437.

Connell, S.

2002   Getting Closer to the Source: Using Ethnoarchaeology to Find Ancient Pottery Making in the Naco Valley, Honduras. *Latin American Antiquity* 13:401–417.

Costin, C.

1991   Craft Specialization: Issues in Defining, Documenting, and Explaining the Organization of Production. In *Archaeological Method and Theory*, Volume 3, ed. M. Schiffer, pp. 1–56. Tucson: University of Arizona Press.

2001   Craft Production Systems. In *Archaeology at the Millennium: A Sourcebook*, ed. G. Feinman and T. Price, pp. 273–327. New York: Kluwer Academic/Plenum Publishers.

Crumley, C.
 1979   Three Locational Models: An Epistemological Assessment of Anthro-
        pology and Archaeology. *Advances in Archaeological Method and Theory*
        2:141–173.
Cusick, J., ed.
 1998   *Studies in Culture Contact: Interaction, Culture Change, and Archaeology.*
        Carbondale: Center for Archaeological Investigations, Southern Illinois
        University.
D'Altroy, T., and T. Earle
 1985   Staple Finance, Wealth Finance, and Staple Storage in the Inka Political
        Economy. *Current Anthropology* 26:187–206.
Dark, K.
 1995   *Theoretical Archaeology.* Ithaca, NY: Cornell University Press.
Demarest, A., P. Rice, and D. Rice, eds.
 2004   *The Terminal Classic in the Maya Lowlands: Collapse, Transition, and Trans-
        formation.* Boulder: University of Colorado Press.
DeMarrais, E., L. Castillo, and T. Earle
 1996   Ideology, Materialization, and Power Strategies. *Current Anthropology*
        37:15–31.
De Montmollin, O.
 1989   *The Archaeology of Political Structure: Settlement Analysis in a Classic Maya
        Polity.* Cambridge: Cambridge University Press.
Diakonoff, I. M.
 1969   The Rise of the Despotic State in Ancient Mesopotamia. In *Ancient
        Mesopotamia: Socio-Economic History, a Collection of Studies by Soviet Schol-
        ars*, ed. I. M. Diakonoff, pp. 173–203. Moscow: "NAUKA" Publishing
        House, Central Department of Oriental Literature.
 1989   General Outline of the First Period of the History of the Ancient World
        and the Problem of the Ways of Development. In *Early Antiquity*, ed. I.
        M. Diakonoff and P. L. Kohl, pp. 27–66. Chicago: University of Chicago
        Press.
Dobres, M., and J. Robb, eds.
 2000   *Agency in Archaeology.* Routledge: London.
Dornan, J.
 2002   Agency and Archaeology: Past, Present, and Future Directions. *Journal
        of Archaeological Method and Theory* 9:303–329.
Douglass, J.
 2002   *Hinterland Households: Rural Agrarian Household Diversity in Northwest
        Honduras.* Boulder: University of Colorado Press.
Dunnell, R.
 1982   Evolutionary Theory and Archaeology. In *Advances in Archaeological
        Method and Theory: Selections from Volumes 1–4*, ed. M. Schiffer, pp. 35–99.
        New York: Academic Press.

Durkheim, E.

2008   *The Elementary Forms of Religious Life*. Oxford: Oxford University Press (originally published in 1912).

Earle, T.

1997   *How Chiefs Come to Power: The Political Economy of Prehistory*. Stanford, CA: Stanford University Press.

Earle, T., and J. Ericson, eds.

1977   *Exchange Systems in Prehistory*. New York: Academic Press.

Ehrenreich, R., C. Crumley, and J. Levy, eds.

1995   *Heterarchy and the Analysis of Complex Societies*. Arlington, VA: Archaeological Papers of the American Anthropological Association, No. 6.

Ekholm, K.

1972   *Power and Prestige: The Rise and Fall of the Kongo Kingdom*. Uppsala: SKRIV Service AB.

Fash, W.

2007   *Scribes, Warriors, and Kings: The City of Copan and the Ancient Maya*. London: Thames and Hudson.

Feinman, G., and J. Neitzel

1984   Too Many Types: An Overview of Sedentary Pre-State Societies in the Americas. *Advances in Archaeological Method and Theory* 7:39–102.

Fish, S., and S. Kowalewski, eds.

1991   *The Archaeology of Regions: The Case for Full-Coverage Survey*. Washington, DC: Smithsonian Institution Press.

Flannery, K.

1968   Archaeological Systems Theory and Early Mesoamerica. In *Anthropological Archaeology in the Americas*, ed. B. Meggers, pp. 67–87. Washington, DC: Anthropological Society of Washington.

1972   The Cultural Evolution of Civilizations. *Annual Review of Ecology and Systematics* 3:399–426.

1973   Archaeology with a Capital "S". In *Research and Theory in Current Archaeology*, ed. C. Redman, pp. 47–53. New York: Wiley.

Flannery, K., ed.

1986   *Guila Naquitz: Archaic Foraging and Early Agriculture in Oaxaca, Mexico*. New York: Academic Press.

Foucault, M.

1982   *The Archaeology of Power*. New York: Pantheon Books.

Friedman, J., and M. Rowlands

1977   Notes towards an Epigenetic Model of the Evolution of Civilization. In *The Evolution of Social Systems*, ed. J. Friedman and M. Rowlands, pp. 201–276. Pittsburgh: University of Pittsburgh Press.

Gailey, C.

1987   Culture Wars: Resistance to State Formation. In *Power Relations and State Formation*, ed. T. Patterson and C. Gailey, pp. 35–56. Washington, DC: American Anthropological Association.

Geertz, C.
  1973   *The Interpretation of Culture: Selected Essays by Clifford Geertz.* New York: Basic Books, Inc.
Geller, P., and M. Stockett, eds.
  2006   *Feminist Anthropology: Past, Present, and Future.* Philadelphia: University of Pennsylvania Press.
Giddens, A.
  1984   *The Constitution of Society: Outline of the Theory of Structuration.* Berkeley: University of California Press.
Glass, J.
  1966   Archaeological Survey of Western Honduras. In *Handbook of Middle American Indians*, Volume 4, volume eds. G. Ekholm and G. Willey, series ed. R. Wauchope, pp. 157–179. New Orleans: Tulane University Press.
Goffman, E.
  1974   *Frame Analysis.* Cambridge, MA: Harvard University Press.
Gosden, C.
  2004   *Archaeology and Colonialism: Cultural Contact from 5000 BC to the Present.* Cambridge: Cambridge University Press.
Green, S., and S. Perleman, eds.
  1985   *The Archaeology of Frontiers and Boundaries.* New York: Academic Press.
Hansen, M., and J. Kelley
  1989   Inference to the Best Explanation in Archaeology. In *Critical Traditions in Contemporary Archaeology* ed. V. Pinsky and A. Wylie, pp. 14–17. Cambridge: Cambridge University Press.
Harris, E.
  1975   The Stratigraphic Sequence: A Question of Time. *World Archaeology* 7: 109–121.
Hawkins, G.
  1963   Stonehenge Decoded. *Nature* 200:306–308.
  1965   Stonehenge: A Neolithic Computer. *Nature* 202:1258–1261.
Hays-Gilpin, K.
  2000   Feminist Scholarship in Archaeology. *Annals of the American Academy of Political and Social Science* 571:89–106.
Healy, P.
  1984   The Archaeology of Honduras. In *The Archaeology of Lower Central America*, ed. F. Lange and D. Stone, pp. 113–161. Albuquerque: University of New Mexico Press.
Hegmon, M.
  2003   Setting Theoretical Egos Aside: Issues and Theory in North American Archaeology. *American Antiquity* 68:213–243.
Helms, M.
  1976   *Ancient Panama: Chiefs in Search of Power.* Austin: University of Texas Press.
  1988   *Ulysses' Sail: An Ethnographic Odyssey of Power, Knowledge, and Geographical Distance.* Princeton, NJ: Princeton University Press.

1993   *Art and the Kingly Ideal: Art, Trade, and Power.* Austin: University of Texas Press.

Hempel, C.
1966   *Philosophy of Natural Science.* Englewood Cliffs, NJ: Prentice Hall.

Henderson, J., I. Sterns, A. Wonderley, and P. Urban
1979   Archaeological Investigations in the Valle de Naco. Northwestern Honduras: A Preliminary Report. *Journal of Field Archaeology* 6:169–192.

Hendon, J.
1996   Archaeological Approaches to the Organization of Domestic Labor: Household Practice and Domestic Relations. *Annual Review of Anthropology* 25:45-61.

Herman, A.
2001   *How the Scots Invented the World.* New York: Three Rivers Press.

Hirth, K. G.
1993   Identifying Rank and Socioeconomic Status in Domestic Contexts: An Example from Central Mexico. In *Prehispanic Domestic Units in Western Mesoamerica,* ed. R. Santley and K. G. Hirth, pp. 121–146. Boca Raton, FL: CRC Press.

Hodder, I.
1990   *The Domestication of Europe.* Oxford: Blackwell.
2006   *The Leopard's Tale: Revealing the Mysteries of Çatalhöyük.* New York: Thames and Hudson.

Hodder, I., ed.
1982   *Symbolic and Structural Archaeology.* Cambridge: Cambridge University Press.
1992   *Theory and Practice in Archaeology.* New York: Routledge.
2001   *Archaeological Theory Today.* Cambridge: Cambridge Polity Press.

Hodder, I., and S. Hutson
2003   *Reading the Past: Current Approaches to Interpretation in Archaeology.* 3rd edition. Cambridge: Cambridge University Press.

Hodder, I., M. Shanks, A. Alexandri, V. Buchli, J. Carman, J. Last, and G. Lucas, eds.
1995   *Interpreting Archaeology: Finding Meaning in the Past.* London: Routledge.

Joyce, R.
1988   The Ulua Valley and the Coastal Maya Lowlands: The View from Cerro Palenque. In *The Southeast Classic Maya Zone,* ed. E. Boone and G. Willey, pp. 269–295. Washington, DC: Dumbarton Oaks.
1991   *Cerro Palenque: Power and Identity on the Maya Periphery.* Austin: University of Texas Press.
1993   Women's Work: Images of Production and Reproduction in Pre-Hispanic Southern Central America. *Current Anthropology* 34:255–274.
2002   *The Languages of Archaeology: Dialogue, Narrative, and Writing.* Oxford: Blackwell.

Kehoe, A.
2008   *Controversies in Archaeology.* Walnut Creek, CA: Left Coast Press, Inc.

Kirchoff, P.
  1952 Mesoamerica: Its Geographical Limits, Ethnic Composition, and Cultural Characteristics. In *Heritage of Conquest*, ed. S. Tax, pp. 17–30. New York: The Free Press.
Kohl, P.
  1981 Materialist Approaches in Prehistory. *Annual Review of Anthropology* 10:89–118.
  1987 The Use and Abuse of World System Theory: The Case of the Pristine West Asian State. *Advances in Archaeological Method and Theory* 11:1–35.
Kroeber, A.
  1939 *Cultural and Natural Areas of Native North America*. Berkeley: University of California Press.
  1940 Stimulus Diffusion. *American Anthropologist* 32:1–20.
Kuhn, T.
  1962 *The Structure of Scientific Revolutions*. Chicago: University of Chicago Press.
LeBlanc, S.
  1973 Two Points of Logic Concerning Data, Hypotheses, General Laws, and Systems. In *Research and Theory in Current Archaeology*, ed. C. Redman, pp. 199–214. New York: John Wiley.
Lloyd, S.
  1980 *Foundations in the Dust: The Story of Mesopotamian Exploration*. London: Thames and Hudson.
Longacre, W.
  1970 *Archaeology as Anthropology: A Case Study*. Tucson: University of Arizona Press.
Lovata, T.
  2007 *Inauthentic Archaeologies: Public Uses and Abuses of the Past*. Walnut Creek, CA: Left Coast Press, Inc.
Lyman, R., and M. O'Brien
  2006 *Measuring Time with Artifacts: A History of Methods in American Archaeology*. Lincoln: University of Nebraska Press.
Lyman, R., M. O'Brien, and R. Dunnell
  1997 *The Rise and Fall of Culture History*. New York: Plenum Press.
Mann, M.
  1986 *The Sources of Social Power, Volume 1: A History of Power from the Beginning to A.D. 1760*. Cambridge: Cambridge University Press.
Mauss, M.
  1990 *The Gift: The Form and Reason for Exchange in Archaic Societies*. London: Routledge.
McGuire, R.
  1983 Breaking Down Cultural Complexity: Inequality and Heterogeneity. *Advances in Archaeological Method and Theory* 7:91–142.
  1992 *A Marxist Archaeology*. New York: Academic Press.

McGuire, R., and R. Paynter, eds.
1991   *The Archaeology of Inequality*. Oxford: Blackwell.
Meillassoux, C.
1981   *Maidens, Meals, and Money*. Cambridge: Cambridge University Press.
Miller, D., M. Rowlands, and C. Tilley, eds.
1989   *Domination and Resistance*. London: Unwin Hyman.
Morley, S. G.
1946   *The Ancient Maya*. Stanford, CA: Stanford University Press.
Mueller, J., ed.
1979   *Sampling in Archaeology*. Tucson: University of Arizona Press.
Nelson, S.
1997   *Gender in Archaeology*. Walnut Creek, CA: AltaMira Press.
Nisbett, R., and L. Ross
1980   *Human Inference: Strategies and Shortcomings of Social Judgment*. Engle-
       wood Cliffs, NJ: Prentice-Hall.
O'Laughlin, B.
1975   Marxist Approaches in Anthropology. *Annual Review of Anthropology* 4:
       341–370.
Ortner, S.
1984   Theory in Anthropology since the Sixties. *Comparative Studies in Society
       and History* 26:126–166.
Parker Pearson, M., and Ramilisonina
1998   Stonehenge for the Ancestors: The Stones Pass on the Message. *Antiq-
       uity* 72:308–326.
Patterson, T.
2003   *Marx's Ghost: Conversations with Archaeologists*. Oxford: Berg.
Paynter, R., and R. McGuire
1991   The Archaeology of Inequality: Culture, Domination, and Resistance. In
       The Archaeology of Inequality, ed. R. McGuire and R. Paynter, pp. 1–27.
       Oxford: Blackwell.
Pitts, M.
2001   *Hengeworld*. London: Arrow Books, a division of Random House.
Pollock, S.
1999   *Ancient Mesopotamia: The Eden That Never Was*. Cambridge: Cambridge
       University Press.
Pollock, S., and R. Bernbeck
2000   And They Said, Let Us Make Gods in Our Image: Gendered Ideologies
       in Ancient Mesopotamia. In *Reading the Body: Representations and Remains
       in the Archaeological Record*, ed. Alison E. Rautman, pp. 150–164. Philadel-
       phia: University of Pennsylvania Press.
Pollock, S., and R. Bernbeck, eds.
2005   *Archaeologies of the Middle East: Critical Perspectives*. Oxford: Blackwell.
Popper, K.
1989   *Conjectures and Refutations: The Growth of Scientific Knowledge*. 4th edition.
       London: Routledge.

Praetzellis, A.
  2000 *Death by Theory: A Tale of Mystery and Archaeological Theory.* Walnut
        Creek, CA: AltaMira Press.
Preucel, R.
  1995 The Postprocessual Condition. *Journal of Archaeological Research* 3:
        147–175.
Preucel, R., ed.
  1991 *Processual and Postprocessual Archaeologies: Multiple Ways of Knowing the
        Past.* Center for Archaeological Investigations, Occasional Papers No.
        10. Carbondale: Southern Illinois University Press.
Price, T., and G. Feinman, eds.
  1995 *Foundations of Social Inequality.* New York: Plenum Press.
Rabb, L., and A. Goodyear
  1984 Middle Range Theory in Archaeology: A Critical Review of Origins and
        Applications. *American Antiquity* 49:255–268.
Rappaport, R.
  1968 *Pigs for the Ancestors: Ritual in the Ecology of a New Guinea People.* New
        Haven, CT: Yale University Press.
Rathje, W.
  1972 Praise the Gods and Pass the Metates: A Hypothesis of the Develop-
        ment of Lowland Maya Rainforest Civilization in Middle America. In
        Contemporary Archaeology, ed. M. Leone, pp. 365–392. Carbondale: Illi-
        nois University Press.
Reed, N.
  2001 *The Caste War of the Yucatan.* Stanford: Stanford University Press.
Renfrew, C.
  1974 Beyond a Subsistence Economy: The Evolution of Social Organization
        in Prehistoric Europe. In *Reconstructing Complex Societies: An Archaeolog-
        ical Colloquium*, ed. C. B. Moore, pp. 69–95. Bulletin of the American
        Schools of Oriental Research, Supplement 20.
Renfrew, C., and P. Bahn
  2008 *Archaeology: Theories, Methods, and Practices.* London: Thames and Hud-
        son.
Renfrew, C., and J. F. Cherry, eds.
  1986 *Peer Polity Interaction and Socio-political Change.* Cambridge: Cambridge
        University Press.
Rice, P.
  2006 *Pottery Analysis: A Sourcebook.* Chicago: University of Chicago Press.
Robb, C.
  1998 The Archaeology of Symbols. *Annual Review of Anthropology* 27:329–346.
Robinson, E., ed.
  1987 *Interaction on the Southeast Mesoamerican Frontier: Prehistoric and Historic
        Honduras and El Salvador.* Oxford: British Archaeological Reports Inter-
        national Series 327.

Roseneau, P.
1992   *Post-Modernism and the Social Sciences: Insights, Inroads, and Intrusions.* Princeton, NJ: Princeton University Press.

Rothman, M.
2004   Studying the Development of Complex Society: Mesopotamia in the Late Fifth and Fourth Millennia BC. *Journal of Archaeological Research* 12:75–119.

Rowlands, M., M. Larsen, and K. Kristiansen, eds.
1987   *Centre and Periphery in the Ancient World.* Cambridge: Cambridge University Press.

Sabloff, J., and C. C. Lamberg-Karlovsky , eds.
1975   *Ancient Civilization and Trade.* Albuquerque: University of New Mexico Press.

Salmon, M.
1982   *Philosophy and Archaeology.* New York: Academic Press.

Santley, R., and K. G. Hirth, eds.
1993   *Prehispanic Domestic Units in Western Mesoamerica.* Boca Raton, FL: CRC Press.

Schiffer , M.
1976   *Behavioral Archaeology.* New York: Academic Press.
1987   *Formation Processes of the Archaeological Record.* Albuquerque: University of New Mexico Press.

Schneider , J.
1977   Was There a Pre-Capitalist World System? *Peasant Studies* 6:20–29.

Schortman, E., and P. Urban
1987   Modeling Interregional Interaction in Prehistory . *Advances in Archaeological Method and Theory* 11:37–95.
1994   Living on the Edge: Core/Periphery Relations in Ancient Southeast Mesoamerica. *Current Anthropology* 35:401–430.
2004   Modeling the Roles of Craft Production in Ancient Political Economies. *Journal of Archaeological Research* 12:185–226.
2011   *Networks of Power: Political Relations in the Late Postclassic Naco Valley, Honduras.* Boulder: University of Colorado Press.

Schortman, E., and P. Urban, eds.
1992   *Resources, Power, and Interregional Interaction.* New York: Plenum Press.

Schortman, E., P. Urban, and M. Ausec
2001   Politics with Style: Identity Formation in Prehispanic Southeastern Mesoamerica. *American Anthropologist* 103:1–19.

Schortman, E., P. Urban, W. Ashmore, and J. Benyo
1986   Interregional Interaction in the Southeast Maya Periphery: The Santa Barbara Archaeological Project 1983–1984 Seasons. *Journal of Field Archaeology* 13:259–272.

Schwartz, G., and S. Falconer , eds.
1994   *Archaeological Views from the Countryside: Village Communities in Early Complex Societies.* Washington, DC: Smithsonian Institution Press.

Scott, J.
1985   *Weapons of the Weak: Everyday Forms of Peasant Resistance.* New Haven, CT: Yale University Press.
Sewell, W.
1992   A Theory of Structure: Duality, Agency, and Transformation. *American Journal of Sociology* 98:1–29.
Shanks, M., and C. Tilley
1987   *Re-constructing Archaeology.* Cambridge: Cambridge University Press.
Sharer, R.
1990   *Quiriguá: A Classic Maya Center and Its Sculpture.* Durham, NC: Carolina Academic Press.
Sharer, R., and W. Ashmore
2002   *Archaeology: Discovering Our Past.* Mountain View, CA: Mayfield.
Sharer, R., and L. Traxler
2006   *The Ancient Maya.* Stanford, CA: Stanford University Press.
Sheets, P.
2005   *The Ceren Site: An Ancient Village Buried by Volcanic Ash.* New York: Wadsworth Publishing.
Sheets, P., ed.
2002   *Before the Volcano Erupted: The Ancient Ceren Village in Central America.* Austin: University of Texas Press.
Shennan, S.
1982   Exchange and Ranking: The Role of Amber in the Early Bronze Age of Europe. In *Ranking, Resources, and Exchange,* ed. C. Renfrew and S. Shennan, pp. 33–45. Cambridge: Cambridge University Press.
Smith, M.
1987   Household Possessions and Wealth in Agrarian States: Implications for Archaeology. *Journal of Anthropological Archaeology* 6:297–335.
Stein, G.
1999   *Rethinking World Systems: Diasporas, Colonies, and Interaction in Uruk Mesopotamia.* Tucson: University of Arizona Press.
2002   From Passive Periphery to Active Agents: Emerging Perspectives in the Archaeology of Interregional Interaction. *American Anthropologist* 104: 903–916.
Stocking, G.
1968   Franz Boas and the Culture Concept in Historical Perspective. In *Race, Culture, and Evolution: Essays in the History of Anthropology,* ed. G. Stocking, pp. 195–233. New York: The Free Press.
Thomas, J.
1999   *Understanding the Neolithic.* New York: Routledge.
Tilley, C., ed.
1993   *Interpretive Archaeology.* Oxford: Berg.

Tosi, M.
1984   The Notion of Craft Specialization and Its Representation in the Ar-
        chaeological Records of Early States. In *Marxist Perspectives in Archaeol-
        ogy*, ed. M. Spriggs, pp. 22–52. Cambridge: Cambridge University
        Press.

Trigger, B.
1980   *Gordon Childe: Revolutions in Prehistory.* London: Thames and Hudson.
2006   *A History of Archaeological Thought.* Cambridge: Cambridge University Press.

Urban, P.
1986   Precolumbian Settlement in the Naco Valley, Northwestern Honduras.
        In *The Southeast Maya Periphery*, ed. P. Urban and E. Schortman, pp.
        275–295. Austin: University of Texas Press.

Urban, P., and E. Schortman
2004   Opportunities for Advancement: Intra-Community Power Contests in
        the Midst of Political Decentralization in Terminal Classic Southeastern
        Mesoamerica. *Latin American Antiquity* 15:251–272.

Wagley, P.
1983   *Welcome of Tears: The Tapirape Indians of Central Brazil.* Prospect Heights,
        IL: Waveland Press.

Wailes, B., ed.
1996   *Craft Specialization and Social Evolution: In Memory of V. Gordon Childe.*
        Philadelphia: University Museum, University of Pennsylvania.

Wallerstein, I.
1974   *The Modern World System*, Vol. 1. New York: Academic Press.
1980   *The Modern World System*, Vol. 2. New York: Academic Press.

Watson, P. J., S. LeBlanc, and C. Redman
1984   *Archaeological Explanation: The Scientific Method in Archaeology.* New York:
        Columbia University Press.

Wattenmaker, P.
1998   *Household and State in Upper Mesopotamia.* Washington, DC: Smithson-
        ian Institution Press.

Webster, D., A. Freter, and N. Gonlin
2000   *Copan: The Rise and Fall of an Ancient Maya Kingdom.* New York: Harcourt
        College Publishers.

Wells, P.
1980   *Culture Contact and Culture Change: Early Iron Age Central Europe and the
        Mediterranean World.* Cambridge: Cambridge University Press.

Whitley, D. S., ed.
1998   *Reader in Archaeological Theory: Postprocessual and Cognitive Approaches.*
        London: Routledge.

Wilk, R., and W. Ashmore, eds.
1988   *Household and Community in the Mesoamerican Past.* Albuquerque: Univer-
        sity of New Mexico Press.

Willey, G.
 1953 *Prehistoric Settlement Patterns in the Viru Valley, Peru*. Bureau of American Ethnology Bulletin 155. Washington, DC: Smithsonian Institution.
Willey, G., and D. Lathrap, eds.
 1956 An Archaeological Classification of Culture Contact Situations. In *Seminars in Archaeology 1955*, ed. R. Wauchope, pp. 3–30. Salt Lake City: Society for American Archaeology.
Willey, G., and P. Phillips
 1958 *Method and Theory in American Archaeology*. Chicago: University of Chicago Press.
Willey, G., and J. Sabloff
 1993 *A History of American Archaeology*. 3rd edition. San Francisco: W. H. Freeman.
Wintle, A.
 1996 Archaeologically Relevant Dating Techniques for the Next Century. *Journal of Archaeological Science* 23:123–138.
Wolf, E.
 1982 *Europe and the People without History*. Berkeley: University of California Press.
 1990 Facing Power—Old Insights, New Questions. *American Anthropologist* 92:586–596.
Wright, H.
 1972 A Consideration of Interregional Exchange in Greater Mesopotamia: 4000–3000 BC. In *Social Exchange and Interaction*, ed. E. Wilmsen, pp. 95–105. Ann Arbor: Anthropological Papers, Museum of Anthropology, University of Michigan, No. 46.
Wright, H., and G. Johnson
 1975 Population, Exchange, and Early State Formation in Southwestern Iran. *American Anthropologist* 77:267–289.
Wylie, A.
 2002 *Thinking with Things: Essays in the Philosophy of Archaeology*. Berkeley: University of California Press.
Yellen, J.
 1977 *Archaeological Approaches to the Present*. New York: Academic Press.
Zagarell, A.
 1986 Trade, Women, Class, and Society in Ancient Western Asia. *Current Anthropology* 27:415–430.

INDEX

ABOUT THE AUTHORS

Patricia Urban began her career in Mesoamerican archaeology as Survey Director for the Naco Valley Archaeological Project, then directed by Dr. John Henderson of Cornell University (1975, 1977). This position also gave her the chance to work closely with students in the Cornell field school. These early experiences convinced Pat that she deeply enjoyed conducting research in Honduras in collaboration with undergraduates. After completing the first stage of the Naco Valley investigations in 1979, Pat directed survey within the Humuya and Sulaco River drainages in central Honduras as part of the Cajon Archaeological Project (Kenneth Hirth, director; 1981). Most of Pat's career, like Ed's, has been devoted to conducting research in the middle Ulua (1983–1986), Naco (1988–1996), and lower Cacaulapa (1999–present) valleys in northwestern Honduras. In addition to being very rewarding research opportunities, these projects gave Pat the chance to once again involve undergraduates in field studies. Beginning with informal collaborations with students over summers in the early 1980s, Pat took the lead in 1988 in developing a more formal field school that came to be known as the Kenyon-Honduras Program in Central American Ethnology and Archaeology. That course of study continues up the present day (2011). Pat's interests in archaeology have evolved over time. Long concerned with the study of ceramics as well as settlement patterns, Pat now interprets these materials in light of, primarily, Marxist theories of political economy. Most recently Pat has been investigating the reflexive relation between structure and agency, a topic addressed most fully in Chapter 9. Pat and

Ed met in graduate school at the University of Pennsylvania and went on to teach together at Kenyon College beginning in 1981. Unlike Ed, Pat was drawn early on to the study of theory, and it has remained a major interest of hers throughout her career.

E DWARD SCHORTMAN has been working on archaeological projects in Mexico and northern Central America since 1972. He has directed or co-directed research in neighboring portions of Guatemala and Honduras, first in the lower Motagua Valley in eastern Guatemala (1977–1979) and later in the middle Ulua (1983–1986), Naco (1988–1996), and lower Cacaulapa valleys (1999–present) of northwestern Honduras. It was in the course of supervising work in the last three areas that Ed, together with Pat Urban, started working with undergraduates in the field. These informal collaborations with young scholars blossomed into the Kenyon-Honduras Program in Central American Ethnology and Archaeology, which has been in operation from 1988 through this writing in 2011. Ed's research interests have long focused on the ways in which interactions among members of multiple cultures shaped the histories of these cultures. As time has gone on, Ed has increasingly taken a Marxist stance in interpreting these cross-border dealings, investigating how political developments, such as the concentration of power in ever fewer hands, have been constrained and enabled by such economic processes as craft production and trade. A current interest is how networks can be used to address these question. Ed has been teaching at Kenyon College since graduating from the University of Pennsylvania in 1981. Being able to do what one wants in life is wonderful; sharing that experience with cohorts of bright young undergraduates is a gift. And yes, Ed was not attracted to archaeology by the prospect of exploring the abstract realm of theory but has grown to appreciate theory's significance in all aspects of fieldwork over the years.

CPSIA information can be obtained
at www.ICGtesting.com
Printed in the USA
FFHW01n1502080718
47348039-50389FF